CENTRE FOR
POPULATION STUDIES

Social Europe

Social Europe

Living Standards and Welfare States

Edited by

Richard Berthoud

Institute for Social and Economic Research, University of Essex, UK

Maria Iacovou

Institute for Social and Economic Research, University of Essex, UK

Edward Elgar
Cheltenham, UK • Northampton, MA, USA

Published by
Edward Elgar Publishing Limited
Glensanda House
Montpellier Parade
Cheltenham
Glos GL50 1UA
UK

Edward Elgar Publishing, Inc.
136 West Street
Suite 202
Northampton
Massachusetts 01060
USA

A catalogue record for this book
is available from the British Library

Library of Congress Cataloguing in Publication Data

Social Europe : living standards and welfare states / edited by Richard Berthoud,
Maria Iacovou.
  p. cm.
  Includes index.
  1. Europe—Social conditions—1945- 2. Europe—1945- 3. Welfare
state—Europe. I. Berthoud, Richard. II. Iacovou, Maria.

HN373.5.S6224 2004
301'.094—dc22

2004046960

ISBN 1 84376 676 0

Printed and bound in Great Britain by MPG Books Ltd, Bodmin, Cornwall

Contents

Figures

Tables

Acknowledgements

This book is based on a programme of research financed by the European Commission, under its Fifth Framework. We are grateful to our liaison officer, Fadila Boughanémi, and to her colleagues in DG Research, for their support of the programme. The data from the European Community Household Panel (ECHP) were supplied by Eurostat. The analysis of the data and the interpretation of the findings are, of course, our own responsibility.

The research team owes many thanks to Marcia Taylor, who manages the European Panel Analysis Group's activities; to Eileen Clucas, who handles the budgetary arrangements; and to Kate Tucker who publishes the series of working papers.

Richard Berthoud and Maria Iacovou owe a special debt of gratitude to Karen Robson, who acted as editorial deputy during a crucial production period when both of the editors were on leave of absence; and to Janice Webb who converted the mass of text into the format required for printing.

Thanks also to the team at Edward Elgar for their efficient production of this volume.

Contributors

The authors are associated with six research institutes, as follows:

Institute for Social and Economic Research, University of Essex (ISER)
Professor Richard Berthoud*
Professor Jonathan Gershuny
Dr Maria Iacovou
Karen L. Robson

DIW Berlin (German Institute for Economic Research)
Dr Joachim Frick
Dr Lutz C. Kaiser (now at Bochum University of Applied Sciences)
Dr C. Katharina Spiess*
Professor Gert G. Wagner*

Economic and Social Research Institute, Dublin (ESRI)
Dr Richard Layte
Bertrand Maître
Professor Christopher T. Whelan*

Tilburg Institute for Social and Socio-Economic Research, Tilburg
University (TISSER)
Professor Ruud J.A. Muffels*
Dr Didier Fouarge
Trudie Schils
Dr Wilfred Uunk

Centre for Labour Market Studies, University of Aarhus (CLS)
Dr Mette C. Deding
Professor Peder J. Pedersen*
Dr Torben D. Schmidt

Department of Sociology and Social Research, University of Milano-
Bicocca (DSSR)
Dr Mario Lucchini
Professor Antonio Schizzerotto*

* Team leader

Preface: The European Panel Analysis Group

This book is based on a three-year programme of research on *The Dynamics of Social Change in Europe* (shortened to '*DynSoc*'), undertaken by the European Panel Analysis Group (EPAG). The programme was funded under the Improving Human Potential heading of the EU's Fifth Framework. Members of the EPAG consortium are the:

- Institute for Social and Economic Research (ISER), University of Essex (co-ordinators);
- DIW Berlin;
- Economic and Social Research Institute (ESRI), Dublin;
- Tilburg Institute for Social and Socio-Economic Research (TISSER), Tilburg University;
- Centre for Labour Market Studies (CLS), University of Aarhus; and
- Department of Sociology and Social Research, University of Milano-Bicocca.

The consortium has collaborated in a series of detailed research projects, each investigating a specific aspect of family, employment and income dynamics. The findings and conclusions of each of the specific projects have been published as EPAG Working Papers. This collection of papers, listed on page 268, make up a substantial body of economic and sociological research literature; the aim of this book is to review the findings from the research programme, and to draw broader conclusions about life chances and welfare regimes in Europe. Bibliographical references to direct outputs from the research programme are denoted by asterisks.

Readers wanting more detailed information about the analytical processes involved in the research can consult the relevant working papers, all of which are freely available on the Internet:

http://www.iser.essex.ac.uk/epag/pubs/workpaps

1. Introduction

Richard Berthoud and Maria Iacovou

This book is concerned with understanding the diversity of people's lives across Europe: documenting differences and similarities between countries and regions, analysing how people's lives evolve over time, and attempting to codify and explain the variations which are observed between countries.

We focus on three major and interconnected aspects of people's lives – their families, their experience of employment, and their incomes – investigating not only the resources, circumstances and behaviour of individuals, but also the interactions between individuals and the wider social frameworks within which they live. We present many examples of differences in lifestyles and behaviour across Europe: differences which, already wide, will become even more pronounced following the enlargement of the EU to encompass as many as ten new countries.

Social scientists have recognised the importance of comparative research for the greater part of a century (Gauthier, 2002). For most of this period the opportunities for this type of research have been limited to comparisons of national indicators, or to more in-depth studies covering only two or three countries. However, the last decade has seen a massive expansion in the possibilities for cross-national research, thanks to the advent of large-scale data sets providing detailed information on individuals across Europe. The research presented here draws on the unique longitudinal and cross-national comparative evidence from the European Community Household Panel survey (ECHP), complemented by results based on various national panel studies.

We seek to answer a number of fundamental questions. To what extent do the patterns of people's lives vary across Europe? What is the impact of these variations on people's well-being? How do different systems of family support and welfare regimes influence income dynamics and changes in living standards? And to what extent do the characteristics of the welfare regime under which people live, rather than the fact that they live in one country or another, determine life outcomes?

The book is structured into three broad sections, covering (in order) families, employment, and incomes. Chapter 2 describes variations in patterns

1

of family living arrangements across Europe. Chapters 3 and 4 consider the interactions between family life and employment at key stages of the life-cycle, with Chapter 3 focusing on young people's parallel transitions from home to partnership/parenthood, and from education to work, and Chapter 4 focusing on the impacts of partnership, parenthood and caring responsibilities on adults' (and especially women's) employment prospects.

Chapters 5, 6 and 7 look at labour market issues, examining, in turn, the trend towards non-standard employment contracts (Chapter 5); mobility in and out of work across the life-cycle (Chapter 6); and the impact of unemployment (Chapter 7).

These work-related issues have obvious implications for household incomes (analysed in Chapter 8), and for the dynamics of poverty (in Chapter 9), and it is here that the social policy programmes embodied in the notion of 'welfare regime' (see below) can be expected to have their most direct effects. The link between household incomes and a family's living standards is unravelled in the final detailed Chapter (10).

The concluding Chapter (11) returns to some of the issues raised in this introduction to ask how far a longitudinal perspective and an international comparative framework have advanced our understanding of the dynamics of social change and of the 'social' dimension in European policy.

A Conceptual Framework for the Analysis of Life Chances

This book reports results from a wide-ranging programme of research undertaken in six institutions, with 18 contributory authors covering a range of disciplines in the social sciences. As such, it does not pretend to be driven by a single unified theoretical perspective. We have adopted a more pluralistic approach, locating the analysis within a broader set of theoretical frameworks with five elements:

- direct links between the dimensions of the family-employment-income nexus at the individual level;
- the impact of social norms, market forces and institutions/policy on people's choices;
- an underlying stability in people's positions, and the importance of a dynamic perspective;
- the pattern of experiences across the life-course;
- the accumulation of 'capital' as a contributor to social mobility.

These theoretical frameworks are brought together in the stylised diagram overleaf (Figure 1.1). The family-employment-income (FEI) nexus, concerned with the circumstances and decisions of the individual, occupies the centre of

Figure 1.1   The family-employment-income nexus

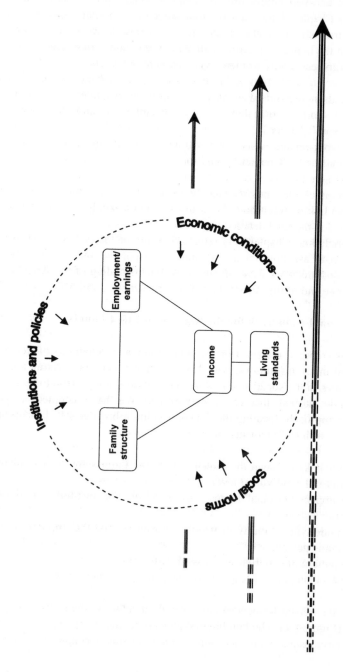

diagram. The influences of institutions, and of the wider social, cultural and economic framework, are shown by the outer ring. Three groups of macro-level influences are depicted, each mediating the FEI nexus, and each also subject to the influence of the other two macro-level factors. Finally, the fact that individuals' lives and institutional factors are subject to change over time are shown by the horizontal lines running across the diagram. All of these factors – the individual-level, the macro-level, and the time dimension, as well as the interactions between them – differ between countries. Part of these differences will be attributable to compositional variations between the populations of different countries – educational levels, experience of unemployment, and so on; and part will be attributable to social, cultural and economic factors which operate at the country level.

Dimensions of social position: the family-employment-income (FEI) nexus
Although families, employment and incomes can be thought of independently, and they are commonly studied in isolation, they in fact form a closely-knit nexus which has to be examined as a whole before any of its parts can be properly understood.[1]

For example, there is a strong and recursive interaction between a person's choices and expectations about family life, his or her own employment prospects, and those of other family members. Historically a man could not marry and start a family until he had a secure enough job to support a wife and children. There are still clear signs that young people wait until after they have entered the labour market to form families (see Chapter 3) and that those who do not do so may experience poverty as a consequence (Chapter 2). The range of available family-and-employment choices is now much wider, and less unequal between husbands and wives, than it was in the past, but (as Chapter 4 clearly shows) women's labour market activities are still strongly affected by their family positions, all over Europe.

The link between family structure and incomes is manifested in several ways. On one level, transfers of cash or in kind may be made between family members. Even if this is not done explicitly, the incomes of all household members are usually aggregated when measuring consumption, and divided by a factor which takes account of the number and ages of people living there, to summarise the whole household in terms of its 'equivalent income' (see Chapter 8). And of course, the incomes available to individuals, both currently and in the future, will affect their decisions in the sphere of the family.

Finally, it goes without saying that people's incomes are largely composed of earnings, and so are mainly determined by their employment – thus, the link between employment and incomes is clear.

External influences on personal choices

One of the perennial issues in the social sciences is how far men and women are in a position to make their own choices, and how far they are in the predetermining grip of social forces.

The external factors examined here are of three distinct types, operating in very different ways. Social norms may be of primary importance as an influence on family structures, economic conditions on employment and earnings, and institutions and policy on final income; but it is clear that all three types of influence have a role to play in all three dimensions of the FEI nexus. The difficulty lies in identifying the nature and extent of these influences – especially in international comparative research, where it is not the effect of a single policy or economic variable which is at issue, but 15 complex bundles of country-level policies, each interacting with other factors operating at the national level.

One option, discussed later in this introduction, is to summarise policy variations between countries in terms of overarching 'welfare-regime types', or in terms of alternative typologies. As we show, this strategy is successful and illuminating in many cases, but there is no single typology which is adequate to explain all the cross-European differences which we observe.

A dynamic perspective

Much social research and policy analysis is based on measures of people's *current* position in the various domains of interest. It is much easier to collect data on that basis, and cross-sectional analysis provides a valuable profile of many important issues. Moreover, measures of the 'stock' of families requiring services or other inputs are of direct interest to policy makers.

Many of the characteristics of interest are essentially stable, at least over the short term. If we want to explain why one person is in work today and another is not, an immediate answer is that this person had a job yesterday, and the other did not. However, if we want to understand the processes involved in employment and unemployment, it is important to look beyond this short-term stability, and identify, instead, the key changes experienced by individuals over a period – *moving* into work and out of work, rather than *being* in or out of work.

Whenever possible, then, we want to follow the important *events* in people's lives: leaving home, getting a job, starting a family, winning promotion, getting sick, giving up work, falling into poverty, entering deprivation. If we can follow the rises and falls of people's fortunes in this way – the opportunities they see, the decisions they take, the risks they face – in a context which also takes account of changes in their households and in the prevailing economic climate, then we are a large step closer to understanding the processes driving change.

The life-course
Any attempt to understand social dynamics also requires a longer-term perspective. The life-course paradigm, as described by Elder (1994, 1998), conceptualises people's lives as the products of their own personal histories, interacting with the social and historical context in which they grow up. Some of the dimensions of social position naturally change across the life-course: people are born, they go to school, start work, have families, their children grow up, they retire, their health deteriorates, they require care, they die. Analysis of these changes only makes sense in the context of a life-cycle framework, and it can be shown that what Shakespeare called 'the seven ages of man' do follow each other in reasonably consistent order (Murphy, 1987; Berthoud and Gershuny, 2000). For other purposes, though, we would ideally want to compare people's social positions over the whole of their life-courses to see how far their situation at each stage was advantaged or disadvantaged relative to others.

This life-course perspective is quite explicit in the analysis of young people's transitions from home to work in Chapter 3, and in the discussion of how training opportunities and job transitions vary between age groups in Chapter 6. It is also implicit in many of the other chapters. There is an underlying assumption, for example, that the period of people's lives when they have family responsibilities coincides with the period when they are in employment (Chapter 4); that their income is likely to fall when they reach retirement age (Chapter 2); and that they are likely to be in need of care towards the end of their lives (Chapter 4).

Accumulating 'capital'
The idea that education, training and experience in the labour market represent an investment in 'human capital' which pays 'dividends' in the form of employment and earnings is so deeply embedded in economic theory that we tend to forget that it is a metaphor. Notions of 'social capital' (Bourdieu, 1986; Putnam, 2000) and 'cultural capital' (Bourdieu, 1986) have also been proposed to help explain some of the processes involved in social stratification.

The theory can be generalised to suggest that people acquire and dispose of all kinds of assets and liabilities in the course of their life. Their family background is an asset to the extent that it encouraged education and provided routes and contacts into higher-level jobs. Education itself is an asset, but a poor school record is a liability. A job is an asset, and unemployment is a liability, in the sense that both these positions have short- and even long-term effects on future employment prospects. A partner may be an asset, or a liability, as indeed may children, depending on the balance of their influence on one's life chances. Citizenship of a prosperous country may be considered an asset, which most residents inherit at birth, but others seek to acquire later in life. Ill health may be considered a liability.

The point is that all these assets and liabilities are stable, though not necessarily permanent, characteristics. Together they make up a balance sheet which adds up to a set of influences on people's current social position, on their future prospects, and on their prospects over the remainder of their lives. It is the stock of such capital, its accumulation (or dissipation) over time, and the ability to access and deploy it in relevant situations, that helps to explain the processes by which people form families, find jobs, and enjoy an income from year to year.

Dynamic analysis in a changing world
We have already highlighted the importance of the individual-level dynamic analysis which forms the bulk of the research in this book – and we will reiterate the arguments in favour of dynamic research based on longitudinal data, later in the chapter. This type of dynamic analysis examines changes in individuals' personal circumstances, over a relatively short period of time: two, three, four or five years[2] – and is therefore represented by the shortest of the horizontal lines in Figure 1.1.

The life-course perspective, which provides a conceptual framework for individual-level changes over a longer period of time – in this case, the lifetime of the individual – is represented by the middle line in Figure 1.1.

However, there is a third aspect of change over time, which is not explicitly dealt with in the research presented in this book, since it has to do not with changes in individuals' lives, but with the evolution over time of the social and institutional factors which constitute the long-term backdrop to people's lives. This aspect of longer-term macro-level change is represented by the longest of the horizontal lines in Figure 1.1. Of course, social and institutional factors do not always change slowly – in fact, social policy may change very fast. However, it may be convincingly argued that the pace of change in a society as a whole tends to be slower than the fluctuations in the lives of individuals within that society.

Although our research does not deal directly with macro-level change, several chapters in the book do highlight the fact that our analysis took place at a particular time – the last years of the twentieth century – and should be viewed against the backdrop of a Europe which has undergone immense changes over the past half-century. Family patterns, employment and incomes have all changed dramatically over this period.

In the sphere of the family, divorce rates have been rising. The age at marriage has been increasing since the middle of last century (though prior to the increase, it was falling), and the incidence of cohabitation rather than formal marriage is rising. Fertility rates have been falling, and the proportion of older people in the population has been rising.

In the sphere of employment, the proportion of women in paid work has risen dramatically, with the rise in mothers' employment being particularly steep. By contrast, unemployment rates among men increased dramatically over the 1970s and 1980s, and despite fluctuations, have not returned to their former low levels. The proportion of younger adults in employment has decreased – partly because of higher youth unemployment, but also because younger people are remaining longer in education. The proportion of adults in short-term and insecure employment has risen.

In the sphere of incomes, GDP and average household incomes have been rising across Europe over the period in question. With respect to income distributions, the picture has been more mixed, with some countries experiencing large increases in income inequality, while levels of inequality elsewhere have been more stable. However, across the EU as a whole, the level of inequality has increased with the accession of more countries, with increasingly diverse levels of income.

Most of the changes described above have occurred across all, or almost all, countries, with a trend in the same direction. So, for example, the trend towards higher incomes has been common across Europe, as has the increase in divorce rates. However, the similarity in trends across Europe does not necessarily indicate that there has been convergence between countries. Two examples from the sphere of the family will make this clear. In the case of fertility rates (which have fallen across Europe since the 1960s), convergence (or perhaps even a cross-over) is evident, since countries where fertility was high in the 1960s (particularly Italy and Spain) are experiencing a faster drop in fertility than countries where fertility was already low. But if we consider births outside marriage, there is a divergence between countries, even though the trend is in the same (upwards) direction in all countries. Although the proportion of births outside marriage has risen in all countries, it has risen faster in countries where it was high in the 1960s (for example, Sweden and Denmark) than in countries where it was low (for example, Greece and Spain) – and thus, on this indicator, the degree of difference between countries has grown.

Longitudinal Analysis and Longitudinal Data

The questions covered in this book have interested scholars and policy makers for many years. However, the opportunity to investigate them at the level of the individual European citizen has arisen only relatively recently, with the development of large comparable cross-national data sets such as the European Community Household Panel (ECHP) – the principal data source for the analysis in this book. In particular, much of our analysis exploits the longitudinal nature of the ECHP, which allows us to adopt the dynamic perspective outlined earlier.

There are several different types of longitudinal data: retrospective recall of events that have already taken place; repeat surveys following up the same sample on two or three occasions; cohort surveys in which a group of people who all experienced an event in a certain period are interviewed again and again at intervals. Each of these methods is highly appropriate for a number of specific analytical purposes, but the longitudinal method with the widest general applications is the household panel survey. A sample representative of all households is identified at the start. Every (adult) member of the household is interviewed. The panel members are then re-interviewed every year, using largely the same set of questions on each occasion. The children of the original panel members are recruited to the survey as they reach the age of 16, and the data therefore remain representative of the population over the years, and even across generations.

The pioneering Panel Survey of Income Dynamics was set up in the United States in 1968; now that it has traversed a generation it is of unparalleled value to US social scientists seeking to understand the processes of social change and the impact of policies over the past decades (see, for example, Bane and Ellwood, 1994).

Data: the European Community Household Panel (ECHP)

In Europe, substantial panels have been launched in several countries, starting with Germany in 1983. Some early comparative analyses have been based on harmonised data from surveys undertaken separately in different countries. But a major development was the introduction in 1994 of the European Community Household Panel (ECHP, also known as the Europanel).

The ECHP was designed as a single purpose-built survey covering the whole of the European Union (EU). In principle (the exceptions are noted below) the same set of questions was asked of a random sample of households and of individuals in every country – covering a wide range of subjects including those relevant to our own interest in family structure, employment patterns, household income and living standards. Each country submits its data to Eurostat, the statistical agency of the EU, which is responsible for checking that the variables are as far as possible consistent with each other, and for deriving summary variables (such as total household income). (For a more detailed description of the survey, see Wirtz and Mejer, 2002.)

The sample totals around 73 000 households across Europe, ranging from 7000 each in Italy and France to just 1000 in Luxembourg; all adults in selected households have been interviewed, providing data about 153 000 individuals.

Members of the sample have been re-interviewed each successive year (thus making it a 'panel' survey), and this means that the data can be used either 'cross-sectionally' to describe the position at any one time, or 'longitudinally' to analyse changes from year to year.

The ECHP was launched in 1994 and the final wave of interviews was in 2001. (The detailed monthly records of employment and income relate to the previous calendar year, so for these data the reference periods are 1993 to 2000.) At the start of the research programme summarised here, three waves of data were available for analysis; at the time of writing, the data for the seven-year sequence 1994 to 2000 have been released for analysis.

Data: comparability

The standard pattern of the purpose-built survey running from 1994 to 2001 is true of only seven of the 15 EU countries: *Denmark, Ireland, France, Portugal, Spain, Italy* and *Greece*. The other eight countries differ in the following ways.

- *Austria* launched the purpose-designed survey in 1995, and *Finland* launched the survey in 1996, so the initial year(s) are missing for these countries.
- *Sweden* provided data from the existing Swedish Living Conditions Survey (ULF), starting in 1997. Thus, the initial years of data are missing for Sweden, and the data are not always consistent with the 'true' ECHP. In particular, the Swedish data do not constitute a panel survey, so certain types of longitudinal analysis are not possible.
- The *Netherlands* and *Belgium* have provided data from existing household panel surveys, known as the Dutch Socio-Economic Panel (ISEP) and Panel Study on Belgian Households (PSBH), which were transcribed into the ECHP format. This means that the data are not always fully consistent with the 'true' ECHP.
- *Germany* and the *UK* ran the true ECHP for three years (1994–96). They then switched to data derived from their existing household panel surveys, the German Socio-Economic Panel (GSOEP) and British Household Panel Survey (BHPS). The latter were backdated to 1994, so there are two sequences of data for these countries for 1994–96, followed by a single sequence from 1997 onwards.
- *Luxembourg's* data for 1994–96 were transcribed from the existing Socio-Economic Panel 'Living in Luxembourg' (PSELL-I); the data for 1997 on were derived from a new survey (PSELL-II), so there is a break in the sequence. The second Luxembourg survey contains no income data.

Table 1.1   *Sources and sample sizes in the ECHP*

Country	Data sources	Years covered by survey	Sample of households	Sample of adults
Finland	ECHP	1996–2001	4 139	8 173
Sweden	Swedish Living Conditions Survey (ULF)*	1997–2001	5 891	9 594
Denmark	ECHP	1994–2001	3 482	5 903
Netherlands	Dutch Socio-Economic Panel (SEP) *	1994–2001	5 187	9 407
UK	ECHP	1994–96	5 779	10 517
	British Household Panel Survey (BHPS)*	1994–2001	5 126	9 028
Ireland	ECHP	1994–2001	4 048	9 904
Belgium	Panel Study on Belgian Households (PSBH)*	1994–2001	3 490	6 710
Luxembourg	S/E Panel 'Living in Luxembourg' (PSELL-I)*	1994–96	1 011	2 046
	PSELL-II*	1995–2001	2 978	6 786
France	ECHP	1994–2001	7 344	14 333
Germany	ECHP	1994–96	4 968	9 490
	German Socio-Economic Panel (SOEP)*	1994–2001	6 207	12 233
Austria	ECHP	1995–2001	3 380	7 437
Portugal	ECHP	1994–2001	4 881	11 621
Spain	ECHP	1994–2001	7 206	17 893
Italy	ECHP	1994–2001	7 115	17 729
Greece	ECHP	1994–2001	5 523	12 492

Notes: Asterisks (*) denote countries where the standard ECHP questionnaire was not used, and where data may not be fully consistent with standard forms.
The last year of data available for our analysis was 1999 in most cases, except where the series terminates earlier, as shown in column 3.

These features of the ECHP, plus data on sample sizes, are summarised in Table 1.1.

Clearly, the mode of data collection means that it is not possible to compare all countries on every indicator for every year. In the chapters which follow, the number of years of the ECHP which are analysed ranges from one (if the focus of interest is on the current situation, rather than changes over time) up to six (depending partly on the number of waves available when particular projects were undertaken, but also on the availability of particular items of data in particular waves).

Additionally, some chapters report findings for the whole EU, while others omit certain countries on grounds of small sample size (Luxembourg), lack of panel data (Sweden), absence of data for a particular year (Austria, Finland, Sweden), the absence of particular questions from the source survey, or for other reasons. Some sections focus on two or three selected countries to illustrate particular issues, and occasionally, results are reported from surveys other than the ECHP: the British Household Panel Survey, the German Socio-Economic Panel, the Dutch Socio-Economic Panel, or Danish administrative data.

As well as straightforward issues of the availability of particular items of data for different year/country combinations, there are also more subtle issues of interpretation which arise when analysing data from a combination of surveys carried out by different organisations, in different languages, in different countries. In particular, questions may have been interpreted differently by respondents in different countries because of linguistic nuances or institutional variations (see Chapter 2). And even when the interpretation of questions appears to be consistent between countries, the interpretation of results by the analyst must be done with care, to avoid making arbitrary and culture-specific assumptions about the meaning of observed patterns.

Data: access and continuity

Despite the difficulties referred to above, which are inherent in any cross-national project of this scope, the ECHP has provided a great leap forward in the availability of data for cross-national comparative research in Europe, and especially in the provision of a longitudinal element.

The more the pity, then, that this outstanding resource has not been disseminated more effectively to the academic community in the European research area. Far from encouraging its availability, Eurostat charges for access to the data at rates beyond the means of many researchers and smaller institutions; and it imposes significant restrictions on the uses to which the ECHP may be put even by those institutions that have paid for a licence. Both of these limitations run quite counter to the trend towards wider availability of micro-data offered by many national statistical offices and academic sources.

It is also to be regretted that the full-scale household panel survey represented by the ECHP will not continue. The final wave of interviews was carried out in 2001, so eight waves of data will eventually be available. Not only will the existing harmonised panel come to an end; it will not be replaced by a new one. The plans for a new set of cross-European Statistics on Incomes and Living Conditions (EU SILC) require member states to provide a much more limited set of longitudinal indicators, leaving each country to devise its own method of collecting the data. The 1994–2001 period may eventually turn out to have been a golden age for comparative analysis of the issues addressed here. All the more reason, then, to take the best advantage of the ECHP while its findings are still up to date.

TWO RESOURCES FOR ECHP ANALYSTS

EPUNet: The EuroPanel Users' Network offers support services and communications for both new and experienced analysts of the ECHP. See http://epunet.essex.ac.uk

CHER: The Consortium of Household Panels in European Comparative Research has combined data extracted from the ECHP with similar data from several other countries to construct a single harmonised data base. See http://cher.ceps.lu/scripts/CherLinks.htm

---

Explaining and Interpreting Differences between Countries: 'Welfare Regimes'[3]

In Figure 1.1, we conceptualised people making choices as individual agents, in the context of three sets of external influences: social norms, economic conditions, and institutions/policies. Within any single country, it is difficult enough to identify the impact of the different types of influence; however, institutional changes and fluctuations in economic conditions can help identify these effects. The difficulties are multiplied when we consider the same set of questions in the context of international comparisons. We may think of the variation in outcomes across the whole of Europe as being partitioned into variations between individuals *within* countries, and variations *between* countries. Key questions, then, are (a) what is the size of the 'country effect' in comparison with the overall range of differences between individuals, and (b) to what factors are these country effects attributable? The relatively small number of countries available for inclusion in any cross-European comparison (15 at present) limits the inferences which may be drawn about the factors behind cross-country variations. With 50 states in the USA functioning as observation points for policy, informed inferences may be drawn from quantitative research on the effects of policy and institutions. With the 15 European countries in the ECHP, this is not possible, and thus, however sophisticated our quantitative techniques, we are often forced to make essentially qualitative judgements about the reasons behind the variations observed between countries.

As an example, we see in Chapter 3 that young people move into the labour market over five years later in Italy than they do in the UK or Austria. The first question we might ask is whether the faster or the slower rate of moving into employment is associated with greater well-being for young people – the answer to this is certainly not clear from the figures alone. Secondly, we might ask why these differences arise. How far can the fact that young Italians are later in getting a job or leaving home be attributed to differences in economic conditions that would apply wherever they lived? How far can the differences between countries be attributed to social policy – for example, on employment and housing – and how far might they be reduced if policy were to converge? How far might they be explained by differences between Italian and British or Austrian social norms? How far does 'country' as such play a role in people's lives?

Of course, there is no reason why 'country' should be the only possible unit of analysis. That would be appropriate if we believed that the current allocation of territories and ethnic groups to nation-states provided the most effective differentiation. But to say that 'country' is the key unit is to assume that, for example, the north of France has much more in common with the Midi than it does with the Walloon (French-speaking) region of Belgium. One can immediately think of all sorts of areas, even within Europe, where the economic or cultural boundaries between regions (within a country) may be as relevant to analysis as the boundaries between countries.

Much of the raw household survey data that has been available in the past has represented a set of countries selected by the availability of data. That leads to an analytical approach which compares 'this' country with 'that' country, or establishes a range of diversity between a number of countries, each considered representative of a category. The ECHP provides, for the first time, a micro-data set that represents the EU as a whole, as well as each of its members. That allows us to interpret the data in terms of an overall distribution (of family types, of employment positions and of household incomes) and distinguish more rigorously between individual variation and country effects.

Typologies
Once we have identified the range of variation between countries, a subsequent question is how far the observable characteristics of countries (political tradition, economic prosperity, religious background and so on) can be used to explain the between-country component.

Perhaps the most useful way of trying to make sense of country-level data is to organise countries into categories that are hypothesised to have some underlying similarity. This is attractive partly because it allows a greater degree of simplicity and parsimony when examining inter-country differences, but mainly because it provides a theoretical underpinning for categorising and interpreting these differences. The most common means for classifying countries has been on the basis of characteristics of their welfare regimes: this idea has been the subject of a good deal of research over the 1990s (Esping-Andersen, 1990, 1999; Goodin et al., 1999; Hicks and Kenworthy, 2003 and others). Basing a schema on welfare regimes provides clear advantages for the analysis of social policy and social welfare, though its relevance to other areas such as family formation or employment patterns is less obvious and not well established. It is part of the task of this book to assess how well a schema based on welfare regimes performs in explaining variations between countries in a number of different spheres of life.

One of the most widely used groupings is the typology of welfare states proposed by Esping-Andersen (1990 and 1999). He identified the following regime types:

1. The 'social-democratic' regime type, with generous levels of state support, with benefits based on individual and universal entitlement, and an emphasis on support from the state, rather than the family or the market. This is typified by the Scandinavian countries.
2. The 'liberal' regime type, with rather modest levels of benefits and an emphasis on the market as the dominant means of support. Benefits are heavily means-tested to target those most in need. This regime type is prominent in English-speaking countries, and is represented in Europe by the UK and Ireland.
3. The 'conservative' regime type, with an emphasis on the central role of the family in support for individuals, with a reduced role for the state, and a predominance of insurance-based benefits. Esping-Andersen includes the countries of continental Europe in this group: the Benelux countries; France, Germany and Austria; plus the southern peninsula countries of Spain, Portugal, Greece and Italy.

Table 1.2 (Esping-Andersen, 1999) summarises the criteria by which countries are allocated between these three regime types.

Esping-Andersen's typology is not without its critics. Of particular importance for those engaged in cross-European research is the lack of a separate category for southern European countries, as proposed by Leibfried (1992), Lessenich (1995) and Ferrara (1999). The case for this was rejected by Esping-Andersen on the grounds that the welfare states of all the countries in his 'conservative' group had certain features in common, in particular their emphasis on the family as a means of support.

Table 1.2   Summary overview of regime characteristics

Factor	Liberal	Social-democratic	Conservative
Role of family	Marginal	Marginal	Central
Role of market	Central	Marginal	Marginal
Role of state	Marginal	Central	Subsidiary
Dominant mode of solidarity	Individual	Universal	Kinship Corporatism Etatism
Dominant locus of solidarity	Market	State	Family
Degree of decommodification	Minimal	Maximum	High (for breadwinner)
Model examples	USA	Sweden	Germany Italy

Source: Esping-Andersen (1999).

However, in spite of the similarities between welfare states across this group of countries, it is undeniable that on virtually all the outcome measures assessed in this book, the southern European countries form a group distinct from the remainder of continental Europe. Thus, we divide Esping-Andersen's 'conservative' group into two:

3a.   The 'corporatist' regime type of Belgium, Luxembourg, France, Germany and Austria.
3b.   The 'residual' regime type of the southern European countries: Portugal, Spain, Italy and Greece.

The Netherlands also requires special attention. Our 'standard' typology contradicts Esping-Andersen (1999) by allocating the Netherlands to the 'social-democratic' (rather than the 'corporatist') regime type. However, Esping-Andersen himself was ambivalent about the position of the Netherlands, and in a number of the chapters which follow, it will be clear that the Netherlands does constitute a hybrid case, having elements in common with both the social-democratic Scandinavian countries and with its corporatist continental neighbours.

This fourfold allocation of countries to groups as explained above and listed again in the first column of Table 1.3 is used as standard throughout the book: this allocation may be assumed to apply unless the text or tables specifically propose a different grouping. Additionally, for ease of reference, tables and charts throughout the book use the ordering of countries in the first column of Table 1.3 as standard, unless stated otherwise.

Table 1.3   Three ways of categorising EU countries

Welfare regime	Geography	Religion	
Social-democratic	*Scandinavia*	*Protestant*	
Finland	Finland	Finland	0
Sweden	Sweden	Sweden	0
Denmark	Denmark	Denmark	0
Netherlands	*North-west islands*	*Mainly Protestant*	
Liberal	UK	UK	15
UK	Ireland	Netherlands	36
Ireland	*Continent*	Germany	37
Corporatist	Netherlands	*Mainly Catholic*	
Belgium	Belgium	Belgium	75
Luxembourg	Luxembourg	Austria	85
France	France	*Catholic/Orthodox*	
Germany	Germany	France	90
Austria	Austria	Ireland	93
Residual	*Southern peninsulas*	Luxembourg	97
Portugal	Portugal	Portugal	97
Spain	Spain	Greece	98
Italy	Italy	Spain	99
Greece	Greece	Italy	100

Note: Percentages in the right-hand column show the proportion of the population of each country affiliated to the Catholic (or Orthodox) church (CIA, 1998).

However, given the aim of this book to provide a critical assessment of the usefulness of welfare-regime typologies in explaining cross-country differences in different spheres of life, a number of chapters *do* explore alternative groupings of countries.

Table 1.3 also illustrates two alternative ways of classifying countries, which produce groupings very similar to the welfare-regime typology:

- *Geography*: It is hypothesised that neighbouring countries are likely to have close social links, and to experience similar economic conditions.

Within Western Europe, a north/south divide is most commonly identified: the Scandinavian countries at one end, the southern (often erroneously referred to as Mediterranean) countries at the other. There is no consensus about how the large group of countries in between should be ordered. Table 1.3 lists them roughly from north-west to south-east.

- *Religion*: The hypothesis here is that a country's historical religious affiliation will have such an important effect on other areas of social and economic life as to be a primary criterion for comparison. Countries are listed in Table 1.3 in order of the proportion of the population reported to be Catholics (or Orthodox in Greece) (CIA, 1998). That objective listing is not always followed by analysts, who tend not to group France, Belgium or Luxembourg among the characteristically 'Catholic' countries.

All of these approaches are of value, and their application will be illustrated in the chapters which follow. It is sometimes helpful to develop a hybrid categorisation, using a combination of these three criteria to define groups of countries that appear to have similar outcomes. There are two main difficulties. One is that, as the listings in Table 1.3 show, there is a strong overlap between the classification systems. The three Scandinavian and the four southern countries appear at the opposite ends of each scale. So it is not possible to say whether differences between them are attributable to social policy regime, geographical position, religious affiliation or some other variable. It is only among the remaining eight countries that the ordering varies from model to model, and these are therefore crucial to the interpretation of processes.

The second difficulty is that analysts do not always establish that all the countries in one group are distinct from all the countries in another group in the outcome under consideration – or if not, how effective the categories are at distinguishing between country outcomes. It is not uncommon for analysts to choose three or four countries each as 'representative' of their hypothesised group; or for data to be pooled across all the countries in a group, so that within-group differences are masked. Both of these approaches help analysts to find differences between groups, but discourage them from testing the validity of the classification system as an explanatory model.

We have not tried to force every analysis in this book into a single model which uses 'welfare regime' to explain differences between countries. Sometimes this typology is a helpful way of comparing country outcomes; sometimes an alternative framework seems more appropriate; sometimes the differences between countries defy generalisation. As often as possible we have allowed readers to form their own views.

The fact that there are substantial differences between countries should not blind us to the fact that there are also important similarities and uniformities in the underlying processes which determine people's lives across Europe. In our investigation of the spectrum of experience across Europe, we highlight both the differences and similarities – and we hope this book goes some way towards helping to illuminate them.

Notes

1. Of course it can be argued that other dimensions in the nexus of life chances – education, health, location and so on – should also be considered. We limit the dimensions directly studied to three simply to avoid over-complicating the analysis.
2. Longitudinal data sets of longer standing, such as the PSID in the USA, enable individuals' lives to be tracked over longer periods. Nevertheless, even with these longer-established data sets, the focus of the analysis is usually essentially short term.
3. See Gauthier (2002), Goldthorpe (1997), Hantrais and Mangen (1996) and Kohn (1989) for more detailed reviews of comparative research methodology.

References

Bane, M. and D. Ellwood (1994), *Welfare Realities: from Rhetoric to Reform*, Cambridge MA: Harvard University Press.

Berthoud, R. and J. Gershuny (eds) (2000), *Seven Years in the Lives of British Families*, Bristol: Policy Press.

Bourdieu, Pierre (1986) 'The forms of capital', in John G. Richardson (ed.) *Handbook of Theory and Research for the Sociology of Education*, New York: Greenwood Press.

CIA (1998), *The World Factbook*, Central Intelligence Agency.

Elder, G.H. (1994) 'Time, human agency, and social change: perspectives on the life course', *Social Psychology Quarterly*, **57**, 4–15.

Elder, G.H. (1998) 'The life course as developmental theory', *Child Development*, **69**, 1–12.

Esping-Andersen, G. (1990), *The Three Worlds of Welfare Capitalism*, Cambridge: Polity Press.

Esping-Andersen (1999), *Social Foundations of Post Industrial Economies*, Oxford: Oxford University Press.

Ferrara, M. (1999), 'The 'southern model' of welfare in social Europe', *Journal of European Social Policy*, **6** (1), 179–89.

*Gauthier, A. (2002), 'The promises of comparative research', *Schmollers Jahrbuch (Journal of Applied Social Science Studies)*, **122** (1), 5–30.

Goldthorpe, J. (1997), 'Current issues in comparative macrosociology: a debate on methodological issues', *Comparative Social Research*, **16**, 1–26.

Goodin, B., B. Healy, R. Muffels and H. Dirven (1999), *The Real Worlds of Welfare Capitalism*, Cambridge: Cambridge University Press.

Hantrais, L. and S. Mangen (eds) (1996), *Cross-national Research Methods in the Social Sciences*, London: Pinter

Hicks, A. and L. Kenworthy (2003), 'Varieties of welfare capitalism', *Socioeconomic Review*, **1**, 27–61.

Iacovou, M. and R. Berthoud (2001), *Young People's Lives: a Map of Europe*, Colchester: University of Essex, Institute for Social and Economic Research.

Kohn, M. (1989), *Cross-national Research in Sociology*, London: Sage.

Lessenich, S. (1995), 'Wohlfahrtsstaatliche Regulierung und die Strukturierung von Lebensläufen: zur selektivität sozialpolitischer interventionen', *Soziale Welt*, **1**, 51–69.

Leibfried, S. (1992), 'Towards a European welfare state? On integrating poverty regimes into the European community', in Z. Ferge and J. Kolberg (eds) *Social Policy in a Changing Europe*, Frankfurt am Main: Campus Verlag.

Murphy, M. (1987), 'Measuring the life-cycle: concepts, data and methods', in A. Bryman et al. (eds), *Rethinking the Life-cycle*, Basingstoke: Macmillan.

Putnam, Robert D. (2000) *Bowling Alone: the Collapse and Revival of American Community*, New York: Simon & Schuster.

Wirtz, C. and L. Mejer (2002), 'The European Community Household Panel (ECHP)', *Schmollers Jahrbuch (Journal of Applied Social Science Studies)*, **122** (1), 143–54.

* Direct output from EPAG's *DynSoc* research programme (see page 268)

2.   Patterns of Family Living

Maria Iacovou

Introduction

This chapter describes how patterns of family living vary across the EU. Its position near the beginning of the book reflects our opinion that an understanding of the variations in family patterns across countries is of great importance in understanding and interpreting variations in other aspects of life. Living arrangements may affect people's behaviour in the labour market; their incomes; and, via their access to shared household resources, their chances of experiencing poverty and hardship.

The chapter begins with some general descriptions of household structures, and proceeds to examine issues of particular interest: young people's living arrangements; the later-life outcomes of women who gave birth as teenagers; the amount of time mothers spend caring for their children; and the family structures of older people. As well as describing family patterns, this chapter also asks *why* they vary so much. Are the big differences across Europe a result of factors such as employment or incomes – or do they have more to do with culture and preferences?

One of the simplest, yet most informative, indicators of family patterns is average household size, which is shown in Figure 2.1 for 14 countries. Household size differs greatly between countries, ranging from 2.1 in Sweden and Denmark to 3.2 in Spain and Ireland. The large differences in this aggregate indicator shows that there must also be substantial differences in underlying household structures at a more detailed level.

Countries in Figure 2.1 are ranked in order of average household size. This ordering reveals certain clusters of countries: the Scandinavian countries have the smallest households in Europe, while the southern countries have some of the largest. These clusters correspond to the welfare-regime-based 'social-democratic' and 'residual' groups, as discussed in Chapter 1. However, the UK and Ireland, which on the basis of welfare-regime typologies would both be allocated to the 'liberal' group of welfare regimes, have very little in common on the household size indicator. The UK has similar-sized households to the 'corporatist' countries, while Ireland's large households are more typical of the southern countries. These differences between the UK and Ireland are not restricted to household size; as will become clear, they run through almost all aspects of family patterns.[1]

Figure 2.1   Average household size

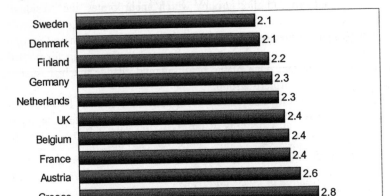

Source: ECHP (1994–99), author's own calculations.

Given that many aspects of family patterns do not fit the standard welfare-regime typology well (and that this may be expected, since welfare state provision is only one of several influences on family structure) it may be more useful to think of family patterns as occupying a continuum, rather than discrete groups defined by a typology based on welfare state characteristics.

A regional/religious gradient, running from northern/Protestant to southern/Catholic or Orthodox, fits observed patterns rather well, and as Table 1.3 in Chapter 1 shows, the ordering of countries under such a gradient is actually rather close to the ordering under a welfare-regime typology. And thinking in terms of such a regional/religious gradient allows us to consider multiple influences on family structure – in particular the role of cultural and religious factors.

For most of the analysis in this chapter, data are displayed for individual countries. However, where for analytical purposes it becomes necessary to divide countries into groups rather than working with the entire continuum, three groups of countries have been defined. First is a 'Nordic' group, consisting of the Scandinavian countries plus the Netherlands – which corresponds to the 'social-democratic' group defined in Chapter 1. The second group is a 'northern/Protestant' group, which incorporates the continental European 'corporatist' countries, as well as the UK. The third group is a 'southern/Catholic' group, which incorporates the 'residual' welfare regimes, plus Ireland. Austria (a member of Esping-Andersen's 'corporatist' group, and not obviously a member of the southern/Catholic group on the basis of geography) is also allocated to this group for pooled analysis – though in fact none of the results would change much if Austria were switched to the 'northern' group.

Figure 2.2 shows the distribution of household types in 14 countries distinguishing between households containing one, two and three or more adults over the age of 18, and for each of these, between those without children under 18 and those with children.

Figure 2.2   Distribution of household types

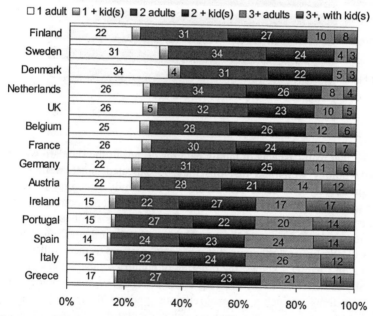

Source: ECHP (1994–99), author's own calculations.

In every country, the commonest household type consists of two adults, with slightly fewer than half of all two-adult households having one or more members under 18 years old. In southern/Catholic countries, the two-adult household is rather less common than in northern/Protestant countries, with the proportion of two-adult households ranging from 46 per cent and 47 per cent in Spain and Italy, up to 58 per cent in Sweden and Denmark.

However, the big differences between countries are in the proportions of smaller and larger households. Single-adult households are much more common in the Nordic countries, accounting for 34 per cent and 39 per cent of the total in Sweden and Denmark. By contrast, they are much less common in southern/Catholic countries, accounting for less than 19 per cent of the total in Italy, Spain, Portugal, Greece and Ireland.

Differences in the proportion of households consisting of three or more adults are even more pronounced. These larger households account for only 8 per cent of the total in Denmark and Sweden, but they form over 30 per cent of the total in the southern/Catholic countries, and close to 40 per cent in Italy and Spain.

Figure 2.3   *Living arrangements of children under 18*

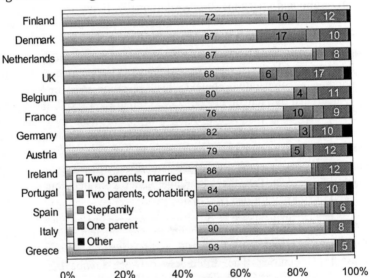

Source: ECHP (1994–99), author's own calculations.

Finally in this introductory section, Figure 2.3 shows the living arrangements of children and young people aged under 18. In all countries, the most common situation is to live with both their natural parents, who are married. The proportions range from 67 per cent in Denmark up to 93 per cent in Greece. The proportion living with both natural parents in a cohabiting relationship ranges from only a few per cent in Catholic/southern countries, up to 17 per cent in Denmark. Stepfamilies are similarly a rarity in the southern/Catholic group of countries, with the proportion rising to 5 per cent or more in Denmark, Finland and the UK. Lone-parent families (which may consist of divorced, separated, widowed or never-married parents) are relatively uncommon in all countries, and the incidence of lone-parent families does not vary systematically across groups of countries. However, lone-parent families are more common in the UK than anywhere else in Europe, accounting for 17 per cent of the families of children and young people.

Young People: Leaving Home, Finding a Partner, Starting a Family

Young people's living arrangements are of particular interest to social scientists because the transition from residential dependence (living with parents) to residential autonomy (living in one's own home) is seen as an important component of the transition to adulthood (Cavalli and Galland, 1995; Schizzerotto and Lucchini, 2002). Additionally, living arrangements in the early years of adulthood are dependent, perhaps more than at any other time of life, on an individual's economic circumstances.

Although many studies of 'youth' and 'young people' concern themselves with individuals aged between (say) 16 and 25 years of age, when studying home-leaving in a comparative context, this age range must be extended upwards – as argued by Iacovou (1999, 2002a). Figure 2.4 shows the age by which half of all young people are living away from home in a range of countries (this is an approximate estimate of the median age at leaving home). As half of all young Italian men have not left the parental home at age 30 (and young men in the other southern/Catholic countries are nearly as slow to leave home) it is clear that the age range under consideration must be extended well beyond 30 for this type of analysis.

Home-leaving occurs a great deal earlier in the northern/Protestant, and particularly in the Nordic, groups of countries. The 'median' age at leaving home for men is 21 in Denmark and 22 in Finland, and even earlier for women in these countries. The differences between groups of countries reported in Figure 2.4 are consistent with earlier work in this area, for example Kiernan (1986).

Women leave home earlier than men in all countries – a year or two earlier in the Scandinavian countries, but a full five years earlier in Greece. Since many young people leave home to live with a partner, this gender difference is at least partly attributable to age differences between men and women in couples. In most countries the man is on average a little over two years older than the woman, while in Greece the average age difference is nearly five years (Iacovou, 1999).

Figure 2.4   *Age by which half of all young people are living away from*
                home

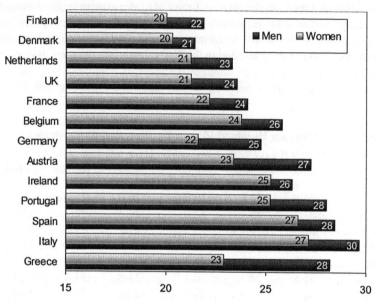

Source: ECHP (1994), adapted from Iacovou (2002a).

Table 2.1 shows the ages by which 50 per cent of young people have made
three important decisions in the domestic sphere: leaving home, living with a
partner, and having children.[2] The age at which men and women leave home
increases from north to south (with a few blips, such as the early age of
leaving home for Greek women). The age at living with a partner also
increases from north to south – although the differences between north and
south are not so stark. This is because the median age at partnering in the
northern countries is a few years higher than the median age at leaving home
– indicating that young people in these countries typically spend some time
unpartnered after leaving home. On the other hand, the median age at leaving
home in the southern countries is virtually identical to the median age at
partnering, implying that these two transitions tend to occur at the same time.
In fact, in Portugal and Spain, the partnering transition tends to occur *earlier*
than the transition to residential independence, indicating the tendency for a
proportion of young couples to live with their parents in at least the first
stages of partnership.

The age of having children also varies throughout Europe, though not
along north/south lines. Looking at the age of living with children for women,
the countries with the latest childbearing are the Netherlands and Italy – while

the countries with the earliest childbearing are Portugal and Finland. One north/south tendency which is evident is the tendency for mean age having children to be much closer to the mean age at partnering for southern countries. In Portugal the difference is less than one year; in Spain it is less than two years. By contrast, in Denmark the gap between partnering and childbearing is over five years, and in the Netherlands it is over seven years.

Table 2.1   *Median ages at leaving home, partnering and living with children*

Country	Men: age by which 50%:			Women: age by which 50%:		
	Have left home	Live with a partner	Live with children	Have left home	Live with a partner	Live with children
Finland	21.9	25.2	30.8	20.0	22.4	25.4
Denmark	21.4	25.4	32.8	20.3	22.2	27.6
Netherlands	23.3	26.1	33.2	21.2	23.2	30.7
UK	23.5	25.5	32.4	21.2	22.8	27.5
Ireland	26.3	28.3	30.5	25.2	26.7	27.2
Belgium	25.8	26.3	30.1	23.8	24.1	27.3
France	24.1	25.9	29.8	22.2	23.7	26.6
Germany	24.8	27.8	31.9	21.6	23.9	28.0
Austria	27.2	27.6	31.1	23.4	23.8	27.9
Portugal	28.0	28.2	28.8	25.2	24.9	25.3
Spain	28.4	29.0	31.3	26.6	26.5	28.2
Italy	29.7	30.3	33.8	27.1	27.4	30.3
Greece	28.2	28.7	31.0	22.9	24.2	26.4

Source: ECHP (1994), adapted from Iacovou (2002a).

This indicates that in southern countries, leaving home, partnering and becoming a parent tend to occur within a very short space of time, while in northern countries they tend to be more chronologically separated. Thus, there are strong and systematic variations in living arrangements in young people's living arrangements across Europe. Are these differences attributable to economic factors, such as the sufficiency of young people's incomes, rates of unemployment, or the degree of protection to which young people are entitled in the labour market?

There is no doubt that these economic factors play a part in determining young people's residential decisions. Smeeding and Ross Phillips (2002) assess the sufficiency of young people's incomes (including incomes from work and from social transfers) across a range of European countries. They show that the incomes of young people in Italy are substantially less sufficient for supporting residential independence, or supporting a family, than young people's incomes in Sweden or the Netherlands. Kaiser (2001) shows that insecure employment is more common (among older as well as younger workers) in southern European countries. Iacovou and Berthoud (2001) show that unemployment among young men is higher in Spain, Italy and Greece, than in all other European countries.

However, Iacovou (2001) suggests that there is also a cultural component to differences in the age at leaving home. In an examination of the dynamics of home-leaving across 13 countries, young people who live with their parents in one year (year *t*) are followed up one year later (year *t*+1), and their living arrangements recorded. In common with other studies (Avery et al., 1992; Clark and Mulder, 2000; and others) it is important to distinguish between different destinations on leaving home, since different characteristics are associated with different destinations. Leaving home as a single person should be distinguished from leaving as part of a couple, and from leaving for educational purposes; leaving to become a homeowner should be distinguished from leaving to become a private tenant or a social tenant.

Many of the results of the analysis are intuitively predictable. For example, in every group of countries, young people with higher personal incomes are more likely to move out of their parents' home, particularly to become homeowners. Young people who live with a partner in their parents' home have an increased probability of leaving the parental home the following year. However, some results are more surprising. Table 2.2 shows the effects of parental income on three possible destinations in year *t*+1: leaving home as a single person, leaving home as part of a couple, and leaving home for educational purposes. The base category is remaining in the parental home at year *t*+1.

For all groups except men in southern countries, higher parental income is associated with an increased probability of young people leaving home for educational purposes. For all groups (except, weakly, men in the Nordic group of countries) there is no association between parental income and a young person's probability of leaving home as a single person. However, looking at exits from home as part of a couple, there are large differences between different groups of countries. In the Nordic countries, higher parental income is strongly and *positively* associated with the probability of leaving home as part of a couple. In the northern group of countries, there is no association between leaving home as part of a couple and parental income. And in southern countries, there is a *negative* association between leaving home as part of a couple and higher parental income.

*Table 2.2   Effect of parental income on home-leaving behaviour
(multinomial logit coefficients)*

	Nordic		Northern		Southern	
	Men	Women	Men	Women	Men	Women
as a single	0.007 *	0.006	0.004	0.001	0.005	−0.001
as a couple	0.010 ***	0.014 **	0.004	0.003	−0.004 **	−0.003 *
for education	0.016 ***	0.018 ***	0.009 **	0.010 **	0.006	0.012 ***

Notes: Parental income at year *t* is measured in centiles within the home country.
Asterisks denote significance of coefficients: *** 1%, ** 5%, * 10%.
Source: ECHP (1994–97), from Iacovou (2001).

What do these results tell us about how preferences differ across countries? One may think of parents and children in all countries as valuing two things: a sense of privacy, which is enhanced by the young person moving out of the family home; and a sense of family closeness, or togetherness, which is enhanced by continuing coresidence. In general, higher incomes give parents and children greater freedom to enter a state which more closely fulfils their own preferences. For example, if parents value privacy more highly than family togetherness, more affluent parents will be able to help their children leave home by providing help with the costs of setting up home independently. If, on the other hand, parents value family togetherness more highly than privacy, more affluent parents may choose to use their resources to induce children to remain at home for longer: for example, by providing access to resources to be consumed at home, such as cars or other consumer durables.

The fact that, controlling for many other factors, the children of more affluent parents in the Nordic group of countries have a much higher probability of moving out of home as part of a couple, suggests that in this group of countries parents have a preference for privacy. By contrast, the fact that the children of more affluent parents in southern countries are *less* likely to move out as part of a couple suggests that in these countries parents have a preference for family 'togetherness'.

This section has shown that there are pronounced differences in home-leaving behaviour across countries, with the age of home-leaving quite closely following a north/south – Protestant/Catholic gradient. These differences are undoubtedly due in part to economic and labour market differences between countries, but they are also due in part to differences in preferences.

Teenage Mothers

Teenage mothers are a minority in all countries: nine out of ten babies in Western countries are born when the mother is in her twenties or thirties (Eurostat, 1999). Nevertheless, despite the relative (and increasing) rarity of childbearing in the teenage years, teenage motherhood is of concern to governments, and thus to researchers, for two main reasons. The first set of reasons is medical: teenage mothers and their babies show higher than average risks of unsatisfactory progress during pregnancy, birth and the baby's early years (Strobino, 1992; Fraser et al., 1995; Cunnington, 2001). The second set of reasons is social and economic, with teenage mothers experiencing social disadvantage on many measures of education, housing, employment and family income (Hoffman et al., 1993; Ribar, 1999; Wellings et al., 1999).

Although teenage motherhood appears to be associated with some adverse outcomes in all the Western countries where these have been studied, the degree of disadvantage varies a good deal between countries. Berthoud and Robson (2003) use the 1996 ECHP to study how later-life outcomes associated with teenage motherhood vary across countries, focusing on a set of five socio-economic indicators. These are: (1) having less than secondary-level education; (2) having no partner; (3) not having a job; (4) living in a family where neither the woman nor her partner has a job; and (5) having household income in the bottom fifth of the distribution in one's own country.

Table 2.3   Five outcomes: teenage mothers compared with women who first became mothers in their twenties

Age of woman at first birth	15–19	20–29	Ratio
Less than upper secondary education	67	34	2.0
Without partner	23	19	1.2
Not working (inactive or unemployed)	59	41	1.4
Neither woman nor partner is working	26	8	3.3
Household income below bottom quintile	45	21	2.1

Notes: All Europe (13 countries), weighted.
All differences between age groups are statistically significant at the 5 per cent level.
Source: ECHP (1994–96), from Berthoud and Robson (2003).

On a Europe-wide level, Table 2.3 shows that the risks of all these outcomes are higher for women who gave birth in their teens. The starkest contrast between the two groups of mothers is on the outcome of living in a family where neither the woman nor her partner is working, which is over three times more common among women who became mothers as teenagers.

The object of Berthoud and Robson's (2003) research is not to estimate teenage birth rates for the EU: these figures are already published in the official statistics, and in fact women who became mothers as teenagers are slightly under-represented in the ECHP. Nevertheless, it is useful to begin with a look at prevalence rates for teenage motherhood; these are shown in Table 2.4.

Table 2.4   *Teenage birth rates: annual rates per 1 000 women under 20*

Finland	9	Germany	13
Denmark	8	Austria	14
Netherlands	6	Portugal	21
UK	31	Spain	8
Ireland	17	Italy	7
Belgium	10	Greece	12
France	9		

Source: UNICEF (2001).

This table shows that annual teenage birth rates range from 6 per 1 000 women in the Netherlands up to 31 per 1 000 women in the UK. Other EU countries with low teenage birth rates are Denmark, Italy, Finland, France and Spain; other countries with high teenage birth rates are Portugal, Ireland and Austria. Clearly, teenage birth rates do not follow the regional patterns that are evident in many other aspects of family formation.

Berthoud and Robson (2003) assess the relationship between the age at first motherhood and the various socio-economic outcomes in each country; the estimated country-specific coefficients are given in Table 2.5. Figures in the first column estimate the relationship between the age at first motherhood and educational qualifications; the figures relate to the increase in the probability of a woman having upper-secondary-level qualifications, with every year that motherhood is delayed up to age 28. For all countries, the coefficients are significant at the 5 per cent level or better.

The figures in the other four columns relate to the difference in the probability of the remaining four outcomes, between two groups of women: those who gave birth as teenagers, and those who first gave birth in their twenties. For each outcome, a positive coefficient indicates that a woman who gave birth as a teenager is more likely (and a negative coefficient indicates that she is less likely) to be in the situation in question. The coefficients indicate that teenage mothers are more likely to be lone parents in later life,

Figure 2.5   *Poverty associated with teenage motherhood, by frequency of*
              teenage motherhood

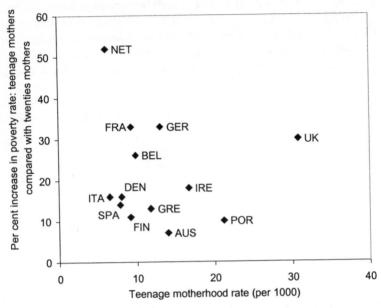

Source: Teenage motherhood rates from UNICEF (2001); per cent increase in poverty rates
           from Berthoud and Robson (2003).

and more likely to live in low-income families; they are also less likely to
have a job themselves or to live with a partner who has a job.

Table 2.5 shows that teenage motherhood is associated with negative later-
life outcomes in all countries, but the extent of the association varies – the
coefficients are not all significant and they do vary in magnitude between
countries. In Ireland, the UK and Belgium, all coefficients are significant, and
the effects tend to be large. In Greece, Austria and Finland, by contrast, the
estimated coefficients are much smaller and not significant. Differences in
impacts do not appear to follow either the north/south gradient used in this
section, nor (with the exception of particularly adverse outcomes in the UK
and Ireland) do they follow the welfare-regime typologies discussed in
Chapter 1.

However, Berthoud and Robson (2003) suggest that the between-country
differences in the *impact* of teenage motherhood are related to differences in
the *prevalence* of teenage motherhood. Figure 2.5 plots the increased
incidence of poverty associated with teenage versus twenties motherhood,
against the prevalence of teenage motherhood in each country.

Table 2.5 Relationship between age at first motherhood and five outcome measures (logistic regression coefficients)

Country	Upper secondary qualifications? (1,2)	Currently a lone parent? (3)	Woman has a job? (2,4)	Someone in family has a job? (2)	Family in lowest income quintile? (2)
Finland	0.20 **	0.76	-0.13	0.25	0.56
Denmark	0.27 **	0.28	-0.14	-0.94 **	1.46 **
Netherlands	0.13 **	0.52	-0.36	-1.63 **	2.29 **
UK	0.21 **	1.33 **	-0.56 **	-0.95 **	1.00 **
Belgium	0.21 **	1.19 **	-0.59 **	-0.70 **	0.49
France	0.23 **	0.36	-0.98 **	-0.83 **	1.45 **
Germany	0.14 **	0.61	-0.96 **	-1.29 **	1.17 **
Austria	0.17 **	-0.04	-0.17	0.09	0.42
Ireland	0.26 **	1.95 **	-0.96 **	-0.96 **	0.94 **
Portugal	0.25 **	0.62 **	-0.09	-0.70 **	0.72 **
Spain	0.20 **	1.22 **	0.18	-0.38	0.52 **
Italy	0.19 **	1.59 **	0.00	-0.77 **	0.41 **
Greece	0.28 **	-0.54	0.03	0.36	0.58 **

Notes: (1) Logistic regression coefficients for every year motherhood is delayed, up to age 28, are reported in the first column. Coefficients in other columns all compare teenage mothers to all other mothers. Figures in bold type denote coefficients significant at 5% level or better.
(2) Also controls for mother's age.
(3) Also controls for years since first birth.
(4) Also controls for age of youngest child.

Source: Adapted from Berthoud and Robson (2003).

This analysis suggests a negative relationship between the prevalence of teenage motherhood and the degree of associated disadvantage. In countries where teenage motherhood is common, its consequences appear to be less severe, and vice versa. The most notable exception is the UK, which has the highest rate of teenage motherhood in the EU, but where teenage motherhood is associated with a high risk of poverty.

Mothers' Time with Children

The tendency for more mothers to enter the labour force has meant that children are spending an increasing amount of time being cared for by people other than their own parents. This has implications both for parental well-being and for children's development: time with parents is considered to be a crucial input into children's cognitive, social-emotional and educational development, and may be regarded as an important intergenerational transfer of wealth (Hill and Stafford, 1985).

There are few studies investigating the amount of time parents in Europe spend with their children, and even fewer which investigate this in a comparative context. Joesch and Spiess (2002) have examined the amount of time European mothers spend looking after their children; how this differs from country to country; and how far these differences may be attributed to different personal and institutional characteristics between countries.

In the ECHP, every individual aged 16 or over was asked whether their normal daily activities, apart from any job or business, included looking after children without pay, and respondents who answered in the affirmative were asked the weekly time spent in this activity. These rather broad questions omit some relevant details (for example, there is no distinction between times when a parent is actively involved in care as a sole activity, as opposed to simply having responsibility for the child while also being engaged in other activities). Additionally, this type of question poses problems in a comparative survey, since it relies heavily on interpretation within a social context. Four countries (Belgium, Finland, France and Portugal) were dropped from the sample because of concerns about the imperfect harmonisation of questions. Even in the remaining countries where the questions appear to be properly harmonised, there is a possibility that responses may be sensitive to respondents' perceptions of cultural norms within their own countries.

However, these concerns aside, the childcare questions in the ECHP do enable a degree of comparison between countries, which has not hitherto been possible. The first column of Table 2.6 shows the mean weekly time that mothers report spending looking after their children. This varies from 37.1 hours in Greece, up to 73.0 hours in the UK.

Table 2.6   *European mothers' reported weekly time spent (in hours) caring for children*

Country	Sample mean	Predicted mean (a)	Predicted mean (b)
Denmark	45.9	43.1	42.1
Netherlands	57.7	57.7	57.0
UK	73.0	71.2	71.8
Ireland	66.9	63.3	63.0
Luxembourg	44.4	44.1	44.0
Germany	51.0	52.7	52.5
Austria	54.9	54.3	54.6
Spain	53.0	52.4	52.5
Greece	37.1	39.9	40.1

Notes: Predictions based on Tobit models estimated separately for each country.
Predicted means represent average weekly hours of childcare predicted in each country, if mothers in each country had (a) the socio-demographic characteristics, and (b) both the socio-demographic and the employment characteristics, of the 'average' European mother.

Source: ECHP (1996), from Joesch and Spiess (2002).

Joesch and Spiess then go on to examine whether these large reported inter-country differences may be explained by differences in family structure, the women's own characteristics, or labour markets. For example, if mothers in one country tend to have more children, or more very young children, than mothers in a second country, this may be reflected in longer hours caring for children in the first country. As well as the numbers and ages of children, the following factors were taken into account as possible covariates of time spent in childcare:

- the number of adult family members present in the household;
- the mother's marital status;
- mother's and father's employment status;
- mother's educational level;
- mother's age;
- mother is 'foreign';
- family financial resources; and
- household technology (measured by presence of a dishwasher).

The influences on the amount of time spent with children were estimated separately for each country, to allow effects to vary between countries.

Having done this, it was possible to calculate how much time the average mother in each country *would* spend caring for children if mothers in each country had the characteristics of the 'average' European mother. These predictions are shown in the second and third columns of Table 2.6, headed 'predicted means'. There are some differences between the actual and predicted means: for example, Greek mothers would spend around three hours more each week caring for children, and Irish mothers would spend around three hours less, if all mothers across Europe had identical characteristics.

However, the proportion of cross-national differences explained by this method is much lower than the proportion which remains after controlling for women's characteristics: thus, it appears that the covariates used to explain time spent caring for children are not particularly effective at explaining cross-national differences.

Joesch and Spiess (2002) repeat this investigation under a more formal methodology (see Oaxaca, 1973) which decomposes differences between populations into (1) a part arising from the populations' differences in characteristics, (2) a part arising from the different effects of these characteristics between populations, and (3) an unexplained residual effect. In common with the results in Table 2.6, this analysis shows that observable characteristics do not explain a very high proportion of inter-country differences in childcare.

Why should this be? Apart from questions which remain about the degree to which ECHP data are properly harmonised, Joesch and Spiess (2002) argue that many of these inter-country differences are attributable to two factors which are not captured by individual-level multivariate models. These are, first, cultural differences with respect to child-rearing, and, second, differences in social policies (such as the provision of childcare facilities, and family-friendly employment policies encouraging part-time or flexible work). Additionally, taking into account time spent by fathers in caring for their children might explain more of the variation in mothers' inputs of time.

Older People's Living Arrangements

The living arrangements of older people are of particular interest. This is in part because older people are forming a larger and larger proportion of the population (OECD, 1996). Additionally, older age may be a time of economic precariousness, with the choice of living arrangements closely related to economic well-being. Older people's living arrangements may also be subject to change due to widowhood, moving in with adult children, or moving into a residential facility – and the decision to move into a residential facility may depend on prior living arrangements (Pendry et al., 1999).

Analysis using the ECHP (Iacovou, 2000a, 2002b) shows that to a large extent older people's living arrangements follow the same regional pattern as those of younger people, with coresidence between the generations more common in the southern/Catholic countries. In the 'southern' group of countries, 33 per cent of women over age 65 live with one or more of their children; in the 'northern' group only 10 per cent live with a child; and in the 'Nordic' group, only 3 per cent live in the same household as one of their children.

It is clear that these residential differences reflect, to a degree, the differences in home-leaving behaviour among the young discussed earlier in the chapter. Thus, in southern/Catholic countries, coresidence with adult children may simply occur because these children have not yet left home, rather than because of any active preference or choice for coresidence.

Table 2.7   Living arrangements: men and women aged 65 and over (row percentages)

Category	Just partner	Partner and children	Just children	Living alone	Other
Women					
'Nordic'	45	1	2	51	1
'Northern/Protestant'	36	4	6	50	4
'Southern/Catholic'	31	11	20	33	6
Average: all	36	5	9	45	4
Men					
'Nordic'	73	3	1	23	0
'Northern/Protestant'	66	9	1	20	3
'Southern/Catholic'	55	25	6	11	3
Average: all	55	25	6	11	3

Notes: Nordic group = Finland, Sweden, Denmark, Netherlands.
         Northern/Protestant group = UK, Belgium, France, Germany.
         Southern/Catholic group = Austria, Ireland, Portugal, Spain, Italy, Greece.
Source: ECHP (1994, or the first available year for late-joining countries), from Iacovou (2002b).

However, as Figure 2.6 shows, this is not the whole story. It is certainly true that southerners experience the departure of their last child from home at a later age than other groups. However, from their early sixties onwards, southern/Catholic Europeans who have no coresident children are more likely to move in with their children than those in the 'northern/Protestant', or (particularly) the 'Nordic' group of countries.

One of the reasons why older people may move in with their adult children is in order to receive care from their children. Although Iacovou (2002b) shows that older people are just as likely to live with their sons as with their daughters in old age (and thus coresidence is not determined along the lines of gender), the bulk of *care* is provided by women. Where older people live with daughters, the daughters provide the care; but where older people live with sons, the care is provided primarily by daughters-in-law.

Figure 2.6   Transitions in older people's living arrangements

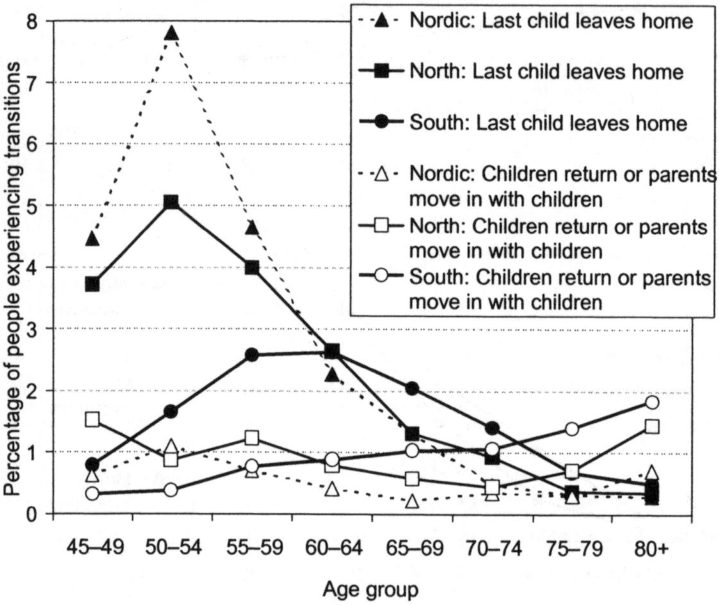

Source: ECHP (1994–97), from Iacovou (2002b).

One of the reasons why older people may move in with their adult children is in order to receive care from their children. Although Iacovou (2002b) shows that older people are just as likely to live with their sons as with their daughters in old age (and thus coresidence is not determined along the lines of gender), the bulk of *care* is provided by women. Where older people live with daughters, the daughters provide the care; but where older people live with sons, the care is provided primarily by daughters-in-law.

Figure 2.7   Proportion of older people giving and receiving care, by age group

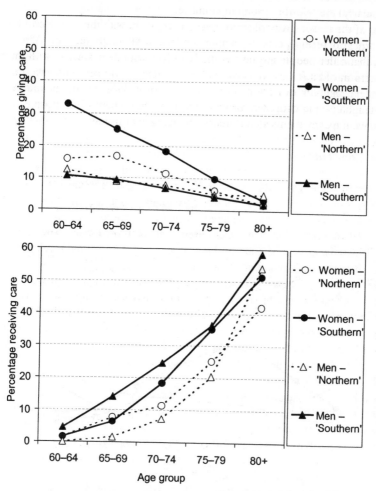

Notes: Based on the sample of older men and women living with their children.
The upper panel denotes the proportion providing childcare within the household; the lower panel indicates the proportion receiving care from another household member. The 'Nordic' group of countries is not shown on the graph as so few older people live with their children.
Source: ECHP (1994), from Iacovou (2002b).

Nevertheless, cohabitation between generations is not simply a case of the younger generation caring for their elderly parents: the older generation also helps the younger generation, by providing childcare. Figure 2.7 takes as its sample people over the age of 60 living with their adult children, and plots (in the upper panel) the proportion providing childcare within the family, and (in the lower panel) the proportion receiving care within the family.

As expected, the proportion receiving care increases with increasing age, while the proportion providing childcare falls with increasing age. Thus, it may be said that the reciprocity in this arrangement is sequential rather than contemporaneous. It is also worth noting that there is far more reciprocity in the arrangements where the elderly coresident is female. Older men receive just as much care as older women, but they provide very little childcare.

So, what makes for these differences in living arrangements? Do they arise as a result of economic differences between countries? Or do they also have a cultural component?

Iacovou (2000a) demonstrates that variations in older women's living arrangements are attributable, at least in part, to observable differences between countries in incomes and other socio-economic factors. The analysis is based on a sample of women aged 70 or over, who have no income from work, and who have one or more children. The likelihood that a woman lives alone is estimated as a function of the woman's age, educational levels, health status, marital history, number of children, and income.

This is done separately for women in 'Nordic', 'northern/Protestant' and 'southern/Catholic' groups of countries. In the 'Nordic' group of countries, it is so uncommon for older women to live with their children that there is little variation in the outcome with *any* explanatory variable. Thus, this group of countries is dropped from the analysis. There are, however, interesting differences between the other two groups of countries. Some of these differences are illustrated in Table 2.8.

Health is an important predictor of coresidence in southern/Catholic countries, where being hampered in daily activities is associated with a seven-point decrease in the probability of living alone. In northern/Protestant countries, by contrast, living arrangements are not significantly associated with health. This may reflect the greater degree of provision of in-home social services for older people with health problems in northern/Protestant countries (see for example Sundstrom, 1994; Blackman et al., 2001).

In northern/Protestant countries, living arrangements are also associated with the number of children a woman has had, with the probability of living alone decreasing with the number of children a woman has. By contrast, there is no association between living arrangements and the number of children in the south. This may be due to the much higher degree of residential mobility in northern/Protestant than in southern/Catholic countries. In countries with little residential mobility, provided a woman has at least one child, she is likely to live close enough to that child to move in with the child in older age without a great deal of disruption. By contrast, in countries with a greater degree of residential mobility, having more children increases the chance that at least one child will live close enough for an easy transition to coresidence in older age.

Table 2.8   Effects on the probability of living alone (marginal effects)

Effect	Northern/Protestant	Southern/Catholic
Health hampers activity	–0.032	–0.071 ***
Number of children	–0.030 ***	0.010
Income: effect of each percentile		
within the lowest quartile	–0.054 **	0.002
within the 2nd quartile	0.101 ***	0.003
within the 3rd quartile	–0.019	0.037 ***
within the top quartile	–0.007	–0.026

Notes: Selected marginal effects from probit regressions on women over 70.
Northern/Protestant group = UK, Belgium, France, Germany.
Southern/Catholic group = Austria, Ireland, Portugal, Spain, Italy, Greece.
Asterisks denote significance of coefficients: *** 1%, ** 5%, * 10%.
Source: ECHP (1994), from Iacovou (2000a).

Income also affects the probability of living alone. The results in Table 2.8 show the effect of increasing income in four sectors of the income distribution. They suggest the existence, in both groups of countries, of lower and upper thresholds for the sufficiency of income. The decision to live alone is not affected by the exact level of income below the lower threshold, or above the upper threshold, since incomes below the lower threshold are insufficient, and incomes above the upper threshold are always sufficient, for independent living – regardless of their exact level. However, the exact degree of income matters more at levels between the upper and lower thresholds, since here the trade-off between residential independence and financial comfort is more pronounced. The coefficients reported in Table 2.8 show that in the northern/Protestant group of countries, the major effect of income occurs in the bottom half of the income distribution, while in southern/Catholic countries it occurs closer to the top of the distribution. Thus, differences in older people's incomes between groups of countries do appear to have an effect on their living arrangements.

This analysis has shown that inter-country differences in living arrangements do depend on measurable economic and policy factors. However, it is interesting to ask whether preferences for independent living versus family living are also important, as we did in the case of young people leaving home.

Iacovou (2002b) suggests that there may again be a cultural component behind older people's choice of living arrangements. An analysis of older women's reported levels of satisfaction with their financial situation and their housing situation reveals that in six countries (Greece, Spain, Portugal, Ireland, Austria and the Netherlands) older women living with their children report significantly higher levels of satisfaction with their financial situation than those who do not live with their children. And in five countries (Greece, Italy, Spain, Portugal and Austria) older women who live with their children are significantly happier with their housing situation than those who do not. Thus, living with one's adult children tends to be associated positively with well-being in countries where this type of coresidence is more common. Caution is needed in interpreting these results, since they may indeed represent positive choices on the part of older people, but they may also represent the lack of viable alternatives to living with one's children in southern/Catholic European countries. In the southern/Catholic group of countries, where older people's financial situation is measurably more precarious, and where social services for older people are much more limited, the situation of older people living alone may be objectively difficult and unsatisfactory, and it may be this which is driving the results.

Patterns Across Europe?

This chapter has explored several aspects of family life across Europe. In this concluding section, we ask how far the typologies discussed in Chapter 1 are useful in the analysis of family patterns.

One particular aspect of family patterns – the timing of childbirth – does not fit any definable typology very well. Table 2.1 shows that countries with early fertility include Finland, France, Greece and Portugal, while the countries with the latest fertility are the Netherlands and Italy. These early- and late-fertility groups are clearly quite heterogeneous in terms of welfare regimes, geography and religion. Looking at rates of *very* early fertility, a faint pattern emerges, with the UK and Ireland (Anglo-Saxon countries with 'liberal' welfare regimes) having the highest rates of teenage motherhood. However, teenage motherhood rates in the rest of Europe do not follow any clear pattern, so the conclusion must be that although fertility patterns in individual countries may be evolving in definable ways, no general regional patterns are observable.

This lack of pattern is also visible when we consider the amount of time mothers spend looking after their children. Although the highest inputs of time are reported by mothers in the UK and Ireland (the 'liberal' regimes) –

the lowest inputs are reported by mothers in Greece, Denmark and Luxembourg, three countries which are very different in economic, cultural and institutional terms. Even controlling for economic and family factors at the individual level, no discernible pattern emerges.

However, in other areas of family structure, clear patterns *do* emerge – though not exactly along the lines of the welfare-regime typologies which are useful in making sense of cross-national differences in many other aspects of life.

The main failure of welfare-regime typologies in capturing variations in family patterns is that the UK and Ireland – both members of the 'liberal' group under a welfare-regime typology – have strikingly different family patterns. Households and families in the UK tend to be similar to those in the continental European 'corporatist' countries, while households and families in Ireland have a good deal in common with those of the southern European 'residual' welfare-regime countries. A threefold typology, based on a north/south Protestant/Catholic gradient and consisting of 'Nordic'; 'northern/Protestant' and 'southern/Catholic' groups, of countries, captures many, though by no means all, variations in family patterns.

The 'Nordic' group is characterised by the smallest households and families in Europe: single-adult households are commoner than they are elsewhere, and households with more than two adults are uncommon. The nuclear family is the norm, and the extended family is uncommon. Young people leave home at an early age, and older people tend to live alone or with a partner – but only very rarely with their children.

The 'southern' group is characterised by the largest households and families in Europe, with coresidence between the generations being common, particularly for families with young adult children, but also for older people Young people remain in the parental home for protracted periods in these countries, and when they do leave, they tend to combine this transition with the transition to marriage and parenthood – unlike in the Nordic and northern/Protestant groups, where the transitions are more widely spaced and allow for a diversity of family forms, particularly for young people in their mid-twenties.

On all the indicators where this threefold typology is applicable, the 'northern/Protestant' group falls between the 'Nordic' and 'southern' groups, with intermediate household sizes and intermediate levels of coresidence between the generations. Therefore, although this threefold typology is very useful for many types of analysis, it may be more accurate to think in terms of a continuum, or a gradient, rather than in terms of three distinct groups.

Notes

1. The UK and Ireland do share some common features, such as high rates of teenage motherhood and a high proportion of young people sharing accommodation with friends. But on most indicators of family patterns, the two countries are very different.
2. This third transition relates to *living with one's own children*, rather than having children. For men in the UK and to a lesser extent in Denmark, this will slightly understate the proportion of men who have fathered a child at any age, and will therefore increase the estimated median age slightly.

References

Avery, R.F., Goldscheider and A. Speare Jr (1992), 'Feathered nest/gilded cage: parental income and leaving home in the transition to adulthood', *Demography*, **29** (3), 375–88.

*Berthoud, R. and K. Robson (2003), 'Teenage motherhood in Europe: a multi-country analysis of socio-economic outcomes', *European Sociological Review*, **19** (5), pp. 451-466, *(EPAG Working Paper 22)*.

Blackman, T., S. Brodhurst and J. Convery (2001), *Social Care and Social Exclusion*, Basingstoke: Palgrave.

Cavalli, A. and O. Galland (1995), *Youth in Europe*, London: Pinter.

Clark, W.A. and C.H. Mulder (2000), 'Leaving home and entering the housing market', *Environment and Planning*, **32**, 1657–71.

Cunnington, A.J. (2001), 'What's so bad about teenage pregnancy?' *Journal of Family Planning and Reproductive Health Care*, **27** (1), 36–41.

Eurostat (1999), *Demographic Statistics 1960–99*, Luxembourg: Office for Official Publications of the European Communities.

Fraser, A.M., J.E. Brockert and R.H. Ward (1995), 'Association of young maternal age with adverse reproductive outcomes', *New England Journal of Medicine*, **332** (17), 1113–17.

Hill, C.R. and F.P. Stafford (1985), 'Parental care of children: time diary estimates of quantity, predictability, and variety', in F.T. Juster and F.P. Stafford (eds), *Time, Goods and Well-being*, Ann Arbor, MI: University of Michigan, Institute for Social Research, pp. 415–37.

Hoffman, S.D., E.M. Foster and F.F. Furstenberg Jr (1993), 'Re-evaluating the costs of teenage childbearing', *Demography*, **30** (1), 1–13.

*Iacovou, M. (1999), 'Young people in Europe: two models of household formation', *EPAG Working Papers*, **6**, Colchester: University of Essex.

*Iacovou, M. (2000a), 'Health, wealth and progeny: explaining the living arrangements of older European women', *EPAG Working Papers*, **8**, Colchester: University of Essex.

*Iacovou, M. (2000b), 'The living arrangements of elderly Europeans', *EPAG Working Papers*, **9**, Colchester: University of Essex.

Iacovou, M. (2001), 'Leaving home in the European Union', *ISER Working Papers*, **2001-18**, Colchester: University of Essex.

*Iacovou, M. (2002a), 'Regional differences in the transition to adulthood', *Annals of the American Association of Political and Social Science*, **580**, 40–69.

*Iacovou, M. (2002b), 'Sharing and caring: older Europeans' living arrangements', *Schmollers Jahrbuch (Journal of Applied Social Science Studies)*, **122** (1), 111–42.

Iacovou, M. and R. Berthoud (2001), *Young People's Lives: a Map of Europe*, Colchester: University of Essex, Institute for Social and Economic Research.

*Joesch, J.M. and C.K. Spiess (2002), 'European mothers' time spent looking after children: differences and similarities across nine countries', *EPAG Working Papers*, **31**, Colchester: University of Essex.

*Kaiser, L. (2001), 'Standard and non-standard employment patterns across Europe', *EPAG Working Papers*, **26**, Colchester: University of Essex.

Kiernan, K. (1986), 'Leaving home – living arrangements of young people in six West-European Countries', *European Journal of Population*, **2** (2), 177–84.

Oaxaca, R. (1973), 'Male-female wage differentials in urban labor markets', *International Economic Review*, **14** (e), 693–709.

OECD (1996), 'Caring for frail elderly people: policies in evolution', *OECD Social Policy Studies*, **19**, Paris: OECD.

Pendry, E., G. Barrett and C. Victor (1999), 'Changes in household composition among the over sixties: a longitudinal analysis of the health and lifestyles surveys', *Health and Social Care in the Community*, **7**, 109–19.

Ribar, D.C. (1999), 'The socioeconomic consequences of young women's childbearing: reconciling disparate evidence', *Journal of Population Economics*, **12**, 547–65.

*Schizzerotto, A. and M. Lucchini (2002), 'Transitions to adulthood during the twentieth century: a comparative analysis of Great Britain, Italy and Sweden', *EPAG Working Papers*, **36**, Colchester: University of Essex.

Smeeding, T. and K. Ross Phillips (2002), 'Differences in employment and economic sufficiency', *Annals of the American Association of Political and Social Science*, **580**, 103–33.

Strobino, D.M. (1992), 'Young motherhood and infant hospitalisation during the first year of birth', *Journal of Adolescent Health*, **13** (7), 553–60.

Sundstrom, G. (1994), 'Care by families: an overview of trends', in caring for frail elderly people: new directions in care', *OECD Social Policy Studies*, **14**, Paris: OECD, 1994.

UNICEF (2001), *A League Table of Teenage Births in Rich Nations*, Innocenti Report Card no. 3, July 2001, UNICEF Innocenti Research Foundation, Florence.

Wellings, K., J. Wadsworth, A. Johnson, J. Field and W. Macdowall (1999), 'Teenage fertility and life chances', *Reviews of Reproduction*, **4**, 184–90.

* Direct output from EPAG's *DynSoc* research programme (see page 268).

3. Transitions to Adulthood

Antonio Schizzerotto and Mario Lucchini

Introduction: Aims of the Analysis

Sociologists have traditionally paid close attention to the process by which individuals become independent of their families of origin and take on adult roles (in other words, occupational, conjugal and parental roles).

There are two main reasons for this interest. First, the process of learning adult roles is crucial for the reproduction of a society over time. Therefore the timing and sequence whereby they are assumed by new generations highlight the cultural aspects, institutional arrangements and workings of that society (Parsons, 1942; Beck, 1986; Kohli, 1986; Elder, 1995). Second, the process of entering adulthood yields interesting insights into social inequality because it connects the social origins of individuals with the social positions they achieve during their lives (Blossfeld, 1986; Hogan and Aston, 1986; Schizzerotto and Lucchini, 2002).

Like many sociological concepts, that of transition to adulthood is rather arbitrary, because it is doubtful whether all the members of a society share a common notion of the adult condition (Modell et al., 1976). Yet every society usually develops a system of rules and expectations regarding the 'appropriate' ages and temporal order for entering the various adult roles (Hogan, 1980; Marini, 1984; Hogan and Aston, 1986; Kertzer, 1989; Shanahan, 2000). In the case of contemporary Western societies, most scholars agree that the passage to adulthood involves five main events which are usually chronologically successive: a) completion of full-time schooling; b) finding a job; c) leaving the parental home; d) forming a stable cohabiting union; and e) becoming a parent (Modell et al., 1976; Iedema et al., 1997).

The pattern of this 'regular biography' is not static, however. The age at which each step towards adulthood is completed may vary according to individual characteristics. Moreover, not all the five events listed above are necessarily experienced by everybody. Becoming an adult is a matter of degree, and an individual does not have to make all the canonical transitions to be regarded as an independent member of his/her society. Furthermore, the complete series of steps towards adulthood may follow a temporal sequence different from that expected on the basis of prevailing social rules. Finally, the typical calendar depicted earlier may change from generation to generation. Obviously, processes of entering adulthood also vary across societies.

In this chapter we analyse the transition to adulthood from the perspectives of both social change and social inequality. Specifically, we focus on the following four questions. Do the different institutional arrangements, welfare regimes, cultural patterns and historical traditions of European countries produce variations in the timing and sequence of transition to adulthood? Do European societies display similarities in the changes, across cohorts, of the pathways to adulthood and in the social norms regulating this process? How do education, gender and generation affect the passage to adulthood? Which theory gives the best account of variations over time in the patterns of transition to adulthood in contemporary societies?

Hypotheses

Starting with the first question, we expected to observe disparities among European countries regarding the ages at which each step towards adulthood is completed and the duration of the entire process leading to adulthood. To be more precise, we expected that young men and women living in most of the southern European countries and in Ireland would display the longest delays in transitions to adulthood, followed by those living in the mid-European nations, the UK and the Nordic countries (Hajnal, 1965; Laslett, 1983; Iacovou, 1999; Corijn, 1999; Iacovou and Berthoud, 2001).

Despite the marked dissimilarities among the patterns of transition to adult condition prevailing in the EU countries, we expected them to display some commonalities as well. Specifically, we hypothesised that in EU nations: a) the sequences of the steps taken to enter adult positions are very similar; and b) the variations, across birth cohorts, of the (median) age at each step display the same trend.

Of course, the features of a country's social structure, institutional arrangements and culture, whether strictly national or common to other nations, are not the only variables affecting patterns, ages and durations of transition to adulthood; these are also influenced by the social characteristics of individuals (Blossfeld and Nuthmann, 1990), among which level of education,[1] gender and birth cohort play a central role.

We believe that the current sociological debate on the variations over time in the pathways to adulthood can be reasonably simplified by contrasting the theory of generation – originally proposed by Mannheim (1952) and subsequently revised by Inglehart (1977) and Becker (1991) – with the thesis of the individualisation of life-courses developed, among others, by Beck

(1986), Kohli (1986), Giddens (1990), and Wallace and Kovatcheva (1998). The theory of generations states that people belonging to a birth cohort are involuntarily placed in a given space of historical life. Consequently, they have access to specific socio-cultural resources and they experience specific combinations of constraints and opportunities. Hence, life-course patterns and pathways to adulthood vary from generation to generation – sometimes speeding up, and sometimes slowing down.

Individualisation theory, on the other hand, maintains that in contemporary societies there are no longer 'normal' biographies, that is, typical sequences in the transition from youth to adulthood. Life-courses have become increasingly fragmented and individualised, most life choices are now reversible, and people are able to decide how to shape their own destinations autonomously. As a consequence, the ties that used to bind the various stages of the life-course together have progressively weakened, and specific life events are no longer associated with specific ages.

We believe that the generation theory is much sounder than the individualisation thesis. Several studies have shown that class, gender and generation still play a crucial role in the educational, occupational and matrimonial destinations of individuals (Erikson and Goldthorpe, 1992; Shavit and Blossfeld, 1993; Shavit and Müller, 1998; Gallie and Paugam, 2000; Jonsson and Mills, 2001; Schizzerotto and Lucchini, 2002). Recent research based on longitudinal data has shown non-monotonic variations throughout birth cohorts in the timing of the events marking the passage to adulthood, without significant alterations in their order of occurrence (Sanders and Becker, 1994; Iedema et al., 1997; Billari, 2000; Jonsson and Mills, 2001; Pisati, 2002; Schizzerotto and Lucchini, 2002; Barbagli et al., 2003).

In the light of the above considerations, we first expected to observe rises and falls during the twentieth century in the ages at which members of different cohorts complete the individual steps towards adulthood, except in the case of school leaving and beginning the first job. Second, we believed that completion of full-time schooling would accelerate the pace of transition to adulthood (Blossfeld and Nuthmann, 1990). Third, we hypothesised that, in the case of men, possession of a job is usually an essential precondition for passage to first union and first parenthood. Finally, we believed that being married increases the probability of entering into parenthood (Thornton et al., 1995).

Data, Methods and Variables

The data used in our analyses are taken from waves 1994 to 1998 of the ECHP. They refer to people born between 1909 and 1983 in 14 EU countries.

We first estimated the median age at which young people reached each of four events: a) attaining their highest educational qualification;[2] b) entering their first job; c) entering their first marriage;[3] and d) having their first child.[4]

We then used event history analysis (Tuma and Hannan, 1984; Yamaguchi, 1991; Blossfeld and Rohwer, 1995) to account for the effects of time, country, and a set of individual characteristics on the probabilities of: a) entering the first job; b) forming the first marriage; and c) having the first child.[5]

Event history analysis is well known to be the most appropriate technique with which to elaborate sound causal explanations of biographical events. Unfortunately, however, the technique obliges the analyst to treat each event individually, and it cannot give an account of the overall shape of the pathways to adulthood. In order to study both the entire sequence of events that lead to adult conditions and the time elapsing between these events, we decided to use sequence analysis (Abbott and Hrycak, 1990; Halpin and Chan, 1998; Rohwer and Trappe, 1997).[6]

For the sake of brevity, only data referring to selected EU countries will be given in most of the graphs and tables presented throughout the chapter. These countries were selected in such a way as to represent: a) the highest and the lowest values of the specific measures used to test our hypotheses; and b) each of the four welfare regimes described in the first chapter of the book.

Ages and Stages in the Transition to Adulthood

As is well known, the twentieth century was characterised by the expansion of school systems, the growth of enrolment rates, and the lengthening of the period spent in education. As a consequence, the median ages at highest school qualification increased almost monotonically across cohorts throughout the EU (Figure 3.1).

A second trend common to all EU countries consists of the progressive reduction of gender disparities in educational opportunities. At the beginning of the twentieth century women had very few chances of obtaining higher education credentials, whereas today they study even longer than their male counterparts (Figure 3.1). Despite the similarities in the overall changes across birth cohorts in the length of educational careers, some marked differences still remain among EU countries. On average, the median ages at the highest educational qualification recorded by the youngest cohorts are lower in southern countries. So a relatively small proportion of southern European youth attend tertiary education and obtain a university degree. Yet these geographical disparities have attenuated in comparison to the past because the southern countries have increased their average levels of education faster than other EU nations (Figure 3.1).

*Figure 3.1   Median ages at attainment of highest school qualification, by
birth cohort and country*

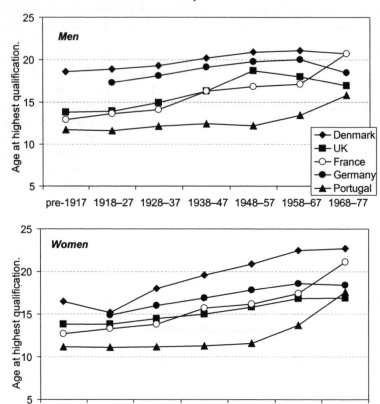

Note: Figures based on Kaplan–Meier estimates.
Source: ECHP (1994–98), authors' own calculations.

During the twentieth century the median ages of starting the first job also
increased steadily across birth cohorts in the whole of the EU (Figure 3.2).
This postponement of the beginning of the work career has usually been
interpreted as the consequence of two events: first, the increased length of
school attendance (it being argued that in western Europe there is a widely
shared social norm to the effect that the workplace must be entered after
completion of schooling); second, a general worsening of occupational
opportunities produced by oil shocks and the de-industrialisation processes
(Blossfeld, 1986; Sanders and Becker, 1994; Iedema et al., 1997;
Schizzerotto and Lucchini, 2002).

Figure 3.2   Median ages at first job, by birth cohort and country

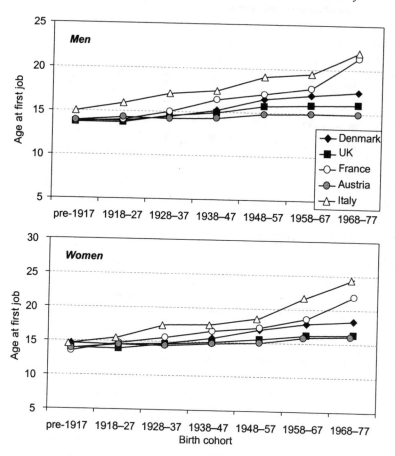

Note: Figures based on Kaplan–Meier estimates.
Source: ECHP (1994–98), authors' own calculations.

Median ages at first job (Figure 3.2) are almost always higher than those at highest school qualification (Figure 3.1), with the exception of the southern EU countries and France. At first sight, this result seems to contradict the prevailing view of increasing delay in the transition to the first job and, on the contrary, to support one of the main contentions of the individualisation thesis, namely that economic activity no longer coincides with the severing of all contacts with the educational system. Actually, the above result derives from the fact that in many countries, students either have occasional jobs during school attendance or carry out practical apprenticeships as a part of their school curriculum.[7] Moreover, our graphs show that among older cohorts, too, median ages at the highest educational credential were greater than those at the first job. Yet, if the theory of fragmented life-courses were valid, only younger cohorts would be characterised by this feature. We may therefore continue to safely interpret the increasingly longer transitions to the first job as mainly being the consequence of lengthening school careers and increasing difficulties in finding first jobs.

It seems that the geographical differentials among the younger cohorts bear out our hypotheses. Southern countries, together with France and Belgium, display the slowest transitions to first job, while the UK, Austria and Germany record the fastest (Figure 3.2). These disparities can be explained in terms of the number of vocation-specific components provided by post-compulsory school curricula, the flexibility of the labour market, and the robustness of the economy. Southern countries possess weaker economic systems and therefore offer fewer occupational opportunities than do the UK, Austria and Germany. Moreover, the former countries and France have rather strongly regulated labour markets, which tend to produce high rates of youth unemployment. The opposite holds for the UK. Although Austria and Germany are characterised by quite rigid labour markets, their school systems largely furnish occupation-specific skills, and this may speed up the first job search. By contrast, the post-compulsory school curricula of southern countries and France are mainly academically oriented. In sum, southern countries are affected by a distinctive combination of factors all of which negatively influence the rapidity of the first job search.

Turning to gender disparities in the chances of entering the labour market, it seems that, today as in the past, EU women transit to their first job later than do EU men. Italy, Portugal, Spain and Greece record the greatest gender differences, while UK and Germany appear to be the most egalitarian countries in this respect (Figure 3.2). Obviously, the mechanisms responsible for geographical differentials in the magnitude of gender inequality in occupational opportunities are the same as those mentioned earlier, to which differences in the gender sensitivity of cultural patterns must be added.

The distribution across cohorts of the median age at first union (Figure 3.3) quite straightforwardly confirms our hypotheses and conflicts rather strongly with the theory of the increasing heterogeneity of life-courses.

In all EU countries and cohorts, the median age for first union proves to be higher than the median ages for both the highest educational qualification and first job. In other words, most people still get married after they have finished school and found a job.

Figure 3.3   Median ages at first marriage, by birth cohort and country

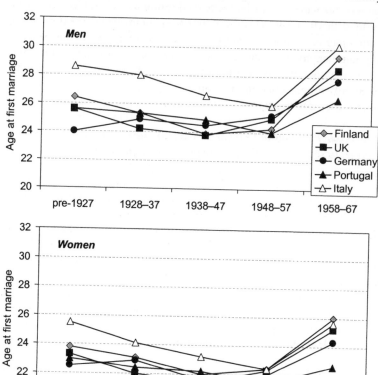

Note: Figures based on Kaplan-Meier estimates.
Source: ECHP (1994–98), authors' own calculations.

These considerations can be extended to ages at first parenthood, although in this case we possess the relevant data only for people born between 1958 and 1967. Everywhere in the EU, men and women have their first child after getting married, and therefore after finishing school and finding their first jobs (Table 3.1).

This means that in the EU as a whole, two widely shared social norms still apply. The first states that the first union should take place when education has been completed and a secure job guaranteeing minimum economic independence has been found (Blossfeld and Huinik, 1991; Iedema et al., 1997, Schizzerotto and Lucchini, 2002). The second states that the first child should be born only when a reasonably stable union has been attained.

Despite the expectations of the individualisation thesis, and in accordance with our hypotheses, median ages at first marriage (and the first baby) do not vary from older to younger cohorts following a linear trend: rather, they display a non-monotonic, U-shaped one.[8] Older cohorts married (and become parents) at later ages than people born between 1938 and 1957; but also the subsequent cohort postponed the formation of the first (legal) union (and the transition to first parenthood).[9]

Table 3.1   *Median ages at first parenthood among people born between 1958 and 1967, by gender (selected countries)*

Country	Gender	
	Men	Women
Finland	30.1	26.6
UK	30.4	26.2
Germany	29.7	25.4
Portugal	29.2	24.0
Italy	33.0	28.5

Note: Figures based on Kaplan–Meier estimates.
Source: ECHP (1994–98), authors' own calculations.

We contend that a weak economy, high unemployment rates, difficulties in finding stable employment, a shortage of suitable housing, and welfare state retrenchment all combine to explain why people born since the late 1950s have delayed their first marriage (and first parenthood). Many of these features characterised the social and economic situations of the oldest cohorts as well, since they too waited as long to get married and assume the parental role as today's young people. By contrast, individuals born between the late 1930s and the late 1950s took advantage of a booming economy, full employment, a rather protective regulation of labour markets, and relatively generous welfare systems. Indeed, they were able to get married (and have their first baby) earlier than their parents and children. However, similarities between the oldest and youngest cohorts should not be exaggerated. The economic situation in which the people belonging to our last cohort grew up was less severe than the one during the first four decades of the twentieth century. Their parents were far more supportive, and the social norms on movements from the parental home to independent living were far less stringent than in the past.

What has changed since the 1960s, however, is the situation of EU women.

On the one hand, modern well-educated young European women are much more inclined to participate in the labour market than their mothers and grandmothers. Yet in most EU countries, and above all in the southern ones, the division of domestic chores between men and women is far from being egalitarian. Moreover, residual, corporatist and liberal welfare regimes do not greatly help young women to reconcile their work obligations with domestic concerns. This is even more the case in southern countries, where part-time jobs are rather uncommon. Difficulties in combining domestic and work schedules make assumption of the role of wife or mother far less desirable today than it used to be in the past – all the more so because contemporary family and couple relationships tend to be rather insecure and unstable. As a consequence, young women are inclined to take their time before assuming a conjugal role. And this, in turn, magnifies the delaying effect of the material constraints mentioned earlier.[10]

It seems that our hypotheses and arguments do not fit very well with the geographical differentials in the median ages at first marriage and first baby. Consider, for the sake of brevity, only the last cohort. People from the Nordic countries and the UK get married and enter the first parental role at higher median ages than do individuals living in several north-central countries. Moreover, while it is true than the majority of southern countries display the most delayed transitions to conjugal and parental roles, it is also true that Portuguese men and women record the most rapid ones (Figure 3.3). We are inclined to maintain that in the case of the Nordic countries and the UK there is no actual contradiction between our hypotheses and reality. The apparent contrast of our convictions with empirical observations quite simply derives from the fact that ECHP does not collect information on the first cohabitation. It is well known that cohabitations everywhere precede formal marriages and that the former are much more widespread in the Nordic countries and the UK than they are in north-central and southern nations. We accordingly contend that inspection of first cohabitation would show that Scandinavian young people and young Britons make the most rapid transitions to conjugal roles. The case of Portugal is different, and we are not really able to explain why it is so.[11]

Social Norms, Economic Environment and Individual Characteristics Affecting the Transitions to Adulthood

Having described differences and similarities between EU countries in the age patterns of transitions to adulthood, we now turn to the causal mechanisms that affect the probabilities of making these transitions. More precisely, we focus on the steps towards adulthood that individuals have already made or not yet made, and on variations between countries.

In all the EU countries, having completed full-time education significantly increases men's and women's chances of finding a first job. Put otherwise: having attained one's highest educational credential enhances the probabilities of being employed (Table 3.2). Obviously, this result confirms that there is a widely held social rule in the EU to the effect that scholastic calendars and work calendars should not overlap.

Table 3.2   *Influences on transitions to first job for EU men and women born between 1969 and1983 (multilevel hazard model coefficients)*

Covariates	Men		Women	
Baseline	−1.51	***	−1.48	***
Age (centred on 18 years)	0.06	***	0.12	***
Highest level of education attained				
Below 2nd level (ISCED 0–2)	1.08	***	0.85	***
2nd level (ISCED 3)	0.92	***	1.03	***
3rd level (ISCED 5–7)	1.27	***	1.31	***
Still studying (reference)	−		−	
Completed transition to first marriage	0.15		−0.71	***
Number of children	−0.48	**	−0.79	***
Annual national unemployment rate	−0.05	***	−0.06	***

Notes: Coefficients from discrete time multilevel hazard models with random baseline. Asterisks denote significance of coefficients: *** 1%, ** 5%, * 10%.
Source: ECHP (1994–98), authors' own calculations.

The level of schooling does not greatly matter in the case of EU men. Among EU women, by contrast, one observes a linear and positive relation between educational qualifications and the chances of getting a first job (Table 3.2).

Being married and having children strongly reduces the probability of getting a job among women (Table 3.2). This result confirms that women still find it difficult to reconcile work and family responsibilities in the contemporary EU.[12]

Obviously, unfavourable economic conditions, as expressed by the national annual rate of unemployment, negatively affect the chances of first job entry among both men and women.

Figure 3.4   *Country variations in the transition to first job (multilevel*
hazard model coefficients)

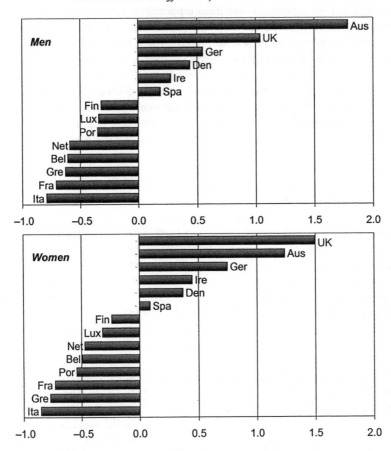

Notes: The graph shows differential hazard baselines from estimates reported in Table 3.2.
              Estimates are based on a sample of those born between 1969 and 1983, and control
              for personal characteristics and national unemployment rates.
Source: ECHP (1994–98), authors' own calculations.

As mentioned earlier, the mechanisms favouring or hampering the
transition to the first job are common to all the EU countries.[13] We stressed,
however, that the chances of finding a job also depend on the economy of
each EU society, its specific institutional arrangements, the nature of its
welfare regime, and its cultural patterns. Figure 3.4 shows the weight and the
direction of the influence exerted by the various EU nations on the probability
of being employed for the first time. In this graph, a positive result (pointing

to the right) shows that the transition is more rapid in this country than elsewhere – that is, it will be made at a younger age. A negative result (pointing to the left) means slower transitions and higher ages at transition. Inspection of these country-specific differentials shows that, other things being equal, young men in Italy, France and Greece find it more difficult to accomplish the transition to first jobs than do their counterparts in other EU countries. By contrast, young Austrian, British and German males enjoy the best chances of rapidly finding a first job. Similar considerations apply to young women. Once again, living in Italy, Greece and France reduces the average EU probability of finding the first job, while the opposite holds for young women living in Austria, Germany and the UK (Figure 3.4).[14]

Table 3.3   *Influences on transitions to first marriage for EU men and women born between 1967 and 1983 (multilevel hazard model coefficients)*

Covariates	Men		Women	
Baseline	–4.56	***	–3.83	***
Age (centred on 22 years)	0.23	***	0.16	***
Highest level of education attained				
Below 2nd level (ISCED 0–2)	1.05	***	1.92	***
2nd level (ISCED 3)	0.82	***	1.63	***
3rd level (ISCED 5–7)	0.66	***	1.47	***
Still studying (reference)	–		–	
Completed transition to the first job	0.63	***	–0.16	***
Number of children	0.53	***	0.04	
Annual national unemployment rate	–0.08	***	–0.06	***

Notes: Coefficients from discrete time multilevel hazard models with random baseline.
        Asterisks denote significance of coefficients: *** 1%, ** 5%, * 10%.
Source: ECHP (1994–98), authors' own calculations.

The models regarding the transition to the first marriage also confirm the presence in all EU countries of social norms regulating the sequence of movements towards adulthood. Not being a student strongly increases the chances of men and women forming a union (Table 3.3). Among men, the same applies to those who have acquired their first jobs. In the case of women, by contrast, having entered the labour market reduces their likelihood of getting married. Which means that, for men, occupation is a preliminary requirement for transition to the first marriage. For women, on the other hand, entering the first job may actually slow down transition to marriage because of the difficulties of reconciling work and family commitments, already stressed.

Having babies has no significant effect on the chances of getting married among women, but it strongly enhances those of men (Table 3.3). In the latter case, a mechanism repairing the sequence error is apparently at work.

Finally, it is interesting to note that the annual national unemployment rate also exerts a negative effect on the transition to marriage which is greater than that exerted on the first employment opportunities.

Country-specific residuals seem quite dramatically to change the picture of transition to first marriage furnished by the analysis of median ages. Among both young men and women, it is the Spanish rather than the Portuguese who receive the strongest push from their country towards first marriage (Figure 3.5). It should be borne in mind, however, that country differentials express the net effect of living in a specific nation and that median ages may be subject to a compositional effect. We may accordingly say that the late transitions to marriage displayed by young Spaniards are not a product of their country's cultural rules on family formation: they are caused by the Spanish level of unemployment. It is well known that Spain records the highest youth unemployment rate in Europe and we showed earlier that the aggregate unemployment rate exerts a strong negative effect on the transition to the first marriage.

A second seemingly strange result emerges from inspection of country influences: the quite remarkable negative influence on the transition to the first marriage derived from living in Denmark (Figure 3.5). However, it should be noted that the information on Denmark is biased by the high proportion of young Danes forming a cohabitation who are not recorded as married by ECHP.

The remaining EU countries display variations quite in accordance with our hypotheses. Suffice it to say that, Spain aside, Finland and the UK are the countries in which family formation rules and institutional arrangements have the strongest positive effect on the chances of getting married (Figure 3.5).

Turning to the transition to parenthood, we briefly reiterate that completing school and attaining a first job enhance the probability of becoming a parent among EU men and women as well (Table 3.4).

Yet, it is worth noting that the higher the level of education, the lower the chances of having a child for both men and women. The reason for this is quite obviously that highly educated people enter the labour market later and invest more in their work careers than do lesser educated individuals. Moreover, it should be stressed that the effect of employment is much more pronounced among men than among women. Of greater interest, however, are the results on the net influence of the transition to the first marriage. Throughout the EU this transition almost automatically paves the way for

parenthood. On average, the chance of having a baby among married young
men and women is 19 times and 13 times higher than those of their respective
counterparts who have not yet married. Obviously, as we have shown
elsewhere (Schizzerotto and Lucchini, 2002), besides formal marriages,
stable cohabitation may also lead to parenthood. The strength of the latter
association is quite close to that of the former.

Figure 3.5   *Country variations in the transition to first marriage (multilevel*
hazard model coefficients)

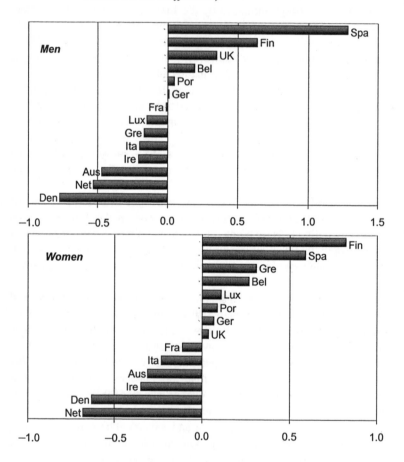

Notes: The graph shows differential hazard baselines from estimates reported in Table 3.3.
         Estimates are based on a sample of those born between 1967 and 1983, and control
         for personal characteristics and national unemployment rates.
Source: ECHP (1994–98), authors' own calculations.

Table 3.4 *Influences on transitions to first parenthood for EU men and women born between 1967 and 1983 (multilevel hazard model coefficients)*

Covariates	Men		Women	
Baseline	−5.44	***	−4.71	***
Age (centred on age 24)	0.12	***	0.06	***
Highest level of education attained				
Below 2nd level (ISCED 0–2)	1.08	***	1.91	***
2nd level (ISCED 3)	0.69	***	1.43	***
3rd level (ISCED 5–7)	0.46	***	1.04	***
Still studying (reference)	–		–	
Completed transition to first job	0.84	***	0.15	***
Completed transition to first marriage	3.01	***	2.62	***
Annual national unemployment rate	−0.01		−0.02	*

Notes: Coefficients from discrete time multilevel hazard models with random baseline. Asterisks denote significance of coefficients: *** 1%, ** 5%, * 10%.
Source: ECHP (1994–98), authors' own calculations.

It is for this reason that, in the case of the transition to parenthood, the distribution of country-specific residuals of the hazard baseline fairly well matches our hypotheses, as well as reflecting ideas widely shared by social scientists on geographical variations in the length and difficulties of the transition to adulthood. Other things being equal, living in the Nordic countries enhances the probability of having a baby, while living in southern ones quite markedly reduces it (Figure 3.6). However, we would point out that the positions of some countries in Figure 3.6 are not immediately understandable. This is the case of Ireland, which has a liberal welfare regime like the UK's, but displays a pronounced positive effect on women's transition to parenthood, while the opposite holds for the UK. It may be that the religious beliefs prevailing in each country account for this difference. But neither religion nor the welfare regime can explain why becoming a parent is so much delayed for young Dutch men or women.

*Figure 3.6   Country variations in the transition to first parenthood
(multilevel hazard model coefficients)*

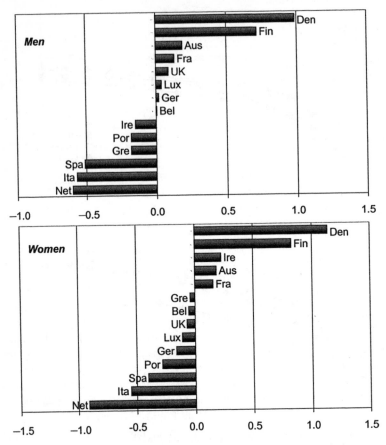

Notes: The graph shows differential hazard baselines from the equation shown in Table 3.5.
             Estimates are based on a sample of those born between 1967 and 1983, and control
             for personal characteristics and national unemployment rates.
Source: ECHP (1994–98), authors' own calculations.

Where are Pathways to Adulthood More Heterogeneous?

As stressed earlier, it might be objected that results from event history
analysis are not a sound basis on which to criticise the individuation thesis. In
order to meet this possible objection, we directly analysed the sequence of
life-course events of people born between 1964 and 1969 in the EU countries.

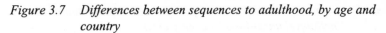

Figure 3.7   *Differences between sequences to adulthood, by age and country*

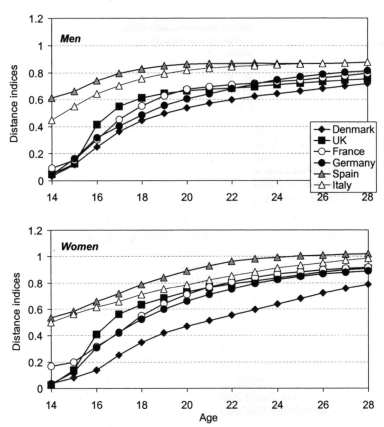

Note: Distance indices derived from optimal matching analysis.
Source: ECHP (1994–98), authors' own calculations.

Most proponents of the individualisation thesis would agree that the events typically making up a contemporary, fragmented life-course – namely, easy passages from school to work and vice versa, cohabitation, out of wedlock births – become more and more frequent as one moves from the southern to the northern EU countries. So one should expect the sequence of transitions to adulthood to be most varied among young people living in the Nordic countries, and most consistent among their counterparts living in the southern ones.

We used a technique called 'optimal matching analysis' to compute an index of dissimilarity showing how differences between young individuals' life-courses change over time (Figure 3.7). High values of the index indicate high levels of heterogeneity between the sequences studied, and vice versa. The graph shows, for example, that in most countries, 14- and 15-year-olds are all doing the same thing (they are all continuing their education, not getting a job, not getting married, and not having children) so they are very low on the index. As they grow older, they do more diverse things (some stay in education, some enter work, some get married, some have children) so the index of dissimilarity increases with age.

But the important question for our analysis is the range of differences between countries. The graph tells a story that profoundly contradicts the individualisation thesis. The countries with the highest difference in the overall pathways to adulthood are Spain and Italy, while young Danes display the most homogeneous trajectories. It might be said that the data on Denmark are not reliable, as we ourselves have pointed out several times. Yet the conclusions do not greatly change if we look at the UK, France and Germany: the degree of dissimilarity between the trajectories to adulthood of those countries' young citizens is less than that observed in the two southern countries.

But why are young Spanish and Italian (as well as Greek) pathways to adulthood more heterogeneous than those of young people living in the remaining EU countries? The reason may lie in the strong educational inequalities that affect the southern EU countries. These inequalities give rise to great differences among the ages at which young men and women enter the labour market. Moreover, even the length of the first job search varies according to the level of education. In their turn, the disparities in the period lasting from completion of school to the first job engender differences in the duration of the transitions to the first marriage and child. The graph seems to provide strong support for this explanation: it is mainly from between the ages of 14 and 22 that the difference in the degree of dissimilarity of life-courses between Spaniards and Italians, on one the one hand, and Britons, French, Germans and Danes on the other, is greater.

Conclusions

We may summarise the main results of our analyses by starting with the question regarding the soundness of sociological theories on the variations in pathways to adulthood in the EU countries during the twentieth century. In accordance with our hypotheses, generation theory has proved to fit the data better than the individualisation thesis. Holistic analysis of both sequences and durations of steps to adulthood has not shown any systematic increase in their heterogeneity as one moves from the southern to the Nordic countries. Event history analysis has shown that in the EU countries, social clocks and widely shared rules governing the chronological order of steps towards adulthood still exist. Moreover, there is very little evidence of steady trends in ages of transition to adulthood throughout the last century in the EU. Only ages on leaving school and on first job entrance display a linear increase over time. By contrast, ages at first marriage and birth of the first child have indeed changed, following a U-shaped trend across cohorts in all EU countries. We have interpreted this similarity between oldest and youngest cohorts as the consequence of: (1) the aforementioned substantial stability over time of the social norms ruling the sequences of steps towards adulthood; and (2) a substantial similarity in the material constraints – stagnant economies, high unemployment rates, strong housing problems – encountered in progress towards economic and social autonomy.

All the above remarks, and even more so the results of our analyses, should demonstrate that the basic logic governing trajectories to adulthood is similar in all EU countries. In our opinion, this similarity derives from the fact that these societies, for most of the twentieth century, had important elements of their respective institutional arrangements in common: namely, a market economy, a pluralistic political regime, a well-developed school system, and the nuclear family as the most common form of household.

Moreover, the net effects of some individual characteristics also prove to be basically the same throughout the EU. We have shown that: (1) high educational credentials lengthen the transitions to first job, first marriage, and first baby; and (2) women find it difficult to reconcile their work commitments with family obligations.

Despite all these similarities, our analyses demonstrate that marked differences still exist among EU countries. By and large, people from southern countries display the slowest and the most delayed transitions to adulthood, while those living in the Nordic countries and the UK exhibit the most rapid ones. This general regularity is the cumulative effect of various economic, institutional and cultural factors, however. The delayed assumption of conjugal and parental roles observed in several southern EU countries, for instance, does not depend only on cultural traditions regarding family formation rules; it also derives from the presence of a weak economy, housing problems, a residual welfare regime, and high unemployment rates among young people. In our opinion, this result has significant policy implications, for it shows that in order to promote easier transitions to independence among young people, integrated measures should be developed. A further result of our research of potential interest from a policy perspective is the existence of some functional equivalents. Rates of aggregate unemployment being equal, a quite rapid attainment of first job, for instance, can be pursued by means of either a flexible labour market or a dual school system with strong vocational components in its curricula.

Notes

1.   In a previous comparative paper on Great Britain, Italy and Sweden (Schizzerotto and Lucchini, 2002) we have shown that the effect of class of origin on the transition to adulthood is almost completely mediated by level of education.
2.   As information on full-time school leaving was lacking for several countries in the ECHP data sets, we use attainment of highest educational qualification as a proxy for it.
3.   We only studied first formal marriage because ECHP does not provide information on cohabiting unions. Moreover, it should be borne in mind that ECHP gives calendar information only on current marriages.
4.   ECHP gives information only on the birth dates of children cohabiting with their parents at the moment of the interview.
5.   Observations began when the selected respondents were 14 years old and ended when transitions were effected. If the transitions did not take place, observation ended either at the last interview or when respondents were 28, 30 and 31 years old for the transition to first job, first marriage and first child, respectively.
6.   Optimal matching analysis was carried out on people born between 1964 and 1969. The observation period for each interviewee lasted from the age of 14 to the age of 28. Some 2000 individual pathways were randomly selected, and 1000 pair-wise comparisons were performed within each elementary subgroup defined by combining country and gender.
7.   Obviously, the latter is the case of countries with a dual school system, like the Netherlands, Germany and Austria.
8.   Germany is the sole exception to this general trend.
9.   In a previous paper (Schizzerotto and Lucchini, 2002), we demonstrated that variations across cohorts of the median ages at the first baby follow, in Great Britain, Italy and Sweden, the same U-shaped trend as the median ages at first marriage.
10.   The U-shaped trend and arguments given in the main text also hold if the first cohabitation, instead of the first formal marriage, is considered (Sanders and Becker, 1994; Iedema et al., 1997; Schizzerotto and Lucchini, 2002).
11.   Tentatively, one could say that in Portugal, like in southern regions of Italy and Spain, the traditional rules of family formation induce people to undertake a rather rapid transition to marriage (Hajnal, 1965).
12.   In the case of men, being married has a small positive effect on the probability of entering the first job, showing that a mechanism designed to repair a sequence error – namely getting married when unemployed – is at work. The coefficient expressing the effect of the number of children is rather unreliable because we found very few cases of men who became fathers before entering the labour market.
13.   We also specified models allowing associations between covariates and dependent variable to change from country to country. These models showed that the strength of these associations varies only slightly among EU countries.
14.   As mentioned earlier, ECHP records apprenticeship episodes of people attending school in countries with a dual school system and the short-term work experiences of students living in the UK as if they are the real beginnings of their work histories. Of course, this means that the parameters of our models regarding the transition to the first job and the values of country-specific hazard baselines may be a little biased. Yet, even on looking at transitions to the first long-run work episode, it turns out that UK youth indeed make very rapid passages to their first job (Schizzerotto and Lucchini, 2002).

References

Abbott, A. and A. Hrycark (1990), 'Measuring resemblance in sequence data: an optimal matching analysis of musicians' careers', *American Journal of Sociology*, **96**, 144–85.

Barbagli, M., M. Castiglioni and Z. Dalla (2003), *Fare Famiglia in Italia: un Secolo di Cambiamenti*, Bologna: Il Mulino.

Beck, U. (1986), *Risikogesellschaft: auf dem Weg in eine andere Moderne*, Frankfurt: Suhrkamp.

Becker, H.A. (1991), 'Aspecten van generaties en cohorten, een overzicht van het onderzoeksprogramma', *Sociologische Gids*, **38**, 212–26.

Billari, F. (2000), *L'analisi delle biografie e la transizione allo stato adulto: aspetti metodologici e applicazioni al caso italiano*, Padova: Cleup editrice.

Blossfeld, H.P. (1986), 'Career opportunities in the Federal Republic of Germany: a dynamic approach to the study of life-course, cohort and period effects', *European Sociological Review*, **2**, 208–25.

Blossfeld, H.P. and J. Huinink (1991), 'Human capital investments or norms of role transitions? How women's schooling and career affect the process of family formation', *American Journal of Sociology*, **97**, 143–68.

Blossfeld, H.P. and R. Nuthmann (1990), 'Transition from youth to adulthood as a cohort process in the FRG', in H.A. Becker (ed.), *Life Histories and Generations*, Utrecht: ISOR, pp. 183–217.

Blossfeld, H.P. and G. Rohwer (1995), *Techniques of Event History Modelling: New Approaches to Causal Analysis*, Hillsdale, NJ: Lawrence Erlbaum Associates.

Corijn, M. (1999), *Transitions to Adulthood in Europe for the 1950s and 1960s Cohort*, Brussels: Centre for Population and Family Studies.

Elder, G.H. Jr (1995), 'The life course paradigm: social change and individual development', in P. Moen, G.H. Elder Jr and K. Luscher (eds), *Examining Lives in Context: Perspectives on the Ecology of Human Development*, Washington, DC: American Psychological Association, pp. 101–39.

Erikson, R. and J.H. Goldthorpe (1992), *The Constant Flux: a Study of Class Mobility in Industrial Societies*, Oxford: Clarendon Press.

Gallie, D. and S. Paugam (eds) (2000), *Welfare Regimes and the Experience of Unemployment in Europe*, Oxford: Oxford University Press.

Giddens, A. (1990), *The Consequences of Modernity*, Cambridge: Polity Press.

Hajnal, J. (1965), 'European marriage patterns in perspective', in D.V. Glass and D.E.C. Eversley (eds), *Population and History*, London: Edward Arnold, pp. 101–46.

Halpin, B. and T.W. Chan (1998), 'Class careers as sequences: an optimal matching analysis of work-life histories', *European Sociological Review*, **14**, 111–30.

Hogan, D.P. (1980), 'The transition to adulthood as a career contingency', *American Sociological Review*, **45**, 261–76.

Hogan, D.P. and N.M. Aston (1986), 'The transition to adulthood', *Annual Review of Sociology*, **12**, 109–30.

*Iacovou, M. (1999), 'Young people in Europe: two models of household formation', *EPAG Working Papers*, **6**, Colchester: University of Essex.

Iacovou, M. and R. Berthoud (2001), *Young People's Lives: a Map of Europe*, Colchester: University of Essex, Institute for Social and Economic Research.

Iedema, J., H.A. Becker and K. Sanders (1997), 'Transitions into independence: a comparison of cohorts born since 1930 in the Netherlands', *European Sociological Review*, **13**, 117–37.

Inglehart, R. (1977), *The Silent Generation: Changing Values and Political Styles Among Western Publics*, Princeton, NJ: Princeton University Press.

Jonsson, J.O. and C. Mills (eds) (2001), *Cradle to Grave, Life-course Change in Modern Sweden*, Durham: Sociology Press.

Kertzer, D.I. (1989), 'Age structuring in comparative and historical perspective', in D.I. Kertzer and K.W. Schaie (eds), *Age Structuring in Comparative and Perspective*, Hillsdale, NJ: Lawrence Erlbaum, pp. 271–92.

Kohli, M. (1986), 'The world we forgot: a historical review of the life course', in W.W. Marshall (ed.), *Later Life*, Beverly Hills, CA: Sage, pp. 271–303.

Laslett, P. (1983), 'Family and household as work group and kin group: areas of traditional Europe compared', in R. Wall, J. Robin and P. Laslett (eds), *Family Forms in Historic Europe*, Cambridge: Cambridge University Press, pp. 513–63.

Mannheim, K. (1952), *Essays on the Sociology of Knowledge*, London: Routledge and Kegan Paul.

Marini, M.M. (1984), 'The order of events in the transition to adulthood', *Sociology of Education*, **57**, 63–84.

Modell, J., F.F. Furstenberg Jr and T. Hershberg (1976), 'Social change and transitions to adulthood in historical perspective', *Journal of Family History*, **1**, 7–32.

Parsons, T. (1942), 'Age and sex in the social structure of the United States', *American Sociological Review*, **7**, 604–16.

Pisati, M. (2002), 'La transizione alla vita adulta', in A. Schizzerotto (ed.), *Vite Ineguali*, Bologna: Il Mulino, 89–139.

Rohwer, G. and H. Trappe (1997), 'Possibilities and difficulties in life course description', in W. Voges (ed.), *Dynamic Approaches to Comparative Social Research: Recent Developments and Applications*, Aldershot: Ashgate.

Sanders, K. and H.A. Becker (1994), 'The transition from education to work and social independence: a comparison between the United States, the Netherlands, West Germany, and the United Kingdom', *European Sociological Review*, **10**, (2) 383–92.

*Schizzerotto, A. and M. Lucchini (2002), 'Transitions to adulthood during the twentieth century: a comparative analysis of Great Britain, Italy, and Sweden', *EPAG Working Papers*, **36**, Colchester: University of Essex.

Shanahan, M.J. (2000), 'Pathways to adulthood in changing societies: variability and mechanisms in life course perspective', *Annual Sociological Review*, **26**, 667–92.

Shavit, Y. and H.P. Blossfeld (eds) (1993), *Persistent Inequality*, Boulder, CO: Westview Press.

Shavit Y. and W. Müller (eds) (1998), *From School to Work*, Oxford: Oxford University Press.

Thornton, A., W.G. Axinn and J.D. Teachman (1995), 'The influence of school enrolment and accumulation on cohabitation and marriage in early adulthood', *American Sociological Review*, **60**, 762–74.

Tuma, N.B. and M.T. Hannan (1984), *Social Dynamics: Models and Methods*, San Diego, CA: Academy Press.

Wallace, C. and S. Kovatcheva (1998), *Youth in Society*, Basingstoke: Macmillan.

Yamaguchi, K. (1991), *Event History Analysis*, Newbury Park, CA and London: Sage.

* Direct output from EPAG's *DynSoc* research programme (see page 268).

4. Family Effects on Employment

C. Katharina Spiess, Maria Iacovou, Karen L. Robson and Wilfred Uunk

Introduction: The Type of Family Effects Analysed

The dramatic changes in family structure, female labour force participation and age structure in European countries have profound implications for the relationship between family and employment. It is well established that partners, children or elders who require inputs of care have an effect on the employment behaviour of the individuals (particularly women) who are called upon to provide care, but the type and size of this effect are likely to have varied with the social changes described. In the other direction, employment behaviour (in particular working time schedules and transitions in and out of employment) have an effect on the time which family members have available to spend on family activities, such as caring for children or elderly relatives.

In this chapter, we focus on three examples of the relationship between family and employment, which may occur over the course of an individual's life. First, there is the individual's requirement to arrange his or her own employment in conjunction with that of another person – their partner. Second, there is the problem of arranging one's own employment when children are present in the family, and third, the problem of arranging employment together with the care of elderly relatives. Thus, first the relationship between couples' employment decisions is analysed, second the impact of children on women's labour supply and future prospects in the labour market are studied, and third the relationship between work hours and informal elderly care is analysed. For each example, some descriptive information is given (on the employment patterns of couples, the hours of work of employed mothers or the care-giving behaviour of employed women). However, the focus of this chapter is on employment changes, and thus each type of effect is discussed in a dynamic framework as well.

Because this is a cross-national study, all of these relationships and transitions are taking place in different institutional settings and in different market environments – and social attitudes towards the combination of family life and work also vary between countries. Thus, throughout the chapter, we highlight the degree of similarity and difference between the countries – either explicitly relating this to the standard welfare-regime typology or, where this does not seem to be appropriate, using other country clusters.

Couples' Employment Decisions

When an individual in a single-adult household decides whether, and for how many hours, to engage in paid work, this decision involves, on the supply side, comparing the streams of income which would be expected under different work/leisure combinations, including that which would arise from zero hours of work. The decision also involves the individual's relative taste for work as compared to leisure; the cost of replacing some of one's own unpaid work in the home (looking after children, cooking, cleaning) with paid inputs; and other costs of going out to work (transport, clothing, equipment).

When people live together in couples, the decision becomes even more complicated, since each member of the couple also has to take into account not only the possible streams of income accruing to the other partner, but also the possibility that the relationship may not continue. The possibility now arises that the members of the couple may specialise in different areas of production: for example, one member may specialise in paid work, while the other specialises in unpaid work in the home.

Becker (1981) argues that such specialised arrangements arise (a) because they generate economic gains to the family, and (b) as a result of inherent differences between men and women. The assumptions underlying this interpretation of neoclassical economics have been vigorously disputed by feminists (Strober, 1993; Wooley, 1993) who point out the importance of issues such as the allocation of resources and bargaining power within relationships. Nevertheless, a specialised allocation of work has, until relatively recently, been the dominant form of organisation within couples across Europe, and despite the enormous growth in female labour market participation in recent decades, a specialised allocation of labour remains common, particularly for couples with young children, as Figure 4.1 illustrates.

Figure 4.1 shows the distribution of work within prime-aged couples, where the man is aged between 25 and 55. Couples are grouped according to which partners have a job: both partners, just the man, just the woman, or neither partner.

Figure 4.1(a) (which forms the basis for analysis later in this section) takes as its sample all couples within the specified age range, and defines having a job as working for 15 hours or more per week. Under this definition of work, the male-breadwinner model is the dominant form of organisation in only three countries: Spain, Italy and Greece. In all other countries, it is more common for both members of a couple to have jobs, particularly in the Scandinavian countries, where two-job couples constitute over 75 per cent of the sample, while male-breadwinner couples constitute only 15–17 per cent.

Figure 4.1(a)   Distribution of work within couples: all couples where the man is aged 25–55, 'work' defined as 15+ hours per week

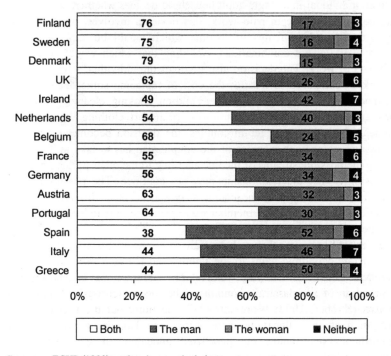

Source: ECHP (1999), authors' own calculations.

The allocation of work varies according to the characteristics of the sample analysed and the definition of work which is used. Figure 4.1(b) examines the distribution of work among couples in the same age group (man aged 25–55) who have at least one child aged under six, and uses a definition of work as full-time employment (working 30 or more hours per week). Among couples with young children, there is clearly a higher degree of specialisation of work. Only in five countries (the Scandinavian countries, plus Belgium and Portugal) do couples with two full-time earners outnumber those with a full-time male worker and a female partner who works part-time or who has no paid work at all.

*Figure 4.1(b)   Distribution of work within couples: couples with children
                   where the man is aged 25–55, 'work' defined as 30+ hours
                   per week*

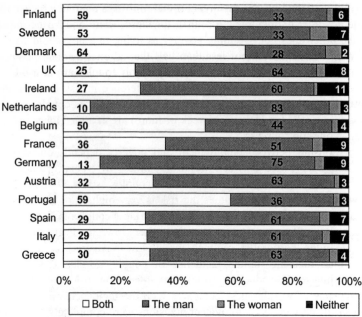

Source: ECHP (1999), authors' own calculations.

To some extent, these employment patterns within couples fall into groups as defined by welfare-regime typology. The 'social-democratic' group is characterised by high employment levels among women in couples; in particular, mothers in the social-democratic group have higher employment levels than mothers in other countries. The 'liberal' group is characterised by low levels of full-time work among mothers. Three countries in the 'residual' group are characterised by the predominance of the male-breadwinner couple, and by low levels of female employment, particularly among mothers. However, Portugal, the fourth member of this group, stands out from the others, in its high levels of labour market participation among women and, particularly, mothers. The 'corporatist' group of countries are a mixed bag – relatively homogeneous on the 15-hour measure among all couples, but very heterogeneous on the 30-hour measure among mothers, with mothers in the Netherlands and Germany among the least likely to work full time.

Couple non-employment and polarisation
The remainder of this section focuses on couples who have no job between

them. The reasons for doing this are twofold. First, there is evidence to suggest that worklessness has been growing at the household level over recent decades (Gregg and Wadsworth, 1996, 2001, 2002). Second, among couples, the risk of poverty and its accompanying social problems are much higher for those where neither partner has a job, than for those where one partner has a job and the other does not. Defining poverty as living in a household with a household equivalent income of less than half the national median income,[1] Iacovou (2003) shows that in every country one-job couples are at a higher risk of poverty than two-job couples, but the difference in risk between the two groups is small. By contrast, workless couples (defined as couples where neither partner works for 15 hours a week or more) are at a *far* higher risk of poverty than one-job couples.

The relationship between employment and poverty depends on welfare benefits, and thus varies between welfare regimes. In 'social-democratic' countries the risk of poverty, even for workless couples, is low, at 18 per cent or less, while in the 'liberal' regimes the risk is very high, at 45 per cent or more (Iacovou, 2003). The risk of poverty for workless couples is also high in the 'residual' welfare regimes (though rather low in Portugal), and intermediate in the 'corporatist' regimes (though low in Austria).

Rather than focusing on the incidence of couple worklessness (which varies according to the economic cycle), it is interesting to look at how the *actual* incidence of worklessness compares with the incidence which would be *predicted* if individuals' employment decisions were completely unrelated to the decisions of their partners. There is no reason why the actual level of couple worklessness should exceed the level of worklessness which would be predicted if members of couples made their decisions independently. After all, if members of couples were to compensate for the other member being out of work by looking for a job themselves, one might expect to see fewer workless couples than an assumption of independence would predict. However, Iacovou (2003) finds that actual levels of couple worklessness exceed the predicted levels of worklessness in every country – sometimes by a large margin.

Figure 4.2 shows actual and predicted levels of couple worklessness in 14 countries, where the predicted level of worklessness is calculated by multiplying the male partners' non-employment rate by the female partners' non-employment rate in each country. Countries are ranked on the graph by predicted levels of worklessness, which vary from 1.2 per cent in Denmark up to 5.7 per cent in Italy. In some countries (such as Greece and Germany) the actual levels of worklessness are only slightly higher than predicted levels. In other countries (such as the UK, Ireland, Belgium and Sweden) actual levels of worklessness are far higher than predicted levels.

*Figure 4.2   Actual and predicted proportion of workless couples, by
country*

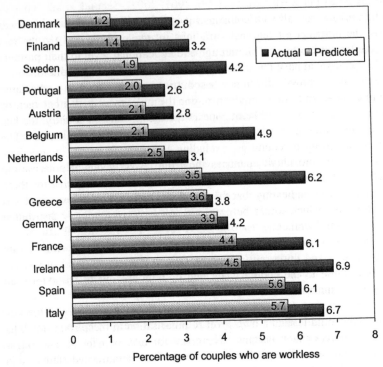

Percentage of couples who are workless

Note: Sample of couples where the man is aged 25–55.
Source: ECHP (1999), from Iacovou (2003).

The difference between actual and predicted levels of worklessness
reflects the extent to which jobs are 'concentrated' among some couples, who
have two jobs, at the expense of other couples who have no job, and thus may
be talked of as 'polarisation'.

There are several ways in which the difference between actual and
predicted worklessness may be translated into an index of polarisation. Gregg
and Wadsworth (2001, 2003) discuss difference-based and proportional
indices; Iacovou (2003) also discusses a covariance-based index of
polarisation for couples. Although these indices are derived differently, they
actually generate very similar rankings between countries, with the highest
levels of polarisation in Belgium, the UK and Ireland, and the lowest levels in
the southern European countries plus Germany.

As well as being robust to different methods of computing polarisation indices, these rankings are also reasonably robust to different definitions of work – for example, if 'having a job' is defined as working for at least one, or 15, or 30 hours per week.

The rankings are also little changed if indices are recalculated to account for (a) the influence of regional variations in employment, and (b) the fact that couples tend to be of a similar age and educational level to their partners – and, of course, to have the same number of children in the household.

Table 4.1 shows difference-based polarisation indices, calculated unconditionally and conditional on regional employment and other factors. On both sets of indices, Belgium appears the most polarised country; the UK and Ireland are next, followed by the Scandinavian countries. The 'corporatist' group of countries, excluding Belgium, forms an intermediate group, while the 'residual' countries show the lowest levels of polarisation. Indeed, polarisation indices in the right-hand column are *negative* for three residual countries, indicating that the actual percentage of workless couples is *lower* than that which would be predicted if jobs were randomly distributed between men and women.

These clusters in polarisation indices have a clear overlap with welfare state regimes – and this is entirely to be expected, since the level of welfare benefits payable to the couple when one or both are out of work form an important consideration in their joint labour supply decision.

It is easy to see why the heavily means-tested welfare regimes in the UK and Ireland should lead to a high level of polarisation in these countries. The lack of incentives these systems have given for one member of a workless couple to move into low-paid work has been well documented (Dilnot and Kell, 1987; Kell and Wright, 1990).[2]

It is also easy to see why the residual welfare regimes of the southern European countries should lead to very low levels of polarisation. In these countries, low income-maintenance benefits mean the partners of workless individuals face every incentive to compensate for the unemployed partner's lack of employment income by finding a job themselves, and little disincentive from the benefits system.

However, it is less easy to understand the connection between the generous and individually based benefit schemes of the Scandinavian countries, and the high levels of polarisation in these countries. It is also difficult to see how the insurance-based welfare programmes of the 'corporatist' countries could be responsible for such large differences in polarisation among this group of countries. Although there are differences between the welfare systems of the different countries in this group (Eardley et al., 1996a, 1996b), there are no differences which immediately illuminate why Belgium should be so highly polarised, while France or Austria, for example, should not. If any explanation for these differences is to be found in the welfare systems of these countries, it must be by looking in detail at the welfare policies of individual countries, rather than at the common characteristics of this cluster of countries.

Table 4.1   Polarisation indices for 14 countries

Country	Unconditional	Conditional on age, education, children and regional employment
Finland	1.79	1.38
Sweden	2.32	1.80
Denmark	1.62	1.36
Netherlands	0.61	0.54
UK	2.72	1.90
Ireland	2.42	1.58
Belgium	2.80	1.98
France	1.76	1.25
Germany	0.27	0.12
Austria	0.72	0.81
Portugal	0.61	0.19
Spain	0.42	−0.49
Italy	0.96	−0.23
Greece	0.15	−0.01

Note: Indices based on the difference between actual and predicted percentages of workless couples.

Source: ECHP (1999), from Iacovou (2003).

Moving in and out of work: the dynamics

Finally, in this section on couples, we discuss whether the polarisation of work discussed above is also observable in a dynamic context: that is, do husbands and wives tend to move into and out of work together?

The longitudinal aspect of the ECHP may be put to good use in addressing this question. The same sample of couples as used above (those where the man is aged between 25 and 55) were observed over consecutive pairs of years (1994 and 1995, 1995 and 1996, up to 1998 and 1999), and the movements into and out of work of continuing couples were studied.

Table 4.2 shows the results of logistic regressions on a sample of couples where neither partner has a job for 15 hours or more in the first year. The probability of the wife having a job in the second year is regressed (a) on the husband's employment status on the second year, and (b) on the husband's employment status plus a large number of controls measured in the first year, including age, marital status, number of children, education of both partners, time since last job, job search activity, and the health of both partners. Results are displayed for 13 countries: Sweden is not shown, since the Swedish ECHP data do not constitute a panel.

Table 4.2   *Relationship between the man moving into work and the woman moving into work, among workless couples (logistic regression coefficients)*

Country	Raw coefficients	Coefficients from multivariate analysis
Finland	0.770 ***	0.703 **
Denmark	0.963 ***	0.201
Netherlands	1.392 ***	0.245
UK	1.399 ***	0.964 ***
Ireland	0.580 ***	0.107
Belgium	2.179 ***	1.412 ***
France	1.322 ***	0.804 ***
Germany	1.304 ***	1.194 ***
Austria	1.283 ***	−0.978
Portugal	1.031 ***	0.493 *
Spain	0.095	−0.000
Italy	0.782 ***	0.244
Greece	1.316 ***	0.938 ***

Notes: Coefficients from logistic regressions on the sample of workless couples.
           Asterisks denote significance of coefficients: *** 1%, ** 5%, * 10%.
Source: ECHP (1994–99), authors' own calculations.

The first column in the table shows that in almost every country, women in workless couples whose partners find a job the following year, are significantly more likely to also find a job themselves. The coefficients are largest in Belgium and the UK (which are also the two countries with the highest degree of work polarisation) and lowest in Spain (which has one of the lowest degrees of polarisation). However, the relationship between cross-sectional polarisation indices and these dynamic coefficients is not clear-cut: for example, Germany and the Netherlands have low levels of polarisation but rather high coefficients in the logistic regression, while Finland and Ireland have high levels of polarisation but relatively small coefficients in the logistic regression.

The second column in Table 4.2 shows the coefficients from the multivariate regressions. As expected, these coefficients are smaller than those in the first column, indicating that some of the dynamic relationship between men's and women's jobs is due to personal characteristics being similar between members of a couple. In six of the 13 countries, the coefficients are still significant at the 1 per cent level. Here, there appears to be little relationship between cross-sectional polarisation and these dynamic coefficients: although Belgium, the UK and Finland retain a strong and significant relationship between men's and women's employment within couples, a significant relationship is also visible in Germany and Greece, which are two countries with low levels of polarisation.

This section has dealt with the relationship between the labour supply of men and women in couples. It has shown clearly that jobs are not spread around in a random fashion, but rather that individuals whose partners have jobs are more likely to have a job themselves. This is the case in all countries, although the effect is far more pronounced in some countries (those of the liberal and social-democratic regime groups, plus Belgium) than others. In all countries, at least some of the effect is attributable to the fact that members of a couple tend to resemble each other in terms of educational attainment and age – and they are subject to the same local labour market conditions. However, even after these factors are controlled for, the relationship between male and female employment status remains strong in those countries where the raw data indicate a strong relationship. We have also shown that this relationship holds in a dynamic sense: women whose partners move into work after being without a job are significantly more likely, in many countries, to move into work themselves.

The Impact of Children on Women's Labour Supply and Social Position

Despite rising rates of female labour force participation, the presence of children remains an important restriction on women's employment. Numerous studies demonstrate that children are negatively associated with women's labour supply. Women with children participate to a much lesser extent in the labour market than childless women, and if mothers are engaged in paid employment, they work for fewer hours than childless women (see, for example, Gornick, 1994; Kurz, 1998; Dekker et al., 2000; Drobnič, 2000; Stier and Lewin-Epstein, 2001). Existing literature suggests, however, that this 'child effect' is not equally strong across Western industrialized countries: there exists a degree of cross-country variation in the extent to which children affect female labour supply (Van der Lippe, 2001).

This section seeks (a) to describe the variation between countries of the European Union (EU) in the impact of children on women's labour supply, (b) to explain cross-country variation in child effects by highlighting the role of institutions aimed at improving the employment situation of mothers, and (c) to analyse social position, illustrating the longer-term effects of marriage and parenthood on women's prospects. Although the literature provides examples of studies describing and explaining cross-country variation in child effects (Gornick et al., 1998; Van der Lippe, 2001), these studies have the important methodological shortcoming of using cross-sectional data to study the impact of children on female employment.[3] Cross-sectional data are not the most appropriate with which to study child effects since the causal order of the relationship between children and labour supply is ambiguous. The presence of children (specifically, the timing) may itself be a consequence of the employment situation of a woman. Estimates of child effects from previous cross-sectional studies are therefore potentially biased.

To investigate the impact of children on women's labour supply in a methodologically appropriate way, this section uses the longitudinal panel data of the ECHP. In this, we follow Uunk et al. (2003). We confine our study to the analyses of the effects of first childbirth on mothers' labour force participation.[4] Although other aspects of the presence of children (such as the birth of other children and the presence of older children) are also interesting to study, such aspects increase complexity. In addition, the association between motherhood and changes in labour supply is likely to be clearer at the time of first childbirth. To study effects of first childbirth on female labour supply, we compare working hours one year prior to first childbirth with working hours two years after first childbirth. The choice of the second rather than the first year after childbirth for the second measure of working hours is based upon our interest in the effect of institutions that are aimed at improving mothers' labour supply. In the first year after childbirth many women are not observed to be in work, even if they remain attached to the labour market, due to parental leave. In the second year after childbirth when in most European countries parental leave arrangements have ended, it becomes interesting to observe how far women have returned to the labour market, compared to the levels at which they participated before childbirth.

We hypothesise that the impact of a young child on a woman's labour supply depends on the institutional arrangements supporting mothers' employment. A general institutional factor is the type of welfare regime. Social-democratic regimes may be expected to have the weakest child effects (that is, the least negative impact of children on labour supply) because of the strong state support for female employment.[5] In the corporatist and residual regimes, child effects are expected to be much larger because there is less state support for mothers to be employed and because the male-breadwinner model is propagated. Countries within the liberal regime type may be expected to occupy an intermediate position: employment is left to the market and therefore women are neither encouraged to work from nor discouraged working for pay.

As well as examining cross-country variations at the level of welfare state regime groups, we will also examine a more specific institutional factor, namely, the level of public childcare provision. The availability of childcare enables mothers to combine paid employment with caring for children. It may reasonably be expected that in countries with a high level of childcare provision, the child effect will be weaker than in countries with a low level of childcare.

Describing cross-country variation in child effects
Table 4.3 describes average weekly working hours of mothers one year prior to the birth of their first child and two years after childbirth for 13 countries of the ECHP data set.[6] Working hours before childbirth show the familiar pattern of low female employment participation in the Mediterranean countries (Spain, Italy and Greece) and much higher participation elsewhere in Europe. Interestingly, women from the Scandinavian, social-democratic countries (Finland and Denmark) do not stand out with the highest level of employment participation before childbirth. Their average pre-birth working hours are comparable to women from liberal regimes (the UK and Ireland), corporatist regimes (the Netherlands, Belgium, France, Germany and Austria) and Portuguese women.

After the birth of the first child this pattern changes dramatically. Whereas women from the Scandinavian countries continue to work at a similar, high level of working hours, women from other countries experience a drop in working hours averaging at least three hours a week. Very substantial reductions in working hours can be observed in the UK (18 hours), the Netherlands (14 hours), Germany (20 hours) and Austria (18 hours). A more modest reduction is observable in Ireland (9 hours), Belgium, France and the countries from southern Europe (3 to 5 hours). Hence, the countries of the EU display a large variation in child effects.

Esping-Andersen's typology of welfare regimes is not well able to explain the observed cross-country variation in child effects. Although countries from the social-democratic regime type (Finland and Denmark) display the weakest child effects, countries belonging to the corporatist regime type do not show unequivocal large child effects. Belgium and France display weak child effects, while the Netherlands and Germany display large child effects. In addition, countries that belong to the residual regime type (southern European countries) have rather weak child effects, despite the central role of the family and the promotion of the male-breadwinner model. In the UK, finally, women withdraw much more heavily from the labour market than could have been expected by their belonging to the liberal regime type.

Table 4.3   *Average weekly working hours of women before and after first childbirth, by country*

Country	Mean working hours before birth	Mean working hours after birth	Change in mean working hours	Number of cases
Finland	29.8	30.4	0.6	29
Denmark	31.8	30.7	–1.1	70
Netherlands	29.3	14.9	–14.4**	93
UK	34.8	17.3	–17.5**	102
Ireland	32.4	24.0	–8.5**	48
Belgium	31.0	26.7	–4.4**	58
France	26.9	22.0	–4.9**	118
Germany	29.6	9.7	–19.9**	123
Austria	33.8	16.0	–17.9**	21
Portugal	31.3	27.9	–3.5	49
Spain	17.3	14.3	–3.0*	120
Italy	20.3	16.0	–4.3**	145
Greece	18.6	14.9	–3.7	86

Notes: Means include non-employed women.
               Asterisks denote significance of coefficients: *** 1%, ** 5%, * 10%.
Source: ECHP (1994–99), authors' own calculations.

Explaining cross-country variation in child effects

These results demand an explanation that goes beyond welfare-regime typology. In this section we relate child effects to an institutional arrangement more specifically aimed at improving mothers' employment situation: the level of public childcare. Before doing this, however, we need to test alternative explanations of the European pattern of child effects.

One alternative explanation lies in the level of pre-birth labour market participation. In some countries where pre-birth labour market participation is low, it may simply not be possible for women to reduce working hours by a large amount after childbirth. This 'floor effect' may help to explain the weak child effects in the Mediterranean countries, where average working hours before first childbirth are already low.

Another alternative explanation concerns the differential composition of mothers in the European countries. Mothers across Europe differ in background characteristics and some of these characteristics may influence withdrawal behaviour. For example, mothers in the Scandinavian countries may continue to participate strongly on the labour market because they are better educated than mothers elsewhere in Europe, assuming that higher education moderates the reduction in working hours after childbirth (due to higher human capital investments).

To test whether these alternative explanations hold, we conducted multivariate regression analyses of the difference in working hours before and after childbirth. Figure 4.3 presents the results. The bars show estimated changes in working hours from three different models. These are (a) a baseline model assuming that hours changes vary only by country ('crude changes'); (b) a model assuming that in addition to country differences there is an effect from the level of pre-birth working hours; and (c) a model assuming that there is an additional effect from compositional factors (woman's age, woman's education and husband's working hours).

The estimated hours changes from model (a) simply repeat the findings from Table 4.3. The estimated hours changes from model (b) are changes in working hours controlling for pre-birth working hours. The model estimates what the changes in working hours would be had all women worked the same number of hours before childbirth (the European average is 26.7 hours). If this had been the case, the child effects would have differed, especially for Spain, Italy and Greece. Women from these countries would have displayed a much larger decrease in working hours accompanying childbirth: about 10 hours instead of the earlier observed 4 hours. Apparently, the low level of pre-birth labour market participation of women in the Mediterranean countries masks larger underlying changes in female labour supply.

As well as controlling for pre-birth working hours, model (c) also controls for compositional factors: age at first childbirth, educational level, and husbands' hours of work. The estimates presented on the graph show the changes in working hours which would be expected if all European women had identical characteristics in these respects. In fact, the graph shows that these estimates are very similar to those from model (b), indicating that differential composition does not explain much of the country variation in child effects. The exceptions are Portugal and Italy, where the reduction in working hours after childbirth would be about 3 hours less if mothers from these countries had 'European traits'. Closer inspection revealed that the relatively low educational level of Portuguese and Italian mothers accounts for their initially greater hours reduction. Differences in women's age or husbands' working hours do not appear to be important.

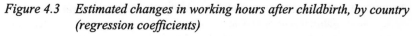

Figure 4.3   *Estimated changes in working hours after childbirth, by country (regression coefficients)*

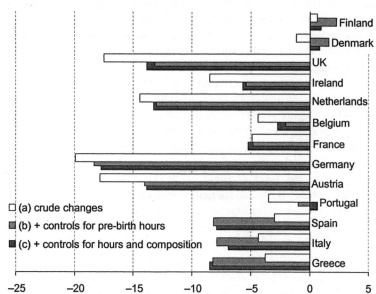

Note: Figures from OLS regressions (three models).
Source: ECHP (1994–99), authors' own calculations.

Now that we know what the child effects would be if women in the EU had a similar starting position and similar background characteristics, the final question is: to what extent are country differences in estimated child effects related to differences in the public provision of childcare? To answer this question, we display in Figure 4.4 the level of public childcare in each country, and the predicted reduction in working hours derived from model (c).[7]

There appears to exist a significant negative relationship between the level of public childcare in a country, and the reduction in working hours accompanying first childbirth. The correlation at the country level is −0.73 – a high degree of correlation. The graph also shows the fitted regression line, with a regression slope of −0.31. This means that a 10 per cent increase in the level of public childcare is associated with a decrease of 3.1 hours in the child effect. Thus, while neither individual-level factors, nor welfare-regime typologies, are good predictors of between-country differences in mothers' labour market participation, the level of childcare provision is much more closely related to mothers' post-birth hours of work.

Figure 4.4 *Reduction in working hours after childbirth, by level of childcare provision*

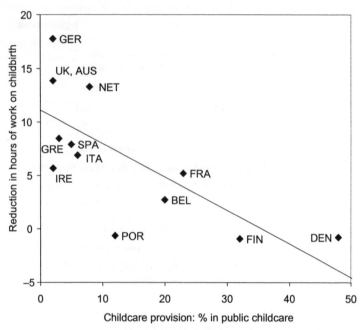

Note: The data points for Austria and the UK coincide.
Source: ECHP (1994–99), authors' own calculations.

It would be possible to interpret this observed relationship between childcare provision and female labour supply in a causally reverse manner, namely as an effect of labour supply on childcare (stronger labour market participation creates demand for care). However, since in our panel design, we measured the provision of childcare *prior* to labour supply (that is, before the measurement of the change in working hours), we believe the relationship may be better interpreted as a causal effect of childcare on mothers' labour supply.

While most countries in Figure 4.4 lie neatly around the regression line, there are a few exceptions, notably Germany and Portugal. Germany displays a larger child effect than can be expected by the level of public childcare and the controls for pre-birth working hours and population composition. This may have to do with the long duration of optional parental leave in Germany, which is partly paid and can last until 36 months after childbirth. Consequently, in the second year after childbirth many German women are non-employed. Alternatively, the large child effect may be attributed to the rather traditional attitudes of Germans regarding mothers' employment (see, for example, Kalmijn, 2003). Portuguese women, on the other hand, display a weaker child effect than might have been expected. Economic necessity may play a role here since Portuguese households are among the poorest in the EU (see Chapter 8). The weaker economic situation may 'force' Portuguese women to stay on the labour market after childbirth, in order to supply household income.

Family effects on women's social position
The analysis so far in this section has traced the impact of motherhood on women's chances of having a job during the period when their children are very young. But absence from the labour market can also have an important influence on people's future earning power, and hence on their overall social position. Robson and Gershuny (2004) have developed a new human capital approach to the measurement of social position, which illustrates the longer-term effects of marriage and parenthood on women's prospects.

Their measure is designed as a composite estimate of every adult's current stock of human capital, or earning power. In practice, the analysis estimates the expected rate of pay (gross hourly earnings) for each working-age adult in the ECHP sample. Four types of predictor variable are used:[8] the mean wage of the respondent's current or most recent occupation, in that country; educational qualifications; age; and the number of months in and out of employment over the past four years. It is this last element – time spent out of the labour market and its association with partnership and having children – which enables us to identify the effects of family formation on a woman's economic prospects.

Figure 4.5 illustrates one common trajectory. It assumes that a single man and a single woman form a partnership, and remain together, without children, for four years. In the first seven countries illustrated, the man can be seen to improve his earning power, and therefore his social position, over that early period of partnership. Only in Spain (and to a lesser extent Italy and Greece) does his position fall. For women, though, most countries show a fall in their social position over the early partnership period; the only exceptions here are Belgium (and to a lesser extent France). In every country men do better over the marriage period than women, but the extent of this gap ranges from only 0.06 or 0.07 index points in Belgium and France, to 0.88 points in the UK.

Figure 4.6 illustrates the next common stage in the family life-cycle – a couple already in a partnership have a first child, and remain together with their child(ren) for four years. Again, men tend to gain social position over this early parenthood period in many northern countries, though they tend to lose slightly in southern countries. It has already been shown (Table 4.3 and

Figure 4.3) that women in most countries reduce their labour market activity following childbirth. The analysis of Robson and Gershuny (2004) shows that in all countries women lose earning power, and social position, as a result. The losses can be substantial, especially in the UK and Germany – much larger than the losses associated initially with forming a partnership. As before, mothers in every country lose ground relative to their children's father: the range of this relative loss this time runs from 0.23 and 0.24 index points in Portugal and Italy, to 1.20 and 1.15 points in Germany and the UK respectively.

Figure 4.5   Impact of partnership on social position (regression coefficients)

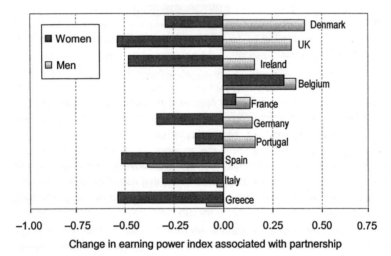

Change in earning power index associated with partnership

Note: The graph illustrates the increase or decrease in earning power associated with single
            people acquiring a partner and remaining together for four years. The effect of
            increasing age is not included.
Source: ECHP (1994–98), from Robson and Gershuny (2004).

In the fairy tale of Cinderella, the prince married a scullery maid and promoted her to princess.[9] The analysis of social position suggests that in real life the contrary tale of 'Allerednic' may be closer to the truth – the prince marries a princess and demotes her to scullery maid (Gershuny, 2000). Over the period of family formation, men typically improve their social position slightly, or it least hold it steady. Over the same period, women typically lose social position – by taking time out from the labour market to undertake family care, and/or by stepping down the occupational hierarchy to combine work and home activities.

Figure 4.6 Impact of parenthood on social position (regression coefficients)

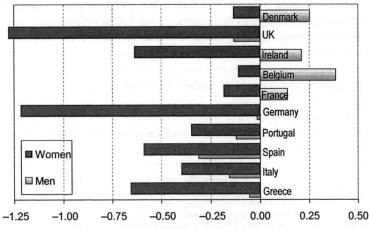

Change in earning power index associated with parenthood

Note:	The graph illustrates the increase or decrease in social position associated with a couple having a baby and remaining parents for four years. The effect of increasing age is not included.
Source:	ECHP (1994–98), from Robson and Gershuny (2004).

The 'Allerednic effect' is strongest in the UK, Germany and Greece – both in terms of the impact of children, and the combined marriage/children effect. Referring back to Figure 4.4, these are three of the countries with the most pronounced hours reductions after childbirth, and also three of the countries with the lowest provision of public childcare. The Allerednic effect is relatively weak in France, Denmark and Belgium – countries where women withdraw less heavily from the labour market after childbirth, and where public provision of childcare is greater. Thus, these findings demonstrate that women's withdrawal from the labour market after having children has consequences extending well beyond the short term: there are implications for the social position of women, in terms of their potential earnings and employment prospects, in the longer term as well.

In summary, this section has shown that there exists considerable variation between the countries of the EU in the impact young children have on female labour supply – the 'child effect' – and in the impact of children on women's future social position, in terms of their human capital. Esping-Andersen's typology of welfare states does not seem very helpful in explaining variations in these effects between countries. Although these effects are weak in social-democratic countries, in line with the strong promotion of, and state support for, female employment, the observed pattern in other European countries is not consistent with our predictions from the welfare state typology. For example, there is great variation between countries within the corporatist regime type, with large negative child effects in the Netherlands, Germany and Austria and much weaker child effects in Belgium and France.

By contrast, there is a strong association between the magnitude of child effects and the provision of public childcare in a country.

Care-giving and Employment of Midlife Women

In the third example of the relationship between family, work and employment we focus on care-giving to adults who need special help because of old age, illness or disability, and the employment of the caregivers. More specifically, we study the relationship between changes in hours of work associated with informal care-giving. So far this research question has been asked by social scientists, mostly within a single-country framework (for a comprehensive overview of past research, see Spiess and Schneider, 2001, 2002, 2003). However, as both care-giving and employment decisions are not only influenced by *personal* factors, such as preferences about caring for one's own parents or commitments to care for them, there is scope for a comparative analysis which takes into account different factors which operate at the level of the country rather than the individual. Many of the factors which influence people's trajectories through life in general also influence the relationship between care-giving and employment. First, different countries offer different *institutional* settings for combining work and care-giving, which relate principally to the possibilities of substituting between one's own care and that of a professional care-giver. Second, countries are characterised by different *social* attitudes towards the care of family members and the labour force participation of women. Third, *market* factors, such as the availability of jobs for care-giving women, affect the relationship between working and care-giving.

Given the empirical fact that care-givers are mainly women, caring for their own parents or other relatives needing care (or the parents or relatives of their partners), our analysis concentrates on women. Furthermore we restrict our study to women aged 45 to 59 as this is the typical age at which more and more women have to cope with the combination of care-giving duties and their own employment. For women younger and older than this, the probability of having a relative or friend needing care is much smaller. Younger women are more likely to be involved in childcare activities, while for older women the probability of leaving the labour market is increasing, meaning the relationship between working and care-giving is a very different one.

The data we use are the 1994 and 1996 waves of the ECHP. This means that 12 European countries may potentially be included in our analysis,[10] yielding a sample of over 12 500 middle-aged women. These women were asked if their present daily activities include, without pay, looking after a person (other than children) who needs special help because of old age, illness or disability. Women who respond positively are defined as care-givers; those who report being involved in paid work are defined as employed, or working.

The raw relationship between care-giving and employment

Figure 4.7 shows the proportion of women involved in paid work, the proportion involved in care-giving, and the proportion who are both working and giving care.

Figure 4.7   Labour force participation and care-giving: middle-aged women

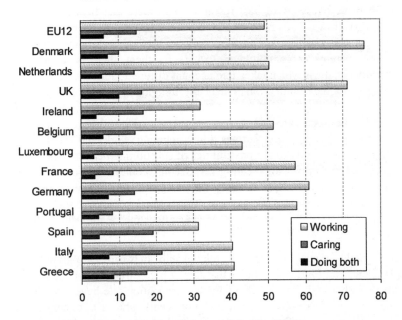

Source: ECHP (1994), adapted from Spiess and Schneider (2002).

In respect of the employment of middle-aged women, Figure 4.7 illustrates something already well known from other studies, namely that labour force participation is relatively high for women in Denmark (76 per cent) while it is the lowest for women in Spain (31 per cent). The highest percentage of middle-aged women who provide care is found in Italy (22 per cent) and

Spain (19 per cent), while Portugal is the country with the lowest percentage (8 per cent), followed by France (9 per cent) and Denmark (10 per cent).

With the exception of Portugal this seems to reflect the living arrangements of older people, as described in Chapter 2: in southern Europe older people live with their children to a much greater extent than elsewhere. The exception of Portugal may be explained by the fact that in this country elders live together with their children but do not receive care from them to the same extent.

Figure 4.8   Percentage of middle-aged care-giving women who are also employed

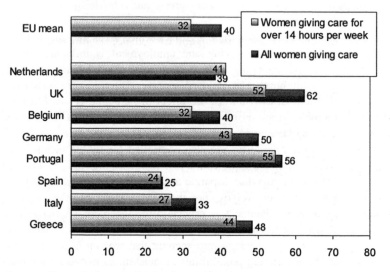

Notes: Denmark, France, Ireland, and Luxembourg are missing due to small sample sizes.
Source: ECHP (1994), adapted from Spiess and Schneider (2002).

One might expect a negative relationship between care-giving and employment, and Figure 4.7 shows that this is partly true. Countries such as Denmark with a high female labour force participation rate have a relatively low percentage of care-giving women (10 per cent), while 19 per cent of the middle-aged women in Spain report some kind of care-giving. However, the UK is an example of a country with a relatively high percentage of middle-aged working women (71 per cent) and a high percentage of care-giving women (16 per cent). Furthermore, the UK is the country with the highest percentage of women involved in both care-giving and working (10 per cent).

Of course, the extent of care-giving varies not only between countries, but also between individuals. One important variation is in the amount of time women devote to caring. Figure 4.8 gives an idea of how the intensity of care is related to employment status, showing the proportion of care-givers who also go out to work – first for all care-givers, and then for those involved in intensive care-giving (defined as 14 hours or more per week).

As it is more difficult to combine more intensive care-giving activity with any kind of employment, it is interesting to see how the percentage of employed women decreases when the sample is first restricted to just care-givers and second to care-givers of more than 14 hours a week. Figure 4.8 shows that the difference is smaller in countries such as Portugal and Greece, and much higher in countries such as the UK and Germany.

The relationship between changes in care-giving and adjustments in women's working hours

In a second step we use a multivariate approach which takes into account that the relationship between care-giving and employment is influenced by a variety of other factors, including *socio-demographic* characteristics (such as, age, education, health, number of children, income, cultural background) and *employment characteristics* (such as, the effect of part-time versus full-time work). Within a multivariate framework, the influence of all these factors may be controlled for simultaneously.

Differences between countries are also controlled for by the inclusion of categorical variables indicating the country of residence. As well as analysis for the whole of Europe together, separate analyses are run for two groups of countries. Since neither the welfare, nor the geographical, nor the religious typologies described in Chapter 1 is especially designed for an analysis of care-giving, we use a different means of grouping countries. This expands the welfare-regime approach by taking into account that women in the different welfare regimes have different possibilities of substituting between their own care-giving, the care-giving of other professionals at home, and institutional care. These possibilities for substitution can be captured by the proportion of elderly people living in institutions, and the percentage of elderly people using formal help at home. The lowest proportion of elderly people receiving long-term care in institutions can be found in Greece (less than 1 per cent), while the highest proportion can be found in Luxembourg and the Netherlands, where more than 6 per cent of the elderly receive long-term care in institutions. The proportion of elderly receiving formal help at home varies, with a relatively low percentage of elderly receiving formal help in southern Europe, and also in Ireland (which is in the middle concerning the receipt of institutionalised care). The highest proportion of elderly receiving formal home help can be found in Denmark, with a percentage of more than 10 per cent (Royal Commission on Long Term Care, 1999: 161).

In contrast to the traditional welfare-regime typology, the country grouping we are using here puts Ireland in the group with the southern European countries, because of fewer substitution possibilities with formal home help. In addition the analysis by Iacovou (see Chapter 2) shows that this grouping can be confirmed if older people's living arrangements are considered. As in the other southern European countries, Irish elders have a much higher probability of living with their children than elders in northern countries. And as is also shown by Iacovou, the percentage of elders receiving care at home is much higher in these countries than in northern Europe. Thus we define two groups of countries: the 'northern' countries (excluding Ireland) and the 'southern' countries (including Ireland).

Rather than using a static analysis of the relationship between care-giving and employment (which gives no information about adjustments and changes in people's behaviour) we use a dynamic approach. This focuses on the relationship between changes in the time spent giving care, and adjustments in working hours between two observation points, two years apart (1994 and 1996).

Adjustments in working hours are measured by the hour, because weekly work hours have been reported in all waves of the ECHP. However, the available measure of hours spent caring is not so fine, so to measure changes in care-giving hours, a set of independent dichotomous variables was defined. These are:

- the respondent did not give care in either year (reference category);
- she provided care in the first year, and stopped;
- she did not provide care in the first year, and started;
- she provided care in both years and increased the level of care;
- she provided cared in both years and decreased the level of care; and
- she provided care in both years at the same level.

Changes in care-giving hours are defined as a move between three levels of care-giving intensity: 1–13 hours per week; 14–28 hours per week; and more than 28 hours per week.

For our estimates, changes in work hours are regressed on changes in care-giving, together with other socio-economic variables and country variables.[11] Of the set of variables indicating adjustments in care-giving, the only ones which have a significant influence on changes in work hours in any of the models are those indicating the *start* of care-giving and an *increase* in hours of care-giving.

Figure 4.9 presents the effects of starting and increasing care-giving on changes in hours of work. Results are presented for Europe as a whole, and also for the two country groups separately.

The first set of bars shows estimates of net changes in hours of work for the whole sample of women, including those who increase, do not change, or decrease their hours of work. Since it may be important to distinguish between increases and decreases in hours of work, the second set of bars focuses on increases in hours of work, displaying estimates of the same regressions, for the sample of women who either increased or did not change their hours of work. The third set of bars focuses on decreases in hours of work, displaying estimates for the sample of women who either reduced or did not change their hours. These three sets of regressions yield 18 relevant coefficients; however, only those which are statistically significant are shown in Figure 4.9.

Figure 4.9   Relationship between changes in care-giving and changes in working hours (regression coefficients)

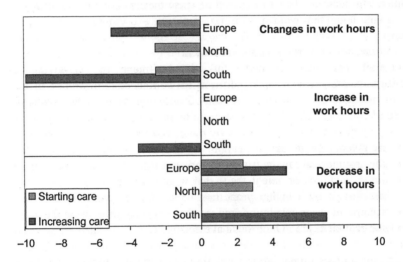

Notes: Figures from ordinary least squares regressions on changes in work hours.
            Statistical significance refers to p<0.10.
Source: ECHP (1994 and 1996), adapted from Spiess and Schneider (2003).

For the regressions based on the entire European sample, women who start giving care change their hours of work by on average 2.4 hours per week more than women with no care obligations. Women who increase their level of care-giving change their hours of work by a much larger average of 5 hours per week. The further distinction between an increase and a decrease in work hours shows that these differences are more or less fully accounted for by women who decrease their hours of work.

We now look separately at the two country groups. Women in the 'northern' countries show a significant relationship between the *beginning* of a care-giving commitment and their working-time adjustment, but there appears to be no effect from *intensifying* an existing care-giving commitment. In more detail, the distinction between an increase and a decrease in work hours shows that women living in the northern countries (that is, those with a higher percentage of elderly receiving formal care) decrease their working hours by 2.9 hours per week more than women without any care obligations.

The regressions based on the 'southern' countries show that both beginning and intensifying a care-giving commitment have a significant effect on changes in working time. In contrast to the northern countries, the dominant effect comes from the intensification of care-giving. The net effect is made up of both a lower probability of women increasing their hours of work, and a higher probability of reducing them. In southern countries, women who increase their care-giving increase their working hours by about 3.5 hours less than women with no care-giving commitment; they also decrease their working time by an average of about 7 hours per week more than women with no care-giving commitment.

Overall, our analysis shows that the beginning of care-giving is significantly associated with a reduction in work hours for women in the 'northern' group of countries. By contrast, female employees in the 'southern' group of countries, including Ireland, respond to an increase in care demands – reducing their hours of paid work by more, and increasing them less, than non-care-givers. There are a number of possible explanations for this including institutional factors, social factors and market factors. Considering *institutional factors*, one might argue that women living in countries which are characterised by a higher proportion of elderly receiving either formal care at home or in an institution, reduce their working time when the care-giving obligation begins. Once they have decided to care for their relatives no significant adjustments in working hours are necessary, as they can rely on a better provision of formal home help. Women living in 'southern' countries do not have this possibility. *Social factors* might play an additional role, as the attitudes in southern countries and Ireland towards the care of a relative might differ from that in northern countries. If the care of a family member is socially more desirable in these countries, it could be that women try to combine their original working time and new care obligations as long as possible. But once their care obligations become too intensive they have to adjust work hours, as they cannot rely on formal home help or institutional care in the same way as women in northern Europe (excluding Ireland). A third explanation might be covered by *market factors*. If the labour market in southern countries, for example, offers less part-time jobs it is more difficult to combine intensive care with any kind of employment.

Outlook for Further Research

The analysis presented in this chapter has shown that there is substantial personal variation in the relationship between family and work; this is true for the employment decisions of couples, mothers and care-giving women. But it has shown, as well, that there are substantial differences between European countries.

The existing welfare-regime typology seems to explain some of these differences. Nevertheless, the majority of between-country differences cannot be explained by this grouping, at least not on the level tested in our analysis.

First, there are certain countries that do not fit in the typical welfare-regime typology. One exception in various contexts is Portugal, which traditionally is grouped with the other southern European countries. But in contrast to the other southern countries, such as Italy, Spain and Greece, Portugal is characterised by a high level of labour market participation among women and, particularly, mothers. The same is true if we consider reductions in working hours after childbirth: the reduction in the working hours of Portuguese women would be less if these mothers had European traits. This result is the exact opposite of that in all other countries. Ireland is another example of a country forming an exception. Under conventional welfare-regime typology, Ireland is grouped with the UK, in the group of the liberal welfare states. However, our analysis of the relationship between care-giving and employment suggests that it makes more sense to group Ireland together with southern Europe, if one is interested in this type of family effect.

Second, we can conclude that some of the family effects we found can in general be better explained by institutional differences than by welfare regime differences. This is particularly true for the impact young children have on female labour supply, and for their mothers' future social position in term of their future prospects in the labour market. The provision of day care seems to explain more than the welfare-regime typology.

Third, our three examples have shown, in various ways, that if any explanation of differences is to be found in the welfare systems, then we must look in more detail at the welfare policies of individual countries. Further research in this direction based on European micro-data seems most promising for analyses of the dynamics of family and work.

Notes

1. This definition follows Jäntti and Danziger (2000) and Smeeding et al. (2002) and others.
2. Initiatives such as the Working Families Tax Credit in the UK have been designed to reduce the disincentives to work for this group, and a lower rate of polarisation may well result from this.

3. An exception is the study by Stier and Lewin-Epstein (2001). This study uses longitudinal data and methods to assess the impact of institutional arrangements on women's employment patterns. However, the study is confined to the child-rearing period and as such does not investigate the impact of the transition into motherhood.

4. We choose to study women in a married or cohabiting union and not single women because the inclusion of the latter group introduces greater complexity. Drobnič (2000), for example, showed for Germany and the USA that the effect of children on the odds of employment exit is weaker for single women than for married women. The reason for this difference is that lone mothers in many countries depend more on paid work than married mothers.

5. In this section, we assign the Netherlands to the corporatist regime type and not the social-democratic regime type because institutional support for working mothers was not very high during the period of investigation. State support for female employment was much more in line with corporatist countries such as Germany and Austria, than with social-democratic countries from Scandinavia (also see Uunk et al., 2003).

6. We exclude Luxembourg and Sweden because the first country has only three panel observations and because the data for the second country do not form a genuine panel. The Swedish data are not derived from a follow-up of the same individuals through consecutive waves, but the data are pooled cross-sections. For the UK and Germany we use the longitudinal panel data from the BHPS and GSOEP. For further details on selection of the sample of analysis, we refer to EPAG Working Paper 39 (Uunk et al., 2003).

7. The level of public childcare is measured by the percentage of children under the age of three in publicly funded day care services (such as daycare centres and kindergartens). It is obtained from the European Commission on Childcare for several countries during the 1990–95 period (see Van Dijk, 2001). Because data for the 1990–95 period lack for Belgium and Germany, for these countries figures from the late 1980s are used (Gornick et al., 1998).

8. The analysis was carried out separately in each country, and shadow wage estimates were standardised in each country to have a mean of 0 and a standard deviation of 1. The model was based on the first five waves of the ECHP, including retrospective data about economic activities during the preceding calendar year.

9. European versions of the tale of Cinderella include Cendrillon (France); Aschenputtel (Germany); Estrellita de Oro (Spain); Assepoester (Netherlands); and Cenerentola (Italy).

10. We could not include Austria, Finland and Sweden, because they joined the ECHP in later waves.

11. These are: age, age squared, education, marital status, nationality, health, household net income, part-time work, full-time work and country dummies.

References

Becker, G. (1981), *A Treatise on the Family*, Cambridge, MA: Harvard University Press.

Dekker, R., R. Muffels and E. Stancanelli (2000), 'A longitudinal analysis of part-time work by women and men in the Netherlands', in S.S. Gustafson and D.E. Meulders (eds), *Gender and the Labor Market: Econometric Evidence of Obstacles to Achieving Gender Equality*, New York: St. Martin's Press, pp. 260–87.

Dilnot, A. and M. Kell (1987), 'Male unemployment and women's work', *Fiscal Studies*, **8**, 1–16.

Drobnič, Sonja (2000), 'The effects of children on married and lone mothers' employment in the United States and (West) Germany', *European Sociological Review*, **16**, 137–57.

Eardley, T., J. Bradshaw, J. Ditch, I. Gough and P. Whiteford (1996a), 'Social assistance in OECD countries: synthesis report', Department of Social Security Research Report No. 46, London: HMSO.

Eardley, T., J. Bradshaw, J. Ditch, I. Gough and P. Whiteford (1996b), 'Social assistance in OECD countries: country reports', Department of Social Security Research Report No. 47, London: HMSO.

Gershuny, J. (2000), 'Social position from narrative data', in R. Crompton, F. Devine, M. Savage and J. Scott (eds), *Renewing Class Analysis*, Oxford: Blackwell.

Gornick, J.C. (1994), 'Women, employment, and part-time work: a comparative study of the United States, the United Kingdom, Canada, and Australia', Ph.D. Dissertation, Cambridge, MA: Harvard University.

Gornick, J.C., M.K. Meyers and K.E. Ross (1998), 'Public policies and the employment of mothers: a cross-national study', *Social Science Quarterly*, **79**, 35–54.

Gregg, P. and J. Wadsworth (1996), 'It takes two: employment polarisation in the OECD', Centre for Economic Performance Discussion Paper no. 304, London: LSE.

Gregg, P. and J. Wadsworth (2001), 'Everything you ever wanted to know about worklessness and polarization at the household level but were afraid to ask', *Oxford Bulletin of Economics and Statistics*, **63**, Special Issue.

Gregg, P. and J. Wadsworth (2002), 'Two sides to every story: measuring the polarisation of work', *Centre for Economic Performance Working Papers*, **1099**, London: CEP.

*Iacovou, M. (2003), 'Work-rich and work-poor couples: polarisation in 14 countries in Europe', *EPAG Working Papers*, **45**, Colchester: University of Essex.

Jäntti, M. and S.H. Danziger (2000), 'Income poverty in advanced countries', in A.B. Atkinson and F. Bourgignon (eds), *Handbook of Income Distribution*, New York and Elsevier: North Holland, pp. 309–78.

Kell, M. and J. Wright (1990), 'Benefits and the labour supply of women married to unemployed men', *Economic Journal*, **400**, Supplement: 119–26

Kurz, K. (1998), *Das Erwerbsverhalten von Frauen in der intensiven Familienphase: Ein Vergleich zwischen Müttern in der Bundesrepublik und in den USA*, Opladen: Leske and Budrich.

*Robson K. and Gershuny, J. (2004), 'Social position in Europe', *EPAG Working Papers* (forthcoming), Colchester: University of Essex.

Royal Commission on Long Term Care (1999), 'With respect to old age: long term care – rights and responsibilities', A report by the Royal Commission on Long Term Care, Chairman: Prof. Sir Stewart Sutherland, Presented to Parliament by Command of her Majesty.

Smeeding, T.E., L. Rainwater and G. Burtless (2002), 'United States poverty in a cross-national context', in S.H. Danziger and R.H. Havemen (eds), *Understanding Poverty*, New York: Russell Sage, pp. 162–89.

*Spiess, C.K. and U.A. Schneider (2001), 'More, less, or all the same? The difference midlife care-giving makes for women's adjustments of work hours', *EPAG Working Paper*, **25**, Colchester: University of Essex.

*Spiess, C.K. and U.A. Schneider (2002), 'Midlife care-giving and employment – an analysis of adjustments in work hours and informal care for female employees in Europe', *ENEPRI Working Paper*, **9**, Brussels.

*Spiess, C.K. and U.A. Schneider (2003), 'Interactions between care-giving and paid work hours among European midlife women, 1994 to 1996', *Ageing and Society*, **23**, 41–68.

Stier, H. and N. Lewin-Epstein (2001), 'Welfare regimes, family-supportive policies, and women's employment along the life-course', *American Journal of Sociology*, **106**, 1731–60.

Strober, M.H. (1993), 'Rethinking Economics Through a Feminist Lens', *American Economic Review*, **84** (2), p. 143.

*Uunk, W., M. Kalmijn and R. Muffels (2003), 'The impact of children on women's labor supply in Europe: a reassessment of the role of institutions', *EPAG Working Papers*, **39**, Colchester: University of Essex.

Van Dijk, L. (2001), 'Macro changes in public childcare provisions, parental leave, and women's employment', in T. Van der Lippe and L. Van Dijk (eds), *Women's Employment in a Comparative Perspective*, New York: Aldine de Gruyter, pp. 37–58.

Van der Lippe, T. (2001), 'The effect of individual and institutional constraints on hours of paid work of women; an international comparison', in T. Van der Lippe and L. Van Dijk (eds), *Women's Employment in a Comparative Perspective*, New York: Aldine de Gruyter, pp. 221–43.

Wooley, F.R. (1993), 'The feminist challenge to neoclassical economics', *Cambridge Journal of Economics*, **17**, 485–500.

* Direct output from EPAG's *DynSoc* research programme (see page 268).

5. Standard and Non-standard Employment: Gender and Modernisation in European Labour Markets

Lutz C. Kaiser

Introduction

Employment is an important social institution that positions individuals within society, both in a monetary and in a non-monetary sense (Solow, 1990). This chapter uses this twofold approach to investigate the socio-economic characteristics that influence standard and non-standard employment, and to analyse job-satisfaction. Since the emergence of non-standard employment is a relatively recent phenomenon, these cross-national comparisons may be assessed in terms of levels of 'modernisation'.

The chapter begins with a discussion of the terms 'standard' and 'non-standard' employment. Data from the European Community Household Panel (ECHP) are then used to describe patterns of non-standard employment in the member states of the European Union (EU), and to show what socio-economic factors influence these patterns. The analysis then compares men's and women's levels of job-satisfaction in the light of their differing employment profiles.

Standard and Non-standard Employment: Conceptualisation and Theoretical Implications

It is striking that the literature on changing patterns of employment offers no common definition or terminology for the new forms of contract. For instance, both the negative label 'marginal' and the positive label 'flexible' have emerged to describe new forms of employment, when a dividing line is drawn between what is said to be 'ordinary' (namely, permanent full-time waged employment) and 'atypical'. A normative interpretation is often assumed, in which the standard pattern is approved, and 'atypical' work is judged to be inferior. There are obvious problems with normatively loaded preconceptions of this nature (Dekker and Kaiser, 2000).

In seeking a more neutral definition of emerging patterns of work, we should also look for a definition which views current patterns of female and male employment in the context of their different starting points. For women, the trajectory has been from economic inactivity towards increasing labour market participation. For men, it has been from permanent full-time employment to disrupted employment profiles that include phases of unemployment. Accordingly, a cross-gender comparison using the terms 'normal/atypical' cannot be applied consistently because part-time employment, for example, would be rather atypical for men but much more common for women. Furthermore, in a cross-national comparison, equivalent or at least similar types of employment might be more typical in one country and less typical in another.

The terms used in this chapter – 'standard' and 'non-standard' employment – are chosen to have neutral connotations, and to mean the same in all countries of the EU and for both genders.

This perspective leads to a more comprehensive view, as female employment patterns have changed even more dramatically over the past decades than those of men. The reasons include greater access to education, declining fertility rates, and a rising employability of women, which is, for instance, a result of the increased importance of the service sector. Therefore, the increasing economic activity of women clearly has to be one of the themes of this chapter.

Because the growth in the number of women entering the labour market is primarily achieved via part-time employment, permanent full-time jobs are declining as a relative share of total employment. However, permanent full-time employment is not decreasing substantially in absolute terms and it is actually increasing in some countries (OECD, 1999), which contradicts the so-called erosion hypothesis (Kaiser, 2001a). Hence, rather than an erosion, the actual development complements the traditional standard employment patterns of men.

These trends contradict traditional theories on differences between male and female labour supply, which are based on the static unitary model of the household with a joint utility function and individuals acting and reacting independently of each other. This approach partially interprets labour supply in terms of biological differences, concluding that 'this sexual division of labor has been found in virtually all human societies . . .' (Becker, 1994: 39).

In contrast, more advanced theoretical approaches suggest that individuals' mutual independent rational choices are not the only factor (Nelson, 1998). An explicit bargaining-oriented dynamic approach can be used, for example, to explain changes in female labour supply over time. A shift in the female's bargaining power within marriage associated with a rise in the opportunity costs of raising children has encouraged women to increase their supply of labour and combine a specialisation in domestic work with market work, mainly by means of non-standard, especially part-time, employment (Ott, 1992, 1995). Accordingly, household structure, the number and age of children, and the relationship between those who bargain for time allocation between market work and domestic work are crucial explanations of the labour supply of women. However, cross-national differences in the institutional background, including the child daycare infrastructure and the shape of tax and social security systems, are likely to affect the EU-wide rise of female economic activity, serving either to promote or hinder the labour market attachment of women (Dingeldey, 2001).

To describe this micro-based development of changing employment patterns in macro terms, the emergence of new forms of employment can be explained in terms of 'modernisation'. One of the leading contemporary commentators on modernisation distinguishes between 'initial', 'catching-up', and 'advanced' modernisation, with the latter describing the most recent stage (Zapf, 1991a, 1991b, 1996). A main feature of advanced modernisation, as emphasized by Zapf (2001: 501), is a 'new gender contract' including the rising labour market orientation of women. Thus, a cross-national comparison may use different levels of modernisation to scale the current structure of welfare and labour market regimes in terms of a new gender contract (Pfau-Effinger, 1999 and 2001). In this sense, modernisation can be described in two ways. One incorporates straightforward improvements in women's access to employment and chances of promotion. The other aims at an optimal match between domestic and market work. However, both perspectives include an augmentation of women's options for market work.

The Variety of Employment Forms across Europe

Standard and non-standard employment patterns are defined by two main characteristics: type of contract and number of working hours. *Standard* employment is defined as permanent full-time work. *Non-standard* employment is defined as jobs which are either fixed-term or part-time (less than 30 hours per week). *Self-employment* is introduced as a third category (not included in non-standard employment) to get at the full range of possible labour market participation statuses.

On average, 65 per cent of European male workers are in a standard employment relationship, with Luxembourg (86 per cent) leading the group of the 15 EU countries (Figure 5.1).[1] Of employed men in Austria, around 77 per cent have a permanent full-time job, with Germany, the Netherlands and France not far behind. In contrast, the four southern countries are clearly, and

Ireland is just, below the European mean value. Between these top and bottom countries, the share of standard employment ranges between 74 per cent for the UK and 67 per cent for Sweden.

On average, 15 per cent of European men work on the basis of a non-standard employment relationship, with Spain leading (28 per cent) and Luxembourg taking last position (5 per cent). Some 20 per cent of EU men are self-employed, ranging from Greece (42 per cent) to the Netherlands (7 per cent).

Figure 5.1   Standard, non-standard and self-employment: men

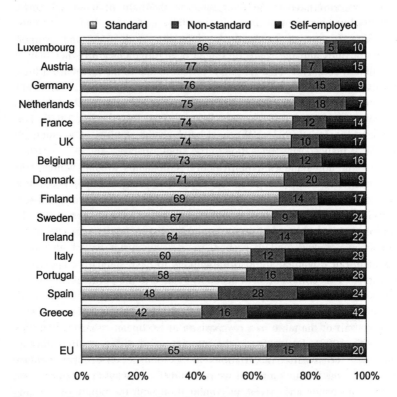

Note: Countries ranked by share of standard employment.
Sources: ECHP (1998), except Germany (ECHP data of the Federal Statistical Office 1996),
              Luxembourg (ECHP 1996), Finland (ECHP 1997), Sweden (ECHP 1997), UK
              (BHPS 1998). Author's own calculations.

The structure is entirely different amongst working women. The overall proportion in permanent full-time jobs falls to 55 per cent (Figure 5.2). At the top of the scale the rates are 67–64 per cent in France, Denmark, Finland and

Sweden. While Germany was third in standard employment among men, for women in non-standard employment it ranks thirteenth out of the 15 countries considered here. At the other extreme the Netherlands, the country with the highest share of women in part-time work world-wide, has only 34 per cent of working women in permanent full-time jobs. However, it is striking that the proportion of women in standard employment in the southern countries is of nearly the same magnitude as the proportion of men. This is particularly true for Portugal (58 per cent for men versus 56 per cent for women) with a female share of standard employment as high as the European average. Nevertheless, these narrower gender differences in the type of jobs held in the southern countries have to be interpreted in the light of the much lower overall employment rates of women, especially in Greece, Italy and Spain. Only Portugal remains exceptional, since for both men and women, employment rates and the share of standard employment are higher than in other southern countries. This finding is probably due to the fact that Portugal possesses the lowest wage level in the entire EU (ILO, 1997; Kaiser, 1997), which forces most of the Portuguese to be attached to the labour market mainly on the basis of a full-time job (Santos, 1991; Ruivo et al., 1998). This economic characteristic places Portugal between the statuses of a 'catching-up' and an 'advanced' modernisation of the labour market.

Concerning non-standard employment relationships among women, the Netherlands takes first place, at 61 per cent, and Portugal the last position at 24 per cent. However, in assessing the data it must be borne in mind that gender differences in the overall employment rate vary widely across the EU. The employment rate gap between men and women is relatively low in the Scandinavian countries and in France. In these countries with high female employment rates, women are also most likely to have standard employment relationships. This combination is probably related to the political support for women's and mothers' employment in these countries, including well-developed child daycare systems. On that score, Germany is placed nearer to the bottom half of the table in a comparison of European countries (Gornick et al., 1997, 1998). Furthermore, the interaction of different child daycare systems with cross-national variations in tax and social security systems clearly shapes the labour supply of women in different ways. Traditional joint taxation of husbands and wives, in combination with the policy of deriving wives' benefit entitlements from their husbands' social security contributions (as in Germany), lower the incentives of women to search for work if their partner possesses a standard employment relationship. In contrast, the Danish example seems to supply both a more appropriate infrastructure and higher incentives for women to be attached to the labour market (Dingeldey, 2001). These examples strongly suggest that employment opportunities in whole countries are shaped by institutions.

Figure 5.2   Standard, non-standard and self-employment: women

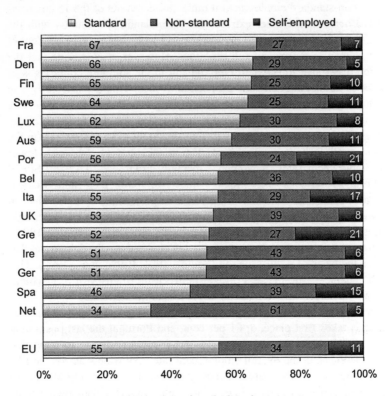

Notes: Countries are ranked by share of standard employment.
Source: ECHP (1998), except Germany (ECHP data of the Federal Statistical Office 1996),
             Luxembourg (ECHP 1996), Finland (ECHP 1997), Sweden (ECHP 1997), UK
             (BHPS 1998). Author's own calculations.

Overall, women make a large contribution to total non-standard employment (Figure 5.3). On average, nearly two-thirds of the EU total non-standard work is attributable to the women's labour force.[2]

In Luxembourg, the UK, Austria, the Netherlands, and Sweden, the proportion ranges between 70 per cent and 80 per cent. Ireland, Germany, Belgium, and France display proportions that are still above the EU mean. The remaining countries' share of women in total non-standard employment is below this threshold. These countries are either members of the Scandinavian (that is, social-democratic) family of nations, namely Finland and Denmark, or can be assigned to the southern (residual regime) group.

Figure 5.3   Women as a proportion of those in non-standard employment

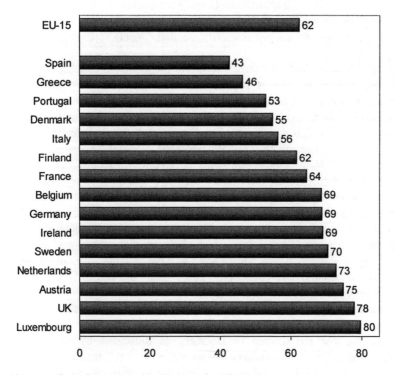

Note: Countries are ranked by the proportion of women.
Source: ECHP (1998), except Germany (ECHP data of the Federal Statistical Office, 1996),
             Luxembourg (ECHP, 1996), Finland (ECHP, 1997), Sweden (ECHP, 1997), UK
             (BHPS, 1998). Author's own calculations.

Socio-economic Determinants of Standard and Non-standard Employment

This section examines the importance of various socio-economic factors as influences on people's choice of standard and non-standard employment.

For this analysis, labour supply is arranged along the working time categorisation only, not distinguishing between 'permanent' and 'fixed-term' or between 'employees' and 'self-employed'. The labour market status 'non-employed' is introduced into the model to cover the various forms of economic inactivity and unemployment. Overall, the definition of employment status is constructed in a fourfold way:

- full-time employment (≥ 30 h/week);
- regular part-time employment (15 to 29 h/week);
- small part-time employment (< 15 h/week); and
- not employed (economic inactivity, unemployment).

In the following analyses, only a subset of the available countries is used. With this restriction, one is put into a 'better position to interpret and understand any developments in the light of their specific institutional frameworks' (Cebrián et al., 2000, 206). The selection of Denmark, the UK, Germany, and Portugal was designed to distinguish between different welfare state regimes (respectively social-democratic, liberal, corporatist and residual). The Netherlands represents a hybrid case between social-democratic and corporatist, but may be seen as a special case because of its very high level of part-time employment. In order to capture socio-economic factors mentioned earlier that are likely to determine labour supply, the analysis takes account of household-related 'bargaining characteristics' (household structure, age/number of children, marital status) and general human capital variables, which are known to have an impact on employment probabilities (years of education, age, state of health, citizenship, unemployment history) (Killingsworth, 1983).

Comparing the effects of family structure on labour supply, the following striking findings emerge (Table 5.1). The impact of different family structures is relatively low for women in Denmark as illustrated by the lack of significant coefficients. By contrast, for the category of full-time employment, the Netherlands, the UK, and Germany display positive effects for women living in a partnership without children. Conversely, women living in a partnership with children are less likely to work full-time. This does not hold for Denmark and Portugal. Hence, in Denmark, female labour force participation seems to be more or less universal, regardless of family structure, and this is similarly true regarding full-time employment for Portuguese women. Concerning the employment probabilities of men, either no significant impact of different family structures emerges (Germany, Portugal) or living in a partnership with children has a positive effect on working full-time (Denmark, Netherlands, the UK).

In terms of the age of children (Table 5.2), the results suggest that very young children reduce Danish women's probability of working full-time, regular part-time or small part-time, and increase their probability of not working at all. By contrast, for the UK, the figures show that children reduce the likelihood of women working full-time, whatever the age of their youngest child. Children increase the probability of part-time employment for British women, though. This finding is in line with the high employment of British women in part-time jobs in the service sector (Böheim and Taylor, 2000).

Table 5.1 *Influence of family structure on men's and women's labour supply (marginal effects)*

Family structure	Denmark		Nether- lands		UK		Germany		Portugal	
	M	W	M	W	M	W	M	W	M	W
Full-time work										
single	-13.7	–	-13.8	15.1	-9.5	–	–	16.1	–	13.8
lone parent	-15.0	–	-13.9	–	-10.8	-8.7	–	–	–	8.8
couple, no kids	-5.4	–	–	20.9	–	15.1	–	15.6	–	–
Regular part-time work										
single	–	–	–	-9.4	–	-7.0	–	-5.3	–	–
lone parent	–	–	–	-7.7	2.5	-6.2	–	–	–	–
couple, no kids	–	-3.0	–	–	–	-9.3	–	-3.3	–	–
Short part-time										
single	–	–	1.5	–	–	-3.2	–	-2.7	–	–
lone parent	–	–	-0.7	-5.9	–	–	–	–	–	–
couple, no kids	–	–	-1.1	-11.5	–	-3.0	–	-5.8	0.8	–
Not employed										
single	11.4	–	10.4	–	10.8	9.0	–	-8.1	-4.9	-17.1
lone parent	14.1	–	10.4	14.6	7.6	15.1	–	–	–	-9.8
couple, no kids	4.5	–	–	-7.7	–	–	–	-6.4	–	-3.5

Notes: Figures are marginal effects from a multinomial logistic regression equation, showing how much more or less likely men and women are to take each employment status, compared with members of a couple with children.
Other controls are included for age of children, marital status, education, own age, health, citizenship, unemployment history, year of interview.
Cells left blank were not significant at the 5 per cent level (robust standard errors).

Source: ECHP (1994–98, pooled across years), author's own calculations.

The Netherlands exhibit a more or less straightforward picture that can be explained in terms of the Dutch part-time employment regime. In general, if children exist in Dutch households, women tend to work in small part-time jobs or are found to be economically inactive, rather than to work full-time. Although the influence of children is in most cases insignificant for Dutch men, there is a tendency to work part-time in the case of children between the ages of seven and 15.

Compared to women's employment probabilities in other countries, very young children in German households have the strongest negative impact on the likelihood of being employed in a full-time job (a reduction of 47 percentage points) and a converse increase in the probability of being out of the labour force (+41 per cent). German women's chances of working in regular or short part-time jobs rise only to a relatively small extent if they have children aged between three and six, but such children have a bigger effect on non-employment (+19.9 per cent) These findings closely reflect the current child daycare gap in Germany, since below the age of three and above the age of six, child daycare facilities are very sparse.[3] Moreover, the current German child daycare facilities have short opening hours, which allow mothers to work only in small part-time jobs. By contrast, children have a much lower impact on Portuguese as well as Danish women's labour supply.

If marital status is taken into account (Table 5.3), both 'unmarried' (includes cohabiters) and 'separated/divorced' are associated with a high likelihood of women's working full-time rather than part-time. This holds for the UK, the Netherlands, Germany, and (with the exception of 'unmarried') for Portugal. However, this straightforward pattern does not appear for Danish women. Concerning men, the opposite is true: unmarried or separated/divorced men tend not to work in a standard job, but are likely to be out of work.

The results obtained from Table 5.3 point to the rationale that 'independence' from marriage is positively correlated with full-time employment for women. This can be interpreted in two ways. On the one hand, it is likely that women need to work full-time if they do not have the support of a partner. On the other hand, independence from a partner may offer a better way to realise one's preferred working time in the labour market.

Overall, Denmark and Portugal appear similar to each other compared to the other three countries, especially concerning Table 5.2. Nevertheless, this finding has to be interpreted on the basis of different welfare state concepts. The Scandinavian-style social-democratic Danish welfare regime generally supports the employment of women and especially fosters labour force participation of mothers. Hence the Danish institutional setting, like an adequate child daycare scheme, is designed to achieve equal employment

Table 5.2 *Influence of number of children by age on men's and women's labour supply (marginal effects)*

Labour supply/ child ages	Denmark		Nether-lands		UK		Germany		Portugal	
	M	W	M	W	M	W	M	W	M	W
Full-time employment										
up to 2	–	–6.0	–	–13.7	–4.4	–28.3	3.0	–47.4	–	–
3–6	–	–	–	–16.3	–	–28.2	–	–27.2	2.7	–3.6
7–15	–3.0	–	–2.1	–9.8	–4.0	–14.9	–	–12.5	–	–5.6
Regular part-time employment										
up to 2	–	–4.4	–	–	–	–	–1.0	–	–	–
3–6	–	–	–	–	–	5.0	–	2.8	–	–
7–15	–	–	10.2	–2.9	–	1.9	–	–	–	–
Short part-time										
up to 2	–	–2.0	–	–	–	1.4	–1.6	6.8	–	–
3–6	–	–2.1	–	–	–	4.2	–	4.5	–	–
7–15	–	–	–	3.1	0.6	3.1	–	1.7	–	–
Non-employed										
up to 2	–	12.5	–	13.9	3.8	26.5	–	40.9	–2.6	–
3–6	–	–	–	17.2	2.6	19.0	–	19.9	–	4.0
7–15	2.5	–	–	9.6	3.1	10.0	–	10.4	–	5.9

Notes: Figures represent marginal effects from a multinomial logistic regression equation, showing how much more or less likely men and women are to take each employment status, compared with those with no children under 16.
Other controls were included for family structure, marital status, education, age, health, citizenship, unemployment history and year of interview.
Cells left blank were not significant at the 5 per cent level (robust standard errors).
Source: ECHP (1994–98, pooled across years), author's own calculations.

opportunities for men and women. In contrast, such institutional settings hardly exist in the residual welfare state of Portugal. On the contrary, child daycare in that country is more or less a private issue. However, the generally low wage level, entailing the necessity to work full-time in order to have a

Table 5.3　Influence of marital status on men's and women's labour supply (marginal effects)

Labour supply/ marital status	Denmark		Nether- lands		UK		Germany		Portugal	
	M	W	M	W	M	W	M	W	M	W
Full–time employment										
unmarried	–8.5	–	–8.5	15.9	–8.3	11.8	–11.9	10.5	–20.3	–10.0
divorced/ separated	–6.6	–	–	18.1	–7.4	9.2	–8.6	11.5	–18.5	8.4
Part–time employment										
unmarried	–	–6.6	–	–	–	–9.9	–	–5.8	1.0	–
divorced/ separated	–	–10.4	–	–	–	–3.8	–	–2.5	–	–
Short part–time										
unmarried	–	–	–	–5.0	–	–	3.4	–	0.9	–
divorced/ separated	–	–	–	–8.3	–	–	3.7	–4.5	–	–
Non–employed										
unmarried	7.7	6.8	6.2	–9.9	5.9	–	–	–5.0	18.4	10.9
divorced/ separated	6.5	7.7	5.2	–12.0	5.0	–4.6	–	–	17.8	–8.0

Notes:　Figures represent marginal effects from a multinomial logistic regression equation, showing how much more or less likely non-married men and women are to take each employment status, compared with married people.
Other controls were included for family structure, age of children, education, age, health, citizenship, unemployment history, and year of interview.
Cells left blank were not significant at the 5 per cent level (robust standard errors).
Source:　ECHP (1994–98, pooled across years), author's own calculations.

second source of household income, seems to have a predominant effect on female labour supply. Thus, in the end, the findings for Portugal fit into the concept of this residual welfare regime, even though one might have assumed that the low level of child daycare facilities and the weak support for mothers' employment should result in a low female labour force participation in that country.

In contrast, the chances of German women being employed are hampered by a conservative welfare state, with childcare obligations severely limiting their opportunities to enter the labour market at all. This contrast is even more pronounced if the results for German men are added. For them, young children coincide with a tendency to work full-time, but overall, the number and age of children shows no crucial importance for the type of employment chosen by German men. Hence, for Germany, the results for men and women complement one another, with a strong emphasis of the male-breadwinner model of the German corporatist welfare state.

In all, if these five countries were assigned to a scale that measures the gender-related level of labour market modernisation, Denmark would lead and Germany would have to be placed at the bottom of such a scale. Even the conservative/social-democratic part-time regime of the Netherlands or the liberal employment opportunities regime in the UK cannot be rated as successful as the performance of the Danish welfare regime. Since Portugal cannot thoroughly be assigned to an advanced modernisation, but still shows some features of a 'catching-up' modernisation, this country cannot easily be placed in relation to the other four.

Another picture can be drawn, if movements between standard and non-standard employment statuses and unemployment are observed. Within such a research frame, Dekker (2001) analyses transition rates in the Netherlands, the UK and Germany. He finds that age is the most important variable in explaining differences in transition patterns. Non-standard employment can be seen as a means of entry into standard employment (mostly in the case of young workers) and an exit option from standard employment (for older workers). The British labour market turns out to be more segmented, but the 'stepping stone' role of non-standard employment is of more relevance in the Netherlands and Germany.

Men's and Women's Views of their Jobs

Job-satisfaction is an important consideration in an analysis of 'inequality in the overall returns to work' (Hamermesh, 2001). Thus, subjective well-being can be assessed as 'the central economic variable driving individuals' decisions' (Sousa-Poza and Sousa-Poza, 2000a) with job-satisfaction playing a key role in overall subjective well-being. Moreover, previous research suggests that job-satisfaction has a positive effect on productivity (Clegg, 1983; Leontaridi and Sloane, 2001).

The analysis here uses a measure of workers' overall job-satisfaction and also satisfaction with two specific aspects which are especially relevant to non-standard employment, namely 'job security' and 'number of working hours'.[4] The following investigates job-satisfaction discrepancies between men and women, and between standard and non-standard employment.

The 'expectation' hypothesis assumes that those who expect comparatively less of a job will be more easily satisfied than those who expect more (Locke, 1969). For instance individuals may have different expectations of what kind of career stage could or should have been reached. The gender/job-satisfaction paradox suggests that women have a higher level of overall job-satisfaction than men despite their obviously disadvantaged position in the labour market in terms of earnings or promotion prospects. According to Clark (1997), '[w]omen's higher job-satisfaction does not reflect the fact that their jobs are unobservedly better than men's, but rather that, perhaps because their jobs have been so much worse in the past, they have lower expectations' (p. 365). However, Clark states that this seeming paradox is only a 'transitory phenomenon', as it has to be expected that gender/job-satisfaction differences will diminish, as employment opportunities of women and men become more equal.

Consequently, the (non-)existence of the gender/job-satisfaction paradox can be interpreted as a proxy for the level of gender modernisation in a labour market regime:

- if no significant gender/job-expectation gap is observed it can be assumed that labour market conditions of women and men are equal to each other ('well-being');
- a gender/job-satisfaction paradox to the seeming disadvantage of men suggests that women hold a disadvantaged position in the labour market ('adaptive'); and
- an obvious gender/job-satisfaction gap to the disadvantage of women occurs if their job-satisfaction level is significantly lower than the job-satisfaction of men ('deprived').

So far, the gender/job-satisfaction paradox has been confirmed for the UK by, for instance, Clark (1996, 1997) and Sloane and Williams (2000), whereas less has been done to test this hypothesis on a cross-national basis. An exception is found in the analysis of Sousa-Poza and Sousa-Poza, who remark that a higher 'overall job-satisfaction' for women occurs especially in Anglo-Saxon countries. Nevertheless, the authors 'have no ready explanation as to why it applies primarily to Great Britain and the United States' (Sousa-Poza and Sousa-Poza, 2000b). There is a suggestion that the paradox is strongest in liberal/English-speaking countries, so the following job-satisfaction analysis includes Ireland in addition to the five countries already discussed.

Table 5.4   Women's satisfaction with their jobs (relative to men)

Aspect	Denmark	Nether-lands	UK	Ireland	Germany	Portugal
Overall	.	.	↑↑↑	↑↑	↑↑↑	↓↓↓
Job security	.	↑↑↑	↑↑↑	↑↑↑	↑↑	↓↓↓
Working hours	.	↑	↑↑↑	↑↑↑	↑↑↑	.

Notes: Results from ordered probit regressions using three indicators of job-satisfaction as
dependent variables.
Arrows indicate the significance of a dummy variable for women. ↑↑↑/↓↓↓ = p
< 0.01, ↑↑↑/↓↓ = p < 0.05, ↑/↓ = p< 0.10.
Additional controls included employment status (standard vs. non-standard),
occupational background, institutional background (public vs. private), job status
(supervisory vs. non-supervisory), job adequacy (self-estimation of skills), number of
jobs, income, household structure, marital status, number and age of children, own
age, state of health, and number of interviews.
Robust standard errors.
Source: ECHP (1994–98, pooled across years), author's own calculations.

Table 5.4 reports gender differences in job-satisfaction, after taking
account of a wide range of job characteristics which might influence workers'
attitudes. For the UK, Ireland and Germany, the expectation hypothesis
cannot be rejected, as women have higher overall job-satisfaction than men.
Hence, women possess an 'adaptive job-satisfaction position' in these three
labour market regimes. These three countries also show a female satisfaction
surplus in terms of 'job security' and 'number of working hours'.

In contrast, Denmark shows no significant gender effects, pointing to the
'well-being' of women in the labour market regarding equal opportunities.
The results for the Netherlands display a positive gender effect regarding 'job
security' and 'number of working hours', but no overall gender job-
satisfaction paradox can be verified. A negative gender effect regarding
'overall job-satisfaction' (and 'satisfaction with job security') is shown by
Portugal. This suggests a 'deprived' position of women in the Portuguese
labour market.

The findings are only partially in line with former research. The Sousa-
Pozas obtained no significant gender effects for Germany and Portugal,
probably because their analysis was based on a cruder measure of job-
satisfaction. However the unexpected findings of Table 5.4 can be explained
by the results of the earlier analysis of men's and women's labour supply. In
Germany, women's employment opportunities are restricted by the relatively
tight 'conservative' frame of the corporatist welfare regime that forces women

to lower their expectations, and to expect less than men concerning employment opportunities. This results in a German gender/job-satisfaction paradox.

In Denmark, the rejection of the expectation hypotheses is due to relatively equal full-time employment opportunities for women and men. The same is true in the Netherlands, but the regime for women is part-time. In contrast, the obvious Portuguese gender/job-satisfaction gap to the disadvantage of women coincides with the welfare state and labour market setting of this southern country. The relatively high employment rate of women in Portugal and the relative high proportion of women working full-time have to be explained in the light of the poor Portuguese wage level. Hence, Portuguese women are urged to combine family obligations and employment, resulting in a double load. There is no effective public support for employment opportunities of women and mothers in the Portuguese welfare state. Therefore, Portuguese women tend towards a level of overall job-satisfaction that is even below that expressed by their male counterparts. So, as Portuguese households are obliged to supply two full-time jobs in order to make ends meet, the wage-related full-time regime in Portugal does not show a significant negative gender effect in terms of 'number of working hours'.

The assumption that the gender/job-satisfaction paradox mainly occurs in liberal labour market regimes is supported, as women turn out to have higher satisfaction than men in the UK and Ireland. Yet this finding still does not serve as conclusive evidence as to why this may be typical of liberal Anglo-Saxon regimes. However, at least for the UK, the relatively high share of non-standard employment among women may provoke a gender/job-satisfaction paradox. Thus, a liberal labour market setting seems to induce higher job-satisfaction for women due to their comparatively low expectations.

The findings for gender job-satisfaction discrepancies are confirmed if the job-satisfaction level of different forms of non-standard employment is compared to the reference group of standard employees (Kaiser, 2002).[5] Among men, part-time workers have a low level of satisfaction with the number of their working hours; but among women, part-timers are more satisfied with their hours than full-timers. Portugal is again the exception. In that country, part-time jobs are associated with a significant lessening of job-satisfaction, not only for men, but also for women. This suggests that Portuguese women want to work full-time, to make full use of their earning capacity.

Summary and Conclusions

In the EU, the contribution of women's economic activity to total non-standard employment is high. On average, nearly two-thirds of all non-standard work is due to the labour market participation of women. To investigate country and welfare state differences in standard and non-standard employment patterns, five EU countries were selected as examples: namely Denmark, the Netherlands, the UK, Germany, and Portugal.

Surprisingly, at first sight, the outcomes for female labour supply in Denmark and Portugal are somewhat similar. However, this similarity turns out to be more superficial than real, because the explanations for the two countries' high levels of full-time employment among women are completely different. The Danish welfare state is deliberately designed to encourage equal employment opportunities for men and women by appropriate child daycare, and tax and social security systems while those institutional devices hardly exist in the residual welfare state of Portugal. On the contrary, the extraordinarily high labour market orientation of Portuguese women has mainly to be explained by the comparatively low wage level that obliges households to obtain a second, preferably full-time, income.

The socio-economic factors that determine standard and non-standard employment enable the five countries to be assigned to a scale that measures gender-related labour market modernisation. Two extreme positions can be identified. On the one hand, Denmark at the top of the scale with an equal opportunity regime that has to be assessed as 'advanced' modernisation. On the other hand, Germany is at the bottom of the scale, with obvious institutional lags that still point to a male-breadwinner regime. In between, we find the conservative/social-democratic part-time regime for women of the Netherlands and the liberal employment opportunities regime of the UK. Although the latter two countries show features of an advanced modernisation, their performance in terms of a gender-related modernisation of the labour market cannot be rated as successful as the Danish case. Since Portugal still shows some features of a 'catching-up' modernisation, the Portuguese case cannot unequivocally be assessed as 'advanced' modernisation. Hence, Portugal cannot really be compared with the other four countries.

The lesson drawn from this example is that varying welfare state settings, like the corporatist of Germany and the social-democratic of Denmark, may result in different outcomes, but that very different welfare state settings, like the Danish and the Portuguese, can yield similar results. At this stage, the Portuguese low wage level is essential to explain similarities in the outcomes of the analyses, even though different welfare concepts underlie their labour markets. Thus, for cross-national research, information that cannot be attributed to a specific welfare state policy, but to a general economic characteristic, is indispensable to evaluate differences and/or similarities.

In terms of gender differences in the level of job-satisfaction, the countries under consideration can be assigned to three different groups.

- Denmark and the Netherlands come up with no significant overall gender/job-satisfaction differences and few gender effects regarding satisfaction with job security and the number of working hours (Netherlands only). From this point of view, Denmark and the Netherlands display job-satisfaction equality.
- Germany, the UK (and Ireland) display a job-satisfaction surplus for women regarding all three categories of job-satisfaction, which clearly points to the existence of a job-satisfaction paradox in these countries.
- Portugal can be assigned to the third group, with a job-satisfaction surplus for men. This finding indicates a job-satisfaction gap to the disadvantage of women in this country.

In all, the objective (socio-economic) determinants of labour market statuses and subjective (job-satisfaction) perspectives are mutually complementary. The more restrictive the labour market access and process is for women, the more likely a gender/job-satisfaction paradox is to emerge in any country. This holds for the UK, Ireland and Germany, but consequently, cannot be applied to Denmark. Again, Portugal has to be evaluated as an outlier due to a state of modernisation that is somewhat different from the other four countries. In conclusion, the findings suggest that there is no universal 'female' attitude towards employment that, as assumed by Gary Becker (1994), arises intrinsically or even biologically. On the contrary, female labour market participation and gender/job-satisfaction differences are due to different employment opportunities that are offered by different welfare state regimes and/or differences in economic characteristics, like wage levels. In this sense, the social-democratic welfare state of Denmark and the Netherlands, the liberal British and Irish welfare state, the corporatist frame of Germany, and the residual welfare regime in Portugal reflect gender-related employment opportunities and job-satisfaction differences.

A joint European strategy is being considered to cope with the expected scarcity of skilled labour resulting from demographic trends. In that context, the increasing educational attainment and rising labour market participation of women offer a unique opportunity to integrate women into European labour markets. Their social rights have been codified legally for decades, but they are still waiting for full implementation in practice. As 'the extension of social rights has always been regarded as the essence of social policy' (Esping-Andersen, 1990, 3), this rationale should be highly relevant for political debate, if the access to and/or exclusion from standard and non-standard employment relationships is on the agenda. The Danish case provides an example of good practice towards gender-related modernisation of the labour market on the bases of equal labour market opportunities. In contrast, the German labour market regime shows distinct features of an institutional lag that is still waiting to be modernised.

Notes

1. All the analyses presented in this chapter are based on the population aged 16 to 64 in order to cover the labour force that is likely to be employed.
2. For the considerable differences between men and women as regards to various forms of non-standard employment, see Kaiser (2001a, 2001b, 2003).
3. For Germany, similar findings arise from the analyses of Spiess, Iacovou and Uunk in Chapter 4 in this book.
4. The ECHP uses a six-point satisfaction scale ranging from '1' (not satisfied at all) to '6' (fully satisfied).
5. Using a fixed-effects panel model.

References

Becker, G.S. (1994), *A Treatise on the Family*, Cambridge, MA.: Harvard University Press.
Böheim, R., and M.P. Taylor (2000), 'Unemployment duration and exit states in Britain', *ISER Working Papers*, **2000–1**, Colchester: University of Essex.
Cebrián, I., V. Gash, G. Moreno, P. O'Connell and L. Toharia (2000), 'Peripheral labour in peripheral markets? Mobility and working time within transitional labour markets among women in Ireland and Spain', in I. Cebrián, M. Lallement and J. O'Reilly (eds), *Working-Time Changes*, Cheltenham, UK and Northampton, MA, USA: Edward Elgar, 205–48.
Clark, A.E. (1996), 'Job satisfaction in Britain', *British Journal of Industrial Relations*, **34** (2), 189–217.
Clark, A.E. (1997), 'Job satisfaction and gender: why are women so happy at work?', *Labour Economics*, **4**, (4), 341–72.
Clegg, C.W. (1983), 'Psychology of employee lateness, absence and turnover: a methodological critique and empirical study', *Journal of Applied Psychology*, **68** (1), 88–101.
*Dekker, R. (2001), 'A phase they're going through: transitions from nonregular to regular jobs in Germany, the Netherlands and Great Britain', Paper prepared for the LoWER Conference on Combining Work, Home, and Education.
*Dekker, R. and L.C. Kaiser (2000), 'Atypical or flexible? How to define non-standard employment patterns – the cases of Germany, the Netherlands and the United Kingdom', *EPAG Working Papers*, **14**, Colchester: University of Essex.
Dingeldey, I. (2001), 'European tax systems and their impact on family employment patterns', *Journal of Social Policy*, **30** (4), 653–72.
Esping-Andersen, G. (1990), *The Three Worlds of Welfare Capitalism*, Cambridge: Polity Press.
Gornick, J.C., M.K. Meyers and K. Ross (1997), 'Supporting the employment of mothers: policy variation across fourteen welfare states', *Journal of European Social Policy*, **7** (1), 45–70.
Gornick, J.C., M.K. Meyers and K. Ross (1998), 'Public policies and the employment of mothers: a cross-national study', *Social Science Quarterly*, **79** (1), 35–54.

Hamermesh, D.S. (2001), 'The changing distribution of job satisfaction', *The Journal of Human Resources*, **36** (1), 1–30.
ILO (1997), *World Employment 1996/1997*, Geneva: ILO.
Kaiser, L.C. (1997), 'Bildung, Ausbildung und Einkommen in der Europäischen Union, International vergleichende Analysen mit Mikrodaten', M.A. thesis, University of Bochum.
*Kaiser, L.C. (2001a), 'Permanent full-time job still dominant form of employment in Europe', *Economic Bulletin*, **38** (4), 119–24.
*Kaiser, L.C. (2001b), 'Standard and non-standard employment patterns across Europe', *EPAG Working Papers*, **26**, Colchester: University of Essex.
*Kaiser, L.C. (2002), 'Job satisfaction: a comparison of standard, non-standard, and self-employment patterns across Europe with a special note to the gender/job satisfaction paradox', *EPAG Working Papers*, **27**, Colchester: University of Essex.
Kaiser, L.C. (2003), 'Entstandardisierte Erwerbsmuster in der Europäischen Union, Eine empirische Analyse für fünf Länder unter besonderer Berücksichtigung von Deutschland', Ph.D. thesis, University of Bochum.
Killingsworth, M.R. (1983), *Labor Supply*, Cambridge: Cambridge University Press.
Leontaridi, R., and P. Sloane (2001), 'Measuring the quality of jobs', *LoWER Working Paper*, April, LoWER: Amsterdam.
Locke, E.A. (1969), 'What is job satisfaction?, *Organisational Behaviour and Human Performance*, **4**, 309–36.
Nelson, J.A. (1998), 'Labour, gender and the economic/social divide', *International Labour Review*, **137** (1), 33–46.
OECD (1999), *Employment Outlook*, Paris: OECD.
Ott, N. (1992), *Intrafamily Bargaining and Household Decisions*, Berlin: Springer.
Ott, N. (1995), 'Fertility and division of work in the family: a game theoretic model of household decisions', in E. Kuiper et al. (eds), *Out of the Margins: Feminist Perspectives on Economics*, London: Routledge, pp. 80–99.
Pfau-Effinger, B. (1999), 'Welfare regimes and the gender division of labour in cross-national perspective: theoretical framework and empirical results', in J. Christiansen, A. Kovalainen and P. Koistinen (eds), *Working Europe – Reshaping European Employment Systems*, Aldershot: Ashgate, pp. 128–56.
Pfau-Effinger, B. (2001), 'Changing welfare policies, labour markets and gender arrangements', in J.G. Andersen and P. Jensen (eds), *Changing Welfare States, Labour Markets and Citizenship*, Vol. 1 of the Publication Series of COST A13 Action Programme of the EU, Oxford, Cambridge: Policy Press.
Ruivo, M., P. Gonzáles and M. Vareao (1998), 'Why is part-time work so low in Portugal and Spain?', in J. O'Reilly and C. Fagan (eds), *Part-time Prospects: an International Comparison of Part-time Work in Europe, North America and the Pacific Rim*, London: Routledge, pp. 199–213.
Santos, B.d.S. (1991), 'State, wage relations and social welfare in the semiperiphery – the case of Portugal', Universidade de Coimbra, Faculdade de Economia, Oficina do Centro de Estudos Sociais, no. 23.
Sloane, P.J. and H. Williams (2000), 'Job satisfaction, comparison earnings and gender', *Labour*, **14** (3), 473–501.
Solow, R.M. (1990), *The Labour Market as a Social Institution*, Oxford: Basil Backwell.
Sousa-Poza, A. and A.A. Sousa-Poza (2000a), 'Well-being at work: a cross-national analysis of the levels and determinants of job satisfaction', *The Journal of Socio-Economics*, **29** (6), 517–38.

Sousa-Poza, A. and A.A. Sousa-Poza (2000b), 'Taking another look at the gender/job-satisfaction paradox', *Kyklos*, **53** (2), 135–52.

Zapf, W. (1991a), 'Die Modernisierung moderner Gesellschaften', in W. Zapf (ed), *Verhandlungen des 25. Deutschen Soziologentages in Frankfurt am Main 1990.* Frankfurt a.M.: Campus, pp. 3–23.

Zapf, W. (1991b), 'Modernisierung und Modernisierungstheorien', in W. Zapf (ed), *Die Modernisierung moderner Gesellschaften. Verhandlungen des 25. Deutschen Soziologentages in Frankfurt am Main 1990.* Frankfurt a.M.: Campus, pp. 24–39.

Zapf, W. (1996), 'Die Modernisierungstheorie und unterschiedliche Pfade der gesellschaftlichen Entwicklung', *Leviathan*, **24** (1), pp. 63–77.

Zapf, W. (2001), 'Modernisierung und Transformation', in B. Schäfers, W. Zapf (eds), *Handwörterbuch zur Gesellschaft Deutschlands*, Opladen: Westdeutscher Verlag, pp. 492–501.

* Direct output from EPAG's *DynSoc* research programme (see page 268).

6. Labour Market Mobility Patterns

Ruud J.A. Muffels and Trudie Schils

Introduction

Concepts of work are changing, with more flexible and diverse patterns of employment emerging. This is not to say that all workers are constantly shopping around for better jobs, but that, on average, mobility from one job into another with different working hours, different levels of permanency or different skill and wage levels is expanding, and working patterns have become more diverse.

The increasing level of social and economic integration, both Europe-wide and globally, together with increasingly rapid changes in the development and application of new technology and knowledge, is likely to give a further impetus to changes in the way people make their work and leisure choices. Over a lifetime, people will probably occupy a larger number of jobs during a shorter period, and many workers will experience longer intermittent periods of unemployment – or they may spend time not in paid work, but engaged in life-long learning activities, caring duties or volunteer work. There is a larger variety of working contracts, and workers are changing jobs more frequently. The notion of a 'transitional labour market' as proposed by Schmid and Gazier (2002) is likely to gain more importance in the light of these ongoing changes. These processes will raise mobility and turnover on the labour market notwithstanding the fact that the majority of jobs are still full-time jobs in paid employment.

It may be argued that this increase in flexibility offers workers greater freedom to construct their lives along different patterns. However, there is another side to the coin of labour market flexibility. Employees' changes of status in the labour market are often not a sign of diversity of choice, but are forced by adverse economic shocks and social risks such as sickness and disability. Increasing flexibility in the labour market means not only more flexibility for workers, but it also means that employers have more room to dismiss employees and more opportunities to hire workers on non-standard contracts – which goes hand-in-hand with rising work insecurity and rising employment instability. Thus, for some employees at least, the trend towards increasing instability of employment patterns over time has led to a deteriorating labour market position.

The increasing degree of labour market mobility and turnover imply that we need to rethink our standard ways of presenting information on labour markets. The standard means of presenting this information is with the use of repeated cross-sectional statistics, presented in the form of time series. They allow us to look at how employment levels are changing over time, or how the labour market situation of particular groups, such as women, the young or the elderly is evolving. However, they cannot tell us whether the changes – if any – are related to changes in the *composition* of groups within the work force, or whether they are due to changes over time in the *choices* which people belonging to particular groups are making, due to changing conditions or opportunities. Longitudinal data permit us to study the underlying processes of change in the lives of real people, and the sorts of events which have an impact on how people fare in the labour market over time. There is a growing need for labour market statistics in which the focus is on such flows and dynamics. This requires longitudinal data, such as the cross-national panel data used in this study.

The aim of this chapter is to provide a deeper insight into flows in the labour market and the factors that might be responsible for the great variations in employment patterns, both within and across countries. The focus is on longitudinal patterns of employment, meaning that we are particularly interested in people's labour market behaviour patterns over a longer time frame. We call these longer-term behavioural patterns 'working profiles'. Over time, people may change their working profiles, moving from unstable working patterns into stable patterns or vice versa. We will show that the degree to which people change their working profiles varies according to factors such as the person's age, or the institutional framework (as defined by regime type) with which he or she is faced.

At a European level, great concern has arisen about the labour market consequences of population ageing. The traditional view derived from human capital theory is that an ageing work force will lead to reduced productivity, increased wage costs and rising unemployment. It is argued that older workers are less mobile, which will reduce labour market mobility. Moreover, older workers who become unemployed face more problems in finding new appropriate jobs, which will lead to an increase in unemployment rates across Europe. However, these predictions from theory have hardly been tested. The aim of the contributions summarised here is to test whether these predictions hold when examining the real evidence for a range of countries over a number of years, using properly comparable data.

This chapter will proceed as follows. The first section presents evidence on the longitudinal labour market attachment of workers – defined as the number of months that people spend employed or unemployed during a three-year period – and how this labour market attachment varies between employment regimes (Muffels and Fouarge, 2002).

The second part of the chapter examines the extent to which transitions in and out of employment differ between age groups and between employment regimes, focusing on two age groups of particular policy interest: younger and older workers. The role of individual and institutional characteristics in determining labour mobility patterns is assessed, using the results of Schils and Muffels (2003) on transitions out of employment across Europe, and of Kaiser and Siedler (2000) on transitions out of unemployment in West Germany and the UK.

Labour Market Attachment and Regime Types

Comparative labour market research should take account of the evidence that labour market stocks and flows are affected not only by demographic and economic factors at the country level, but also by cross-national institutional differences reflected in labour market policies and social security systems (Muffels et al., 2002). Looking at the national settings, it appears that there is a wide variety in goals, objectives, tools, institutions and policies affecting the labour market.

Our starting point is Esping-Andersen's classification (1990) into social-democratic, liberal and corporatist regime types, amended to incorporate a fourth, residual, regime type (see Table 1.3 and discussion in Chapter 1). Since the analyses involve the labour market performance of these welfare regimes, the term 'employment regime' instead of 'welfare regime' is used.

We expect that liberal regimes, with less labour market protection and more incentives built into their benefit systems, will have less temporary labour and higher labour mobility rates than social-democratic and corporatist countries, with their stricter labour protection rules and more generous benefit systems with higher replacement rates and less incentives.

Although Esping-Andersen allocates the southern (or residual) European countries to the corporatist regime type, there is evidence (European Commission, 1999; OECD, 1999) that labour markets in residual countries are quite different from those in the continental European countries in terms of employment regulation, unemployment levels, non-standard jobs, and the informal economy. With this in mind, Muffels and Fouarge (2002) test whether the residual or southern countries should indeed be considered as a separate welfare state or employment regime, rather than part of the corporatist type. They find that residual labour markets face stronger employment protection regulations, which may explain why their share of non-standard jobs is much higher (see Chapter 5 in this book). In addition, it emerges that their employment levels are lower and their unemployment rates higher – suggesting that the role of the informal economy is indeed much larger and more widespread in these countries.

One way in which attachment to the labour market may be measured is in terms of the proportion of workers in non-standard employment at a given time. However, this is essentially a static indicator. Muffels and Fouarge (2002) take a dynamic view of labour market attachment, using data from the first three waves of the European Community Household Panel (ECHP). At the European level, three years seem sufficient to observe a substantial number of transitions from one employment status into another.[1]

Stability or volatility in the labour market?
Table 6.1 gives an indication of the stability and volatility of different labour market states. Six distinct states are defined: employment, self-employment, unemployment, education or training, retirement, and other non-working. For each regime type, the labour market status in the first year is shown down the left-hand side, and status in the second year is shown across the top of the table.

It is clear from this table that there is both a degree of stability and a degree of mobility in the labour market. Employment is the most stable state in three out of four regime types (retirement is most stable in residual regimes). Across all regime types, unemployment and education are the least stable states. Retirement and other non-working seem to be more or less absorbing states, with rather low mobility rates except for mobility between the two.

Many of the observed differences between regime types are as we predicted beforehand. The stability of employment is greatest in the social-democratic and corporatist regimes, and lower in the liberal and (particularly) residual regimes. The stability of retirement is highest in corporatist and residual regimes, whereas it is much lower in social-democratic regimes. However, a closer look at the figures shows that a large fraction of the retired in social-democratic regimes move into the state of non-working the following year, which is most likely a move from early retirement into full retirement at the legal retirement age. The magnitude of the retiree flow might be the result of the generous early retirement benefits in this regime, which seem to attract a rather large share of older workers.

Considering the non-employed states of unemployment and being out of the labour force, the corporatist regimes show the highest stability whereas again, the highest volatility is observed in liberal regimes. This high volatility in liberal regimes is accounted for by the very high year-on-year transitions out of unemployment and education/training into employment in these regimes. This corroborates our conjectures about the more efficiently

Table 6.1   *Percentage of people moving between main activity statuses between 1993–95: year-on-year transitions (row percentages)*

	Destination state					
Regime type	Emp-loyed	Self-emp-loyed	Unem-ployed	Educa-tion/training	Retired	Other non-working
Origin state						
Social-democratic						
Employed	**91**	1	3	1	1	3
Self-employed	10	**77**	2	1	3	7
Unemployed	28	2	**39**	5	3	23
Education/training	33	1	6	**58**	0	2
Retired	1	0	0	0	**72**	26
Other non-working	4	1	8	1	1	**85**
Liberal						
Employed	**86**	3	2	1	2	4
Self-employed	13	**78**	1	0	2	5
Unemployed	39	4	**35**	3	4	15
Education/training	48	0	11	**32**	1	8
Retired	1	0	0	0	**88**	11
Other non-working	10	2	3	2	18	**65**
Corporatist						
Employed	**89**	2	4	1	3	2
Self-employed	8	**81**	1	0	4	6
Unemployed	32	4	**45**	3	6	10
Education/training	22	1	11	**59**	0	6
Retired	0	0	0	0	**96**	3
Other non-working	7	1	3	1	9	**79**
Residual						
Employed	**83**	3	8	0	2	3
Self-employed	9	**75**	4	0	4	7
Unemployed	33	6	**41**	3	2	15
Education/training	15	2	14	**63**	0	6
Retired	0	1	0	0	**90**	8
Other non-working	5	3	6	0	8	**77**

Note: The sample comprises 102 788 observations; Finland, Austria and Sweden are excluded. Bold figures indicate people whose activity status remained the same.
Source: ECHP (1994–96), authors' own calculations.

functioning labour markets in liberal regimes. With more mobility into and out of employment, the liberal regimes also seem to have the most flexible labour markets of the four regime types.

Longitudinal employment status
The flows presented in Table 6.1 represent annual mobility rates between the main activity states measured at the time of the interview. We now proceed to examine longitudinal indicators of employment status and employment mobility. To do this, we use monthly calendar information on the usual activity status of the respondent in each month. Our measure of longitudinal employment status is based on the number of months for which people are employed over a 36-month observation period. We define four categories as: persistently employed (100 per cent in employment), mainly employed (50–99 per cent in employment), mainly non-employed (1–49 per cent in employment) and persistently non-employed (0 per cent in employment). Longitudinal employment statuses for the 36-month period covering the calendar years 1993–95 are tabulated in Table 6.2.

Table 6.2   Longitudinal employment status over 36 months (row percentages)

Regime type	Persistently employed	Mainly employed	Mainly non-employed	Persistently non-employed
Europe	44	14	11	30
Social-democratic	48	17	13	23
Liberal	47	18	12	24
Corporatist	49	15	10	26
Residual	36	11	12	41

Notes: Sample contains all people of working age.
Data not available for Sweden; for Austria and Finland the employment status variable is defined over the last 24 and 12 months respectively.
Source: ECHP (1994–96, covering calendar years 1993–95), from Muffels and Fouarge (2002).

Across Europe, 58 per cent of the working-age people in all countries are persistently (44 per cent) or mainly (14 per cent) employed, whereas 41 per cent are mainly (11 per cent) or persistently (30 per cent) non-employed. More than one in four persons in Europe is experiencing what we might term 'precarious' employment (that is, they are mainly employed or mainly non-employed, but not persistently employed). It might be expected that longitudinal attachment to the labour market would be weaker in residual employment regimes due to higher levels of unemployment compared to the social-democratic and corporatist regimes.

Looking at the evidence for the different employment regimes, it indeed seems true that the number of people persistently non-employed is substantially higher in the residual regime, at 41 per cent against 23 per cent in the social-democratic regime. In addition, the number of persistently employed is much lower in the residual regime, at 36 per cent against 49 per cent in the corporatist regime. Hence, attachment to the labour market seems weaker in the residual regime. However, unexpectedly, it turns out that the prevalence of precarious employment (mainly employed plus mainly non-employed) is higher in the liberal and social-democratic regimes (30 per cent), as opposed to the residual regime (23 per cent). We suspect that this has to do with a higher share of female part-time labour in the liberal and social-democratic regimes compared to the residual regimes of Italy, Spain and Greece.

The extent to which the different employment regimes are capable of guaranteeing that people move from unstable employment into full employment should be an important indicator of their labour market performance. Transitions between longitudinal employment statuses over three years are depicted in Table 6.3, by regime cluster.

The percentages on the diagonal of the transition matrix show that there is a good deal of stability in the labour market position of workers and job seekers. In liberal, social-democratic and corporatist regimes, people in full, secure employment in 1993 have a slightly higher chance of remaining in stable jobs in 1995 than they have in the residual regime. In the residual regime, more people in persistent employment are likely to move into persistent non-employment the following year (10 per cent, as opposed to 5 or 6 per cent in the other regimes).

Furthermore, mainly employed and mainly non-employed people have a much lower chance of escaping from unstable jobs and moving into stable jobs in the residual regime than in the other regime types. Only about 42 per cent of those mainly employed in the residual regime move into stable jobs, against almost 60 per cent in the liberal countries, 52 per cent in the corporatist countries and 46 per cent in the social-democratic countries (the European average is 50 per cent). Furthermore, the proportion of people moving from being mainly employed into persistent non-employment is higher in the residual regime than in the other regimes (34 per cent against 21 per cent in the social-democratic countries and 28 per cent in the liberal and corporatist countries). The conclusion must be that from the state of mainly employed, upward mobility is lower in the residual regime and downward

Table 6.3 Percentage of persons moving between employment status between 1993 and 1995, by regime type (row percentages)

Regime type	Destination state			
	Persistently employed	Mainly employed	Mainly non-employed	Persistently non-employed
Origin state				
Europe				
Persistently employed	87	4	2	7
Mainly employed	50	15	6	29
Mainly non-employed	41	15	12	32
Persistently non-employed	11	4	5	81
Social-democratic				
Persistently employed	88	5	2	5
Mainly employed	46	25	9	21
Mainly non-employed	41	18	14	28
Persistently non-employed	12	6	7	75
Liberal				
Persistently employed	87	5	2	6
Mainly employed	59	10	4	27
Mainly non-employed	47	16	8	29
Persistently non-employed	13	6	6	75
Corporatist				
Persistently employed	88	4	2	7
Mainly employed	52	14	6	28
Mainly non-employed	48	14	8	30
Persistently non-employed	12	4	5	79
Residual				
Persistently employed	85	4	2	10
Mainly employed	42	17	8	34
Mainly non-employed	28	13	20	39
Persistently non-employed	8	3	4	86

Notes: Sweden, Finland and Austria excluded.
Figures are row percentages, that is percentages of all persons belonging to the category in 1993.

Source: ECHP (1994–96, covering calendar years 1993–95), from Muffels and Fouarge (2002).

mobility is higher. From a review of the evidence on the labour market performance of these employment regimes, it might be concluded that the residual regime performs worse in terms of enhancing job mobility and preventing labour market exclusion.

This issue is further examined in Muffels and Fouarge (2002), by estimating models to explain why some people are more likely to be in or to move into persistent employment whereas others are more likely to be non-employed.

Different levels of human capital endowments (measured by education level) may be expected to lead to differences in labour market opportunities (Becker, 1964; Mincer, 1993). Furthermore, the well-known 'job search' theoretical approach (Lipmann and McCall, 1976; Mortensen, 1986; Narendranathan and Nickell, 1986) predicts that human capital will play a role in the outcome of the search process for a better job, with more highly educated people more likely to be successful in getting their preferred job.

Our results from preliminary estimations of the probability of belonging to a given employment longitudinal status (not shown here in detail) illustrate that people with higher levels of education do indeed have higher chances of being persistently or mainly employed and lower chances of being persistently non-employed. Being married has the same effect. The odds of being mainly or persistently employed rather than mainly non-employed are lower for households where more children are present, and for households in social-democratic or residual employment regimes. Living in a residual regime and having more children also increases the relative probability of being persistently non-employed.

Women are more likely than men to be persistently non-employed, while older workers and people living in countries with a social-democratic employment regime are less likely to be persistently non-employed. A higher life satisfaction score is associated with being in stable employment.

We turn now to a model which estimates the dynamics of longitudinal employment status across time. Table 6.4 presents estimates of factors affecting the probability of moving from being mainly employed in 1994 into the other three states in 1996, relative to the probability of remaining in the same situation.

Increasing age has a negative effect on the movement into persistent non-employment – and age squared has a positive effect. The probability of becoming persistently non-employed decreases with age up to a certain point 30 and increases thereafter. This most likely reflects the effect of work experience and tenure. The older people are, the more likely they are to have more work experience and longer tenure up to a certain age – thus, they are less likely to become persistently non-employed. However, after a certain age, workers become more likely to leave the labour market through retirement.

Table 6.4   *Factors associated with moving out of being mainly employed (multinomial logit coefficients)*

Factor	Movements out of being mainly employed		
	Into persistent employment	Into being mainly non-employed	Into persistent non-employment
Female	0.058	0.239	0.558***
Age	0.011	−0.050	−0.239***
Age squared	−0.000	0.000	0.004***
Low education level	−0.070	−0.062	−0.198*
High education level	0.813**	0.425	−0.238
Non-standard household	0.840*	1.005*	−0.299
Widowed	2.819*	0.955	1.160
Poor health	−0.221	−0.027	0.782***
Engaged in job search	−1.032**	0.002	−0.163
Home-owner	−0.321*	−0.571**	−0.180
Regime type			
Social-democratic	−0.829***	−0.623***	−0.620**
Corporatist	−0.154	−0.262**	−0.074
Residual	−1.315***	−1.134***	−0.218
Household changes from 1994–96			
Separated	−0.079	0.727	1.089**
More adults in household	0.575*	0.788*	0.321

Notes: Asterisks denote significance of coefficients: *** 1%, ** 5%, * 10%.
Coefficients are from multinomial logit regressions, relative to staying mainly employed (N = 2 928, Pseudo R^2 = 0.132).
Coefficients are effects relative to reference category: male, with medium education, living in a liberal regime, in a standard household (single or couple, with or without children) with no change in household composition between 1994 and 1996.
Sample: those aged 15–65 in all countries except Sweden, Austria and Finland.
Source: ECHP (1994–96), from Muffels and Fouarge (2002).

There is no significant impact of household composition (that is, of being a single, a couple with or without children or a lone parent) on changes in labour market attachment, except for non-standard households (such as a brother and a sister living together). These families are more likely to move into continuous employment, and less likely to drop out of employment entirely.

Having a higher education level, as expected, raises the likelihood of making a transition into persistent employment. This effect seems to signal the impact of the knowledge economy in which higher-skilled workers have a strong labour market position and ample opportunities to improve their work prospects by moving into more stable jobs.

The probability of moving into a secure or stable job varies greatly across employment regimes. The likelihood of moving from being mainly employed into persistent non-employment is lower in social-democratic regimes than in the liberal regime. The probability of moving into a more stable job is higher in the liberal regime (which acts as the reference regime) than the social-democratic and particularly the residual regime. This observation, that upward mobility into more stable employment is significantly lower in the residual regime, corroborates our earlier results.

Although only three waves were available for analysing transitions across the various employment regime types, the results of Muffels and Fouarge (2002) show remarkable differences across the three distinct 'ideal types' of employment regime. The next section investigates the extent to which labour mobility differs between regimes over a longer period; additionally, it will show that labour market patterns are different for younger and older workers.

Labour Market Mobility Patterns of Younger and Older Workers

In the previous section we examined labour mobility patterns across all age groups, observing both a degree of stability and at the same time a degree of mobility. Using ECHP data for the late 1990s, the annual mobility rate (the proportion of people in a particular state moving into another state the following year) is calculated as around 16 per cent, on average. Apart from movements into and out of the labour market due to unemployment, disability or (early) retirement, the highest degree of mobility is found into and out of non-standard and part-time jobs. New forms of labour have increased the magnitude of mobility between firms. Additionally, there is reason to believe that there is also a degree of mobility within firms due to the need for firms to enhance flexibility in order to cope successfully with rapidly changing market conditions. The rise of the knowledge economy poses new demands in terms of life-long learning and multi-skilling.

In addition, the ageing of the population will substantially affect mobility rates and labour market performance in a number of European countries. The dominant view in academic and policy circles is that the ageing of the population and particularly the ageing work force will have significant effects on the performance of the European economies. Wage costs are likely to rise due to the payment of seniority wages in a number of countries, and labour productivity will fall. This will be a barrier to economic growth. In some sectors of industry there will be a shortage of juvenile labour for jobs requiring skills that older workers generally do not possess (for example, physically demanding jobs).

Many of these expectations are derived from human capital theory that predicts that investments in human capital will be lower for older workers than for younger workers because the pay-off time is too short to make these investments profitable or efficient (Becker, 1964; Mincer, 1962). The traditional view derived from human capital theory is therefore that an ageing work force will result in reduced productivity, increased wage costs and rising unemployment. It is argued that due to the low investment in their human capital, older workers will be less mobile, and therefore labour market mobility will fall as a result of an ageing work force. Moreover, low levels of human capital or lack of investment in maintaining the value of human capital endowments (such as during periods of unemployment or disability) are expected to reduce re-employment probabilities, especially for older workers.

For these reasons, we examine the level of human capital investment in terms of the training provided to older and younger workers, and the impact that the level of training has on the labour mobility patterns of different age groups. In Schils and Muffels (2003) and Kaiser and Siedler (2000), the predictions derived from human capital theory have been examined. In this chapter, we show particular interest in transitions in and out of employment and unemployment, respectively. Due to limitations in the data, we could not investigate internal labour mobility (that is, mobility within firms) but instead examined investments in training and external mobility patterns across age groups.

The transitional labour market patterns of older workers are analysed and compared with those of younger workers. In addition, institutional differences across countries are examined, particularly with respect to training facilities and early retirement schemes and how these affect age-related labour mobility patterns.

Training
First, we examine how patterns of investment in human capital vary by age and regime type. Figure 6.1 depicts, for four age groups, the share of employed people receiving training or education.

One striking feature of Figure 6.1 is the high percentage of young people receiving training in corporatist regimes. In Germany, one of the largest corporatist countries, a dual system operates, where young people work while still in formal training or education. This may explain the relatively high percentage of young people in training and the large difference between the young and the prime-aged category.

In the liberal regimes, a fairly high percentage of workers of all ages participate in training. This might be explained by the larger turnover on the labour market (higher job-to-job mobility) which encourages employers to

Figure 6.1 Percentage of employed people receiving training, by regime type

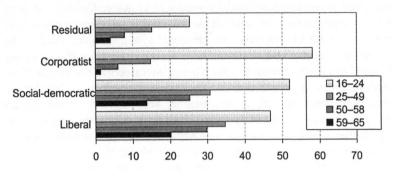

Notes: For the Netherlands, no information is available for 1994.
            Sweden is excluded from this analysis due to a high percentage of missing
            observations (about 40 per cent).
Source: ECHP (1994–98, pooled across years), from Schils and Muffels (2003).

invest more in training in order to enhance commitment to the job. Also, employees might be more willing to invest in training in order to be more employable and hence to maintain their standard of living through working, particularly because they know that if they lose their job they will be entitled to rather poor benefits. In residual countries, benefits are also poor but the need to commit workers to a job through training is less because of strong employment laws protecting workers from dismissal. For employees, the expected pay-off to training is lower, due to worse employment opportunities – and indeed, the figures show that fewer people are engaged in training in this regime.

Across all regime types, the percentage of people receiving training while employed declines with age. This might be due to a shorter time during which firms expect to receive the pay-off from their investments in older workers, or to 'discrimination' against older workers with respect to access to training.

As well as the probability of receiving training, the *type* of training received (not shown on graph) also differs across age groups: older workers are more likely to receive vocational training which will most likely be firm-specific training, whereas younger workers are more likely to receive general training. Interestingly, older workers are more likely to receive training paid for by their employers (which again indicates that their training is more likely to be firm-specific).

Theoretically, employers face risks in paying for such firm-specific training: if the worker leaves the firm, the employer must hire a new worker to fill the empty position. The investment in the worker who has left is hence lost to another firm. Workers also face risks when paying for firm-specific training: if the worker is laid off, he or she will have paid for specific skills which are not transferable to another job. Thus, the theory does not predict clearly whether employers or workers will be most likely to pay the costs of training. Empirical analysis in Schils and Muffels (2003) shows that most training is paid for by employers, which indicates that, to an extent at least, employers are not reluctant to invest in the human capital formation of their older workers and do not intend to lay them off as quickly as possible.

Investment in the training of older workers is highest in the liberal regimes, followed by the social-democratic, residual and corporatist regimes in that order. We predict that the lower the investment in training of older workers, the higher will be the rate of mobility from employment to unemployment.

Transitions for different age groups
To examine whether annual transition rates between the main labour market states (employment, unemployment and inactivity) are different for workers of different ages and in different regimes, transition rates between 1994 and 1998 are shown in Table 6.5.[2]

For those employed in one year, the probability of remaining in employment is highest in the 25–49 age group and lowest in the 59–65 age group in all employment regimes. Over 90 per cent of 25–49s who are employed in one year are still employed a year later, against 67–75 per cent for the oldest age group. The lowest percentages for the oldest group were found in the corporatist and social-democratic regimes, which might be explained by the generosity of their early retirement arrangements.

The likelihood of workers remaining in employment is highest in liberal regimes for all age groups. This does not imply that labour market mobility is lower in liberal regimes – on the contrary, job-to-job mobility might be higher but intermittent periods of unemployment shorter, due to less generous benefit levels and more efficient labour markets.

Transitions from employment to unemployment (job-to-non-job mobility) are quite low for all age groups. In corporatist and social-democratic countries relatively high percentages are found for the 50–58 age group. This demonstrates that unemployment benefit arrangements are functioning as hidden routes into early retirement. For other age groups, the highest percentages of people moving into unemployment are found in the residual regimes, which might be due to the generally higher unemployment rates in these regimes.

In all regime types, re-entry rates into employment after unemployment decline with age. This appears to support the hypothesis that older people experience more barriers to finding a new job than young people, for reasons already explained in this chapter.

Table 6.5   *Transition rates between employment, unemployment and*
                   inactivity, by regime type and age (row percentages)

	Destination state											
Origin state	Aged 16–24			Aged 25–49			Aged 50–58			Aged 59–65		
	E	U	I	E	U	I	E	U	I	E	U	I
Social-democratic												
E	**81**	4	15	**93**	3	5	**89**	3	8	**67**	2	31
U	40	**28**	32	27	**46**	27	14	**54**	31	10	**25**	64
I	29	4	**67**	20	17	**63**	7	7	**86**	5	1	**95**
Liberal												
E	**88**	4	8	**94**	2	4	**91**	2	7	**76**	1	23
U	44	**38**	18	34	**41**	25	25	**42**	33	15	**29**	54
I	29	6	**64**	18	3	**79**	8	2	**90**	3	1	**97**
Corporatist												
E	**84**	8	8	**93**	3	3	**89**	4	7	**67**	2	30
U	37	**46**	17	33	**52**	15	13	**71**	16	1	**39**	61
I	16	5	**78**	16	5	**78**	4	4	**91**	1	1	**98**
Residual												
E	**83**	10	7	**94**	4	3	**89**	3	9	**74**	2	23
U	26	**55**	20	30	**52**	18	19	**59**	22	11	**41**	47
I	9	12	**79**	10	7	**83**	4	2	**94**	2	0	**98**

Notes: E = employed, U = unemployed, I = inactive.
           Rows do not necessarily sum to 100%, since the destination category of 'missing' is
           not reported.
Source: ECHP (1994–98, pooled across years), from Schils and Muffels (2003).

Whether these declining re-entry probabilities are due to employers being reluctant to hire elderly workers or to the elderly themselves not searching hard enough to find a job remains unclear. Across all age groups, the probability of re-employment is highest in liberal regimes, where benefits are less generous and incentives to work are therefore strong. Spell analysis by Kaiser and Siedler (2003) shows that 12 months after the unemployment spell started, one-third of the West German males are still unemployed and did not escape unemployment whereas only one quarter of the British males were still unemployed. For the females the differences between the two countries are even larger: 35 per cent of the West German females and only 13 per cent of the British females were still unemployed 12 months after the start of the unemployment spell.[3]

The transition figures show that the oldest age group (those aged 59–65) has the highest probability of moving out of the labour force after unemployment, across all regime types. But the lowest transition rates from unemployment into inactivity are found in the liberal regime (54 per cent) and particularly in the residual regime (47 per cent) whereas these percentages are 61 per cent and 64 per cent for the corporatist and social-democratic regime respectively. The rather large differences in the exit patterns of older unemployed across the various regimes may be attributed to the differences in the attractiveness of exit gateways to retirement. Liberal regimes (such as that in the UK) and residual regimes (such as those in Spain, Greece or Portugal) tend to have less attractive exit routes out of the labour force.

Multivariate models
These findings provide only a general picture of the background of these employment transitions. Kaiser and Siedler (2000) and Schils and Muffels (2003) have estimated more detailed models for explaining these transitions, incorporating both individual and institutional factors.[4] Table 6.6 presents the findings of Schils and Muffels (2003) on the factors explaining transitions from work into unemployment or inactivity. Models were estimated separately for men and women because the labour market behaviour of men and women differs markedly. The models include individual- and household-level variables, human capital and institutional characteristics.

Looking first at the role of personal characteristics, the oldest age group has a significantly higher probability of moving out of employment, into either unemployment or inactivity, compared to the prime-aged reference group. Older men and women tend to leave employment to withdraw from the labour market but older women tend also to move into unemployment. The effect for men suggests that the generosity of the early retirement arrangements exerts a positive effect on the transition into inactivity.

With respect to gender differences, young women have a significantly higher probability of becoming unemployed than prime-aged women. We suspect that this group of young women in most European countries as yet have no children to care for; they most likely have children at later ages and withdraw at that later stage due to caring duties. On the other hand, young men tend to move out of the labour force significantly more than young women, most likely due to moving into further education. These results are further supported by the positive effect of the number of children on withdrawal from the labour market for women. Being divorced or widowed, as well as never having been married, have a negative effect on women moving out of the labour market – probably for economic reasons.

Table 6.6   *Factors affecting transitions out of employment into unemployment or inactivity (multinomial logit regression coefficients)*

Variable	Men		Women	
	Unem-ployment	Inactivity	Unem-ployment	Inactivity
Individual characteristics				
Aged 16–24	–0.23	0.61***	0.40*	0.22
Aged 50–65	0.36	1.34***	0.83***	0.84***
Number of children	0.07	0.00	0.00	0.09**
Divorced/separated/widow	0.25	–0.14	0.15	–0.25***
Never married	0.30***	0.02	0.13	–0.35***
Good health	–0.17***	–0.24**	–0.13	0.06
Poor health	0.41**	0.81***	0.62***	0.50***
Human capital variables				
High education level	–0.17	0.08	–0.25**	0.12
Low education level	0.44***	0.02	0.11	0.00
Tenure current job (years)	–0.21***	–0.07***	–0.19***	–0.07***
Receiving training?	–0.26**	0.29***	–0.02	0.05
Job characteristics				
Hours worked per week	–0.01***	0.03***	–0.00	–0.03***
Public sector employee?	–0.29***	0.02	–0.39***	–0.29***
Non-supervisory level	0.04	0.30**	0.02	0.25**
Supervisory level	0.01	0.58***	–0.05	0.40**
Unemployed before this job	0.78***	–0.08	0.40***	0.09
Personal labour income	–0.05***	–0.05***	–0.09***	–0.10***
Other h/hold labour income	–0.01***	–0.00	–0.01**	–0.00
Regime effects				
Social-democratic	–0.09	–0.72***	1.07***	–0.40***
Corporatist	0.15	–0.72***	1.17***	–0.19*
Residual	0.45***	1.10***	1.22***	–0.15
Soc-dem if aged 16–24	–0.01	1.20***	–1.18***	1.13***
Soc-dem if aged 50–65	0.73**	0.261	–0.24	–0.01
Corporatist if aged 16–24	0.91***	0.57**	–0.29	–0.19
Corporatist if aged 50–65	0.28	0.19	–0.88**	–0.53**
Residual if aged 16–24	0.09	1.29***	–0.399*	–0.06
Residual if aged 50–65	0.17	1.04***	–1.05***	0.28
Year				
1995	0.00	–0.05	–0.24***	–0.21**
1997	–0.19**	–0.06	–0.22***	–0.21**
Constant	–1.02***	1.90***	–2.02***	–0.73***

Notes: The reference person is aged 25–49, married, in medium health, with medium educational levels, an intermediate-level job, and living in a liberal regime in 1996. Asterisks denote significance of coefficients: *** 1%, ** 5%, * 10%.

Source: ECHP (1994–98), from Schils and Muffels (2003).

Never-married single men are more likely to move into unemployment, which may either point to their lower human capital and worse labour market prospects or the disincentive effect of the benefit system. Having poor health is associated with a higher probability of moving out of employment into either of the non-employed states, for both men and women. Having good health is associated with a lower probability of moving out of employment, but this effect is observed only for men.

Human capital variables also play their expected role. A high education level lowers the probability of moving to unemployment, especially for women, whereas a low education level raises the likelihood of becoming unemployed, particularly for men. This mirrors the less favourable employment situation of low-educated people in the knowledge economy.

Longer tenure in one's current job is negatively related to the probability of moving out of employment into either unemployment or inactivity. Longer tenure is indicative of a good match between job and worker; additionally, people with longer tenure are most likely to have trained on the job and therefore have a more stable employment situation. For both men and women, the effect of tenure is much smaller for exits into inactivity, which might be attributed to early retirement schemes providing better benefits the longer the tenure in the current job.

Currently receiving training reduces the likelihood of a transition into unemployment, but only for men. It appears that being engaged in training pays off, at least for men, since the probability of becoming unemployed is reduced. The positive effect for men of training on withdrawal from the labour market appears counterintuitive. Further analysis shows that the effect holds only for young workers, indicating that young workers receiving training are more inclined to leave the labour force to follow further education.

Job characteristics are also important. The more hours a man works, the less likely he is to become unemployed, or to withdraw from the labour market. A similar effect, at least for moving into inactivity, is found for women. The longer hours a woman works, the less likely she is to withdraw from the labour market. These findings show that the longer one works in a job the better the labour market position of the holder of that job.

Working in the public sector reduces the probability of moving out of employment into unemployment, reflecting the better employment protection situation within the public sector. The effect holds for men as well as for women. Women working in the public sector are less likely to withdraw from the labour market, which is not the case for men.

Workers occupying a lower-level job (non-supervisory) or a higher-level job (supervisory) compared to jobs at the intermediate level, are both more inclined to withdraw from the labour market. It requires further scrutiny to examine the reasons for the higher withdrawal rates of these particular groups. In either case it might be associated with a higher probability of becoming disabled or moving into early retirement schemes.

The findings also show that male and female workers who were unemployed before their current job are more likely to re-enter unemployment, though no more likely to withdraw from the labour market. People with higher earnings are less likely to quit employment to either destination – possibly because the opportunity costs of losing a well-paid job are higher.

Effects of employment regimes are shown for each regime type compared to the liberal regime. In corporatist and social-democratic regimes, both men and women are less likely to withdraw from the labour market and to move into inactivity than they are in liberal regimes, while women are more likely to move into unemployment. In the residual regime, both men and women are more likely to move into unemployment, and men are also more likely to become inactive. This reflects the worse employment situation in the residual countries.

The interaction effects between regime type and age group are shown to be significant in many cases. The odds of becoming unemployed are significantly lower for the youngest female workers in social-democratic regimes compared to the odds in liberal regimes. Note, however, that the odds of *withdrawing* from the labour market are *larger* for both young female and male workers in this regime. This holds for young men in the other regimes too, but the strongest effect is found in the residual regime, indicating again that the labour market position of young men is rather weak in this regime. These regime-type effects on the withdrawal of young workers from the labour market suggest that more often in social-democratic than in liberal regimes the youngest workers leave their jobs to move into education. The reason for the move into inactivity might be their worse labour market situation in conjunction with the more active labour market policy in the corporatist and social-democratic regimes offering them more opportunities to raise their human capital and improve their labour market prospects through education. The results also indicate that in residual regimes both the youngest and the older generations of male workers have a higher probability of withdrawing from the labour market compared to their counterparts in liberal regimes. The results for the youngest age group might, apart from the poor unemployment benefits, mirror the typical familial features of the residual regimes where large fractions of young people still live in their parents' home, for which reason the economic need to earn a living is less pressing. Looking at the data more carefully, it is shown that more than 80 per cent of the young who are observed to make a transition from employment into inactivity in residual regimes are living in households with at least three adults. For the oldest generation, a similar effect might be responsible for their higher withdrawal rate; incomes are shared within the larger multiple-generation households.

For the youngest and oldest generations of female workers in the residual regime, the findings show that they are more likely to move into unemployment, signalling again their worse employment situation. In corporatist regimes the youngest generation tend to move into unemployment whereas the oldest generation tend to either move into unemployment or to withdraw from the labour market. In both cases it might reflect the worse employment conditions for which reason they either receive unemployment or retirement benefits.

Finally, we measured differences between years to account for business cycle effects. In 1995 and 1997, the odds of women becoming unemployed or withdrawing from the labour market are significantly lower than in 1996, probably due to the improved employment conditions.

Transitions from unemployment into employment
Kaiser and Siedler (2002) examine transitions from unemployment into employment in the UK and West Germany.[5] Estimates from their models are reported in Table 6.7.

There are significant positive effects on the probability of moving into employment for some of the household composition variables. For example, being married increases the likelihood of moving into employment for men in the UK. The presence of children has a strong negative effect for German women. This corroborates the findings presented in Chapter 4, that women in corporatist regimes tend to withdraw from the labour market when children arrive in the household. Results for the UK show a negative effect of the existence of children for men, which seems slightly odd. The positive effect for married men indicates that the unexpected negative effect for men with children may be caused by a negative effect for single unmarried men with children. Unmarried men who have responsibility for the care of their children need, just like women, to reduce their working commitments – which may result in withdrawal from the labour market.

The results for the combination of education level and age show a clear picture. The higher an unemployed person's education level and the younger they are, the more likely they are to get a job. This holds both for males and females in West Germany. Similar effects were generally found in the UK, but with a striking difference. Those in the UK who are both low-educated and young are no more likely than their low-educated older counterparts to move into employment; this is true both for males and for females. This corroborates our earlier results for the liberal UK, finding that young unemployed people have a rather unfavourable labour market position

Table 6.7   Main effects on the likelihood of a transition from unemployment into employment

Variable	West Germany		UK	
	Men	Women	Men	Women
Household variables				
Married	0.172	0.096	0.181*	0.192
Having children	−0.075	−0.511**	−0.236**	0.043
Human capital variables				
Low educ if young	0.697**	0.311*	0.093	0.060
Med educ if young	0.709**	0.373**	0.285**	0.308**
High educ if young	0.484**	0.387*	0.247**	0.298**
Low educ if older (ref)				
Med educ if older	0.082	0.236	0.108	0.230
High educ if older	0.340	0.358	0.332**	0.304*
Receiving training	0.726**	0.627**	0.11	−0.50**
Immigrant	−0.33***	−0.46**		
Unemployment variables				
Number of spells	0.481**	0.756**	0.438**	0.331**
Duration spells in months	−0.058**	−0.099**	−0.054**	−0.047**
Receiving u/e benefit	−0.334**	−0.154	−0.170**	−0.199*
Receiving u/e assistance	−1.274**	−1.047**		

Note: Parameter estimates shown are from a Cox proportional hazard rate model. Asterisks denote significance of coefficients: *** 1%, ** 5%, * 10%.
Source: ECHP (1994–97), adapted from Kaiser and Siedler (2000).

because they seem to have low education levels. For older people in both Germany and the UK, a high level of education exerts a positive effect on the rate of leaving unemployment – though coefficients are significant for the UK only.

Another assumption of human capital theory relates to the question of whether training during unemployment shortens its duration. Earlier it was shown that training during employment may reduce the probability of becoming unemployed, and the findings in this study show that, at least for Germany, receiving training has a positive effect on the probability of leaving unemployment and moving into employment.

In both countries, and for both sexes, there is a negative relationship between the duration of preceding unemployment spells and the probability of moving into employment: thus, the longer the duration of previous unemployment spells the lower the likelihood of moving into employment.

For each additional month of previous unemployment, the probability of leaving unemployment decreases by about 6 to 9 per cent in Germany and 5 per cent in the UK. This may be because human capital loss during unemployment lowers re-employment probabilities. It might also signal the selection strategies of risk-averse employers, who opt for workers with lower risks of a bad match. The positive effect of the number of spells seems at first to be counterintuitive, but it might signal the better re-employment probabilities of people experiencing multiple (and hence also shorter) spells of employment.

The effects of receiving unemployment benefits on the duration of unemployment are consistently negative, both in Germany and the UK. People are less inclined to search for jobs when the financial burden of remaining unemployed is lower. This reflects the standard disincentive effect of unemployment benefits. In the end, when unemployed people find a job the match might be better due to this longer search, but the data do not provide evidence on this issue. The significant negative effects seem to be stronger in Germany than in the UK, suggesting that the disincentive effects are stronger in Germany. This might mirror the higher replacement rates of unemployment benefits in the corporatist Germany compared to the liberal UK.

Finally, the results show most strongly for Germany that immigrants tend to have lower re-employment probabilities than native-born residents. In the UK the effect is significant for unemployed women only.

Summary and Conclusions

The world of work is changing. There is a larger variety of working time arrangements and labour contracts; workers change jobs more rapidly, and they tend to experience more intermittent periods of unemployment. Working career patterns have changed in the context of rapidly changing economic and cultural influences. These ongoing changes will raise mobility and turnover in the labour market. The aim of this chapter is to provide a deeper insight into labour market mobility patterns and compare them across different employment regimes and across different age groups. In the first part of the chapter we showed how people's attachment to the labour market, measured both at a point in time and over a longer time horizon, varies across the different policy regimes.

Examining year-on-year transition matrices for the various labour market states, we notice that employment is the most stable, while self-employment is less stable, and unemployment and education/training are less stable still. The less stable the labour market status is, the higher the volatility and the more frequently people occupying these states experience a transition into another state. The states of retirement and 'out of the labour force' are relatively stable, with rather low mobility rates out of these states except for mobility between the two. Across regimes, it turns out that stability of employment is largest in social-democratic and corporatist regimes and lowest in residual and liberal regimes.

Looking at longitudinal working profiles we again observe a high degree of stability in persistent employment, a lesser degree of stability in the state of persistent unemployment, but much more mobility when people are mainly employed or mainly non-employed (what we might call insecure or intermittent employment). These findings show that both stability and mobility coexist in the labour market. The image of a segmented labour market with stable jobs on the one hand and unstable jobs on the other is far from reality in any employment regime.

Examining transitions from one longitudinal employment profile into another shows that upward mobility (into a more stable job) is higher in the liberal and social-democratic countries and lowest in the residual countries. In addition, downward mobility (into a less stable job) is higher in the residual countries. Therefore, we conclude that the residual regime is performing worst in terms of enhancing job mobility and safeguarding employment stability. These findings indicate that the residual regime does indeed stand out as a separate and distinct regime type, with a poorer record as far at its labour market performance is concerned. The liberal regime performs best across all regimes in terms of efficiency, but this is likely at the cost of safeguarding secure and stable jobs and stability of income position over time. With respect to guaranteeing a stable income position over time and more work security, the corporatist and social-democratic regimes perform better than the liberal regime, but apparently with some cost in terms of efficiency (see also Goodin et al., 1999).

In the second part of the chapter we examined labour mobility patterns by age group. First we investigated the extent to which investments in training differ between age groups. In general, older workers in all employment regimes are less educated and receive less training than younger workers. Our conjecture that investment in human capital would be lower for older workers is shown to be largely correct. We expected that investment in human capital would be highest in social-democratic and corporatist regimes. We suspected that in these regimes, the existence of more employment protection rules and social security arrangements in tandem would provide incentives for employees to engage in training and for employers to supply training. However, no support is found for this hypothesis. In social-democratic and corporatist regimes the negative effect of being older on the likelihood of receiving training is largest, which might point to the typical pattern of early retirement in these regimes. Older workers move out of the labour force rather than engaging in training.

Second, we looked at the impact which this reduced investment in older workers' training might have on the labour mobility of older workers compared with younger workers. The evidence suggests that in all employment regimes, prime-aged workers move the least of all three age groups. Both the young and the old have the highest job-to-non-job mobility. It must be noted that although older workers do have a lower probability than young workers of becoming unemployed, once they become unemployed their probabilities of remaining in unemployment are higher. Our conjecture that job-to-non-job mobility in social-democratic and corporatist regimes is highest because of the use of social security arrangements as early retirement pathways is supported by the data.

Finally, we examined the transition from unemployment into employment in two large countries representing different employment regimes: the UK and Germany. Most of the predictions following from human capital theory are confirmed by the hazard rate models estimated here. More highly educated people have much better chances of getting a job. Receiving training during unemployment increases the likelihood of moving into another job. A longer duration of previous unemployment spells lowers the likelihood of getting a job offer. Disincentive effects of generous benefit levels are more pronounced in the corporatist Germany than in the liberal UK, where benefit levels are relatively low.

These results, which were based on national panel surveys as well as the five-wave ECHP panel data set, have shown to be very promising and to support most of the theoretical conjectures made. Given the limited number of years of data in the ECHP, we were not really capable of tackling economic cycle effects. Though the ECHP unfortunately ended in 2001, we can add some more waves of data and more countries will permit us to enrich our analyses and to improve our model specifications by allowing us to control for economic cycle effects and improving the corrections made for selection bias. That the impact of regime type remains significant in most models even after the inclusion of a very rich set of covariates supports the theoretical significance of including institutional variables that may account for differences in policy settings in the various countries under scrutiny. Policies are indeed important in improving the performance of labour markets in reducing unemployment and fostering economic welfare for all.

Notes

1. Considering the relatively short observation period in the mid-1990s, it cannot be ruled out that the mobility patterns observed are influenced by differences in the business cycle across countries. At the time of observation, however, all countries under scrutiny were in the same (upward) phase of the business cycle.
2. People are classified into four different age categories: 16 to 24 being young workers; 25 to

49 being prime-aged workers; 50 to 58 as well as 59 to 65 being older workers. This distinction in the older workers' category is made because evidence is found that people aged 50–58 have other labour market patterns than their older coworkers (Bercovec and Stern, 1991; Guillemard and van Gunsteren, 1991; Blau, 1994; Antolin and Scarpetta, 1998; Blondahl and Scarpetta, 1998; Kapteyn and de Vos, 1998; Heyma, 2001).
3. For their study, Kaiser and Siedler used the German Socio-Economic Panel Study (GSOEP) from 1991 to 1995 and the British Household Panel Study (BHPS) from 1992 to 1996.
4. Kaiser and Siedler (2000) estimated a semi-parametric competing risks Cox-proportional-hazard model for the transition out of unemployment into employment or inactivity, whereas Schils and Muffels (2003) estimated a multinomial logit model for the transitions from employment to unemployment or inactivity. For more details on the methods used, see the original working papers.
5. For Germany, the original model was estimated for both East and West Germany. Here, however, only the results for West Germany are discussed, since East Germany should be considered a special case.

References

Antolin, P. and S. Scarpetta (1998), 'Microeconomic analysis of the retirement decision: Germany', *OECD Working Paper*, **204**, Paris: OECD Economics Department.

Becker, G. (1964), *Human Capital: a Theoretical and Empirical Analysis, with Special Reference to Education*, New York: National Bureau of Economic Research.

Bercovec, J. and S. Stern (1991), 'Job exit behaviour of older men', *Econometrica*, **59** (1), 199–210.

Blau, D.M., (1994), 'Labor force dynamics of older men', *Econometrica*, **62** (1), 117–56.

Blondahl, S. and S. Scarpetta (1998), 'The retirement decision in OECD countries', *OECD Working Paper*, **202**, Paris: OECD Economics Department.

Esping-Andersen, G. (1990), *The Three Worlds of Welfare Capitalism*, Cambridge: Polity Press.

Esping-Andersen, G. (2002), *Why We Need a New Welfare State*, Oxford: Oxford University Press.

European Commision (1999), *Employment in Europe 1998*, Brussels: European Commission, Directorate V/A.

Goodin, B., B. Headey, R. Muffels and H.J. Dirven (1999), *The Real Worlds of Welfare Capitalism*, Cambridge: Cambridge University Press.

Guillemard, A.M. and H. van Gunsteren (1991), 'Pathways and their prospects: a comparative interpretation of the meaning of early exit', in M. Kohli (ed.), *Time for Retirement*, Cambridge: Cambridge University Press.

Heyma, A. (2001), *Dynamic Models of Labour Force Retirement; an Empirical Analysis of Early Exit in the Netherlands*, Amsterdam: Thela Publishers.

*Kaiser, L.C. and T. Siedler (2000), 'Exits from unemployment spells in Germany and the United Kingdom – a cross-national comparison based on institutional background information and the use of panel-data (1990–96)', *EPAG Working Papers*, **7**, Colchester: University of Essex.

Kapteyn, A. and K. de Vos (1998), 'Social security and retirement in the Netherlands', in J. Gruber and D.A. Wise (eds), *Social Security and Retirement Around the World*, Chicago: Chicago University Press, pp. 269–303.

Lipmann, S.A. and J.J. McCall (1976), 'The economics of job search: a survey',

Economic Inquiry, **14**, 155–89.

Mincer, J. (1962), 'On-the-job training: costs, returns and some implications', *Journal of Political Economy*, **70** (5), 50–79.

Mincer, J. (1993), *Studies in Human Capital*, Aldershot, UK and Brookfield, US: Edward Elgar.

Mortensen, D.T. (1986), 'Job search and labor market analysis', in O. Aschenfelter and R. Layard, *Handbook of Labor Economics Vol. II*, Amsterdam: Elsevier Press, pp. 849–920.

*Muffels, R.J.A. and D.J. Fouarge (2002), 'Working profiles and employment regimes in Europe', *Schmollers Jahrbuch (Journal of Applied Social Sciences)*, **122**, 85–110.

Muffels, R., P. Tsakloglou and D. Mayes (eds) (2002), *Social Exclusion in European Welfare States*, Cheltenham, UK and Northampton, MA, USA: Edward Elgar.

Narendrathan, W. and S. Nickell (1986), 'Estimating the parameters of interest in a job search model', in R. Blundell and I. Walker (eds), *Unemployment, Search and Labour Supply*, Cambridge: Cambridge University Press.

OECD (1999), *Employment Outlook 1999*, Paris: OECD.

Schmid, G., and B. Gazier (2002), *The Dynamics of Full Employment: Social Integration Through Transitional Labour Markets*, Cheltenham, UK and Northampton, MA, USA: Edward Elgar.

*Schils, T. and R. Muffels (2003), 'The ageing workforce and labour market mobility – do mobility patterns differ between age groups and welfare regimes?', *EPAG Working Paper*, **44**, Colchester: University of Essex.

* Direct output from EPAG's *DynSoc* research programme (see page 268).

7. Unemployment and Welfare Regimes: Measurement, Search Activity and Income Distribution

Mette C. Deding, Peder J. Pedersen and Torben D. Schmidt

Introduction

The countries of the European Union (EU) are approaching the 30th anniversary of the start of a period of persistently high unemployment in most of the member states. Since the mid-1980s, average standardised unemployment rates for the EU as a whole have remained between 8 and 10 per cent, without any noticeable trend. There has, however, been a sizeable range in unemployment rates between member countries, peaking at a difference of 13 percentage points between Spain and Austria in 1994. In 2001 the range was down to around 8 percentage points.

In this chapter, we discuss several aspects of this persistent European unemployment problem. First, we chart the development of unemployment in the EU since the mid-1980s, focusing on unemployment profiles across different welfare state regime types. Next, we examine the concept of unemployment itself. Is the term 'unemployment' clear and well defined? Are estimates of the rates of movement out of unemployment sensitive to different methods of defining unemployment? And, as well as the standard categories of 'unemployed' and 'out of the labour force', is there a case for defining a third category of non-workers, in between these two?

We turn next to the issue of labour market search – an important aspect of labour market flexibility. We examine to what extent active search is undertaken among the unemployed, and whether search activity improves unemployed people's chances of finding a job. Since search activity also plays a part in job-to-job changes without intervening spells of unemployment, which are important for a well-functioning labour market, we also examine the factors connected with on-the-job search in the different European labour markets.

Next, we turn to the relationship between unemployment levels and incomes. We present evidence that the distribution of disposable incomes is surprisingly stable, even in the face of major swings in the distribution of market incomes as unemployment levels fluctuate. Finally, we examine the extent of unemployment traps across Europe: that is, the situation which unemployed people may face, in which their disposable income from working full-time may be only slightly higher – or even possibly lower – than the income from collecting unemployment benefits and saving the fixed costs of work.

Unemployment in the EU: Differences by Welfare State Regime

In Figure 7.1, we show average unemployment rates across the 15 current EU countries, divided into the four different welfare state regime types defined in Chapter 1.

Figure 7.1   Unemployment rates in four welfare state regimes, 1986–2001

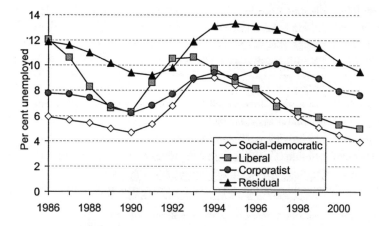

Note: Population weighted averages.
Source: OECD (2002).

Over the 15 years shown in Figure 7.1, average EU unemployment has moved without any clear trend between 8 and 10 per cent. It peaked in 1994 and has since then declined by about 3 percentage points. There are large differences in unemployment profiles between the four welfare state regimes, as well as differences within the individual regime types.

In the social-democratic group, unemployment rates were low during the 1980s, and jumped dramatically around 1990. This reflects the fact that Finland and Sweden were islands of near-full employment until 1990, when the collapse of the Soviet Union resulted in unemployment in Finland making a record jump from 3 to 17 per cent. Since 1993, unemployment in the social-democratic group has declined to half its peak level. The average for the liberal group, dominated by the UK unemployment rate, was (marginally) the highest in 1986, but is now close to the same low level as in the social-democratic group. The countries of the corporatist group had relatively low rates of unemployment in the late 1980s and early 1990s, but these have increased over the latter part of the 1990s, peaking at close to 10 per cent in 1997. As in the social-democratic group, the within-group variance is high, with overall low unemployment in Austria and fairly high unemployment in France, Germany and Belgium. Finally, the residual group has had the highest average rate of unemployment throughout the period. The only country with relatively low unemployment in this group is Portugal.

Figure 7.2   Unemployment rates in 15 EU countries, 2001

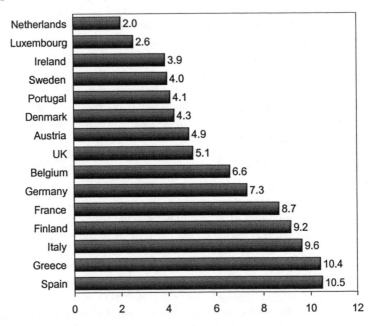

Source: OECD (2002).

Figure 7.2 illustrates the wide range in EU unemployment rates in 2001, from over 10 per cent in Spain down to 2 per cent in the Netherlands. Figure 7.2 also shows that there are clear exceptions to the welfare state classification as far as unemployment is concerned, with the main group outliers being Finland, Austria and Portugal.

Concepts of Unemployment

The concept of unemployment, as used in everyday language, may seem well defined to most people. However, a moment of reflection will change this consensus. The perception of unemployment may vary across individuals, countries and groups of countries – and of course, it may vary over time.

Formal versus informal definitions of unemployment

The usual criterion for distinguishing 'unemployment' from 'economic inactivity' is that the unemployed want work, while the inactive do not. However, there are different ways in which one may distinguish between unemployment and inactivity. The International Labour Office's (ILO's) formal definition of unemployment defines a person as unemployed who (1) is out of work, (2) has been searching actively for work within the last four weeks and (3) is able to start work within two weeks.[1] An example of an informal definition of unemployment is self-defined status, where a person defines his or her own labour market status as 'unemployed' without specific reference to whether they are currently looking for work. Any differences in the rates of transition into employment between individuals in these two groups would also indicate differences between the two concepts of unemployment, as a precise measure of individuals available for vacant jobs.

Figure 7.3 shows transition rates from unemployment into employment on the one hand, and into inactivity on the other, under these two definitions. The upper bar for each country shows those who are unemployed according to the ILO definition, and the lower bar shows those who are self-defined as unemployed.

There are marked differences in many countries in the transition rates, depending on the definition of unemployment being used. Those defined as unemployed under the ILO definition are more likely to move into work than those self-defined as unemployed. This difference is particularly marked in Austria, Belgium and the Netherlands, and is less pronounced in Italy, Greece and Spain. Transition rates into inactivity, on the other hand, are higher among the self-defined unemployed than the ILO unemployed. This difference is observed in almost all countries to a greater or lesser extent, and the differences do not seem to follow any clear pattern on the basis of welfare state regimes.

A hidden labour force?

Another issue in the definition of unemployment lies in distinctions between different groups of non-working people. Flinn and Heckman (1982, 1983) test the extent to which 'unemployment' and 'out of the labour force' are distinct labour market states in the USA. Their findings indicate that the two states are indeed quite different, which has implications both for theories of the labour market and for the formulation of policy.

Figure 7.3   *Percentage of unemployed people entering employment and inactivity the next year, under two definitions of unemployment*

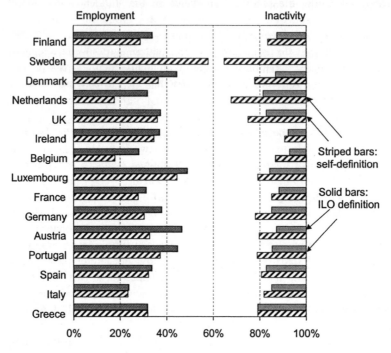

Source: ECHP (1994–98, pooled across years), authors' own calculations.

In a European context, a similar issue has been addressed by Holst and Spiess (2001, 2002), who analyse the concept of the *hidden labour force*. Traditionally, being unemployed is defined as meeting the formal criteria of not having a job, actively seeking work, and being available to start work – while being out of the labour force is defined as not having a job, but not actively seeking work or not being available to start work.

Holst and Spiess characterise a person in the 'hidden labour force' as lying somewhere between these groups – having a looser attachment to the labour force than the formally unemployed, but with at least a potential attachment to the labour force (in contrast to persons who are completely outside the labour force). They define the group as consisting of people who (a) would like to take on a job, but are not able to start the job within a shorter period, (b) are for some other reason not currently searching for a job, and (c) are not searching for a job due to discouragement after a long spell of unemployment.

This group fails to fulfil the criteria for being classified as unemployed (because they are not actively looking for work), but they may nevertheless have sufficient aspiration to get a job that entry or re-entry to the labour force might be the outcome.

Table 7.1 shows the relative importance of the 'hidden labour force', giving the proportion of men and women in this group for each country. There are large differences between countries in the share of the hidden labour force, but they do not follow any clear pattern across welfare regimes. The major systematic variation is between men and women – in nearly every country, women are substantially more likely than men to be members of the hidden labour force.

Table 7.1   Percentage of working-age adults in the hidden labour force

Regime/Country	Women	Men
Social-democratic		
Denmark	3.9	(1.7)
Netherlands	1.7	(0.8)
Liberal		
UK	1.5	(0.9)
Ireland	1.9	3.5
Corporatist		
Belgium	3.3	2.1
France	2.4	0.8
Germany	1.8	(0.9)
Residual		
Portugal	2.6	1.6
Spain	3.3	1.7
Italy	6.0	3.4
Greece	1.3	–

Note: – denotes ten or fewer cases; ( ) 11–30 cases
Source: ECHP (1996, weighted), adapted from Holst and Spiess (2002).

Holst and Spiess (2002) compare transition rates to employment from three different non-employed states: being unemployed, being in the hidden labour force, and being out of the labour force (inactive). Table 7.2 summarises the results. There is a clear overall ranking, with transition rates to employment being higher for the unemployed than for those in the hidden labour force, and lowest for the 'inactive' group. Transition rates into employment for the 'hidden' group tend to be closer to those of the formally unemployed than to those of the inactive group, indicating that the concept of the hidden labour force may indeed be relevant as far as their labour market behaviour is concerned.

Table 7.2   Transitions into employment for three groups of non-working people (percentages)

Status in initial year	Unemployed	Hidden labour force	Inactive
		% who move into employment the following year	
Social-democratic			
Denmark	49	–	–
Netherlands	40	(32)	(9)
Liberal			
UK	48	39	16
Ireland	31	19	11
Corporatist			
Belgium	34	–	(9)
France	31	28	(5)
Germany	39	39	14
Residual			
Portugal	43	32	18
Spain	30	18	4
Italy	24	18	5
Greece	32	(17)	6

Note: – denotes ten or fewer cases; ( ) denotes 11–30 cases.
Source: ECHP (1994–96, weighted), from Holst and Spiess (2002).

Transition rates into employment follow no clear pattern between the regime types. The only exception is that in the residual regime type, the behaviour of those in the hidden labour force is somewhat closer to that of the inactive group, and somewhat further away from that in the unemployed group, than in other countries. Thus, being in the hidden labour force may be thought of as closer to being inactive in these countries.

Labour Market Search

Labour market flexibility is high on the political agenda in most European countries, as an important precondition for economic efficiency and growth.

Flexible labour markets ensure that workers are quickly relocated in response to disturbances and shocks, for example from new technology and globalisation. A key issue regarding labour market flexibility is job search behaviour among workers, since the extent of active search among different groups of workers may be expected to influence labour market flexibility. A high propensity to search will increase the probability of finding a match in the job market: see, for example, the classical search models of McCall (1970) and Mortensen (1970).

The flexibility of labour markets may also be important in terms of income inequality. Search by workers and firms on the labour market increases the allocative efficiency of the labour market, and search is also related to the incidence and duration of spells in low income or poverty. For unemployed workers, it is well established that spells of unemployment have a long-run negative impact (known as 'scarring') on subsequent earnings: see for example Gregory and Jukes (2001) and Arulampalam et al. (2001).

Figure 7.4   *Proportion of unemployed people engaged in active job search*

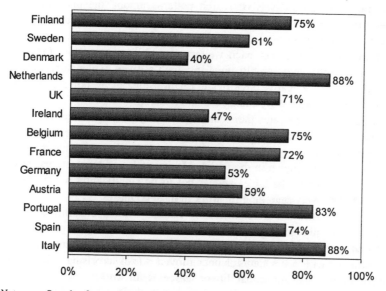

Notes: Sample of unemployed people, based on self-definition.
Figures represent averages over four years.
Source: ECHP (1994–97), authors' own calculations.

Search activity is undertaken not only by unemployed people, but also among people in work searching for better opportunities. Both types of search are analysed in Pedersen and Schmidt (2002). In the present chapter, we concentrate first on unemployed search and the obvious purpose of this activity, measured by succeeding in getting a new job. Next, we discuss search activity among employed workers.

Search activity among the unemployed

In the previous section, we mentioned two approaches to defining 'unemployment'. Here, the informal definition is used: unemployment is defined as considering oneself to be unemployed, since it is an individual's self-perceived situation which may be expected to guide his or her behaviour, including the extent of active search.

Among the unemployed in the European Community Household Panel (ECHP) under this criterion, the proportion engaged in active job search varies widely across the European countries, ranging from around 40 per cent in Denmark and Ireland, up to 80 per cent in Italy, Portugal and the Netherlands (see Figure 7.4). This may be taken as a first indicator of very different search incentives across Europe, which do not fall into clear patterns on the basis of welfare regime type.

A more detailed analysis of search patterns among the unemployed is found in Pedersen and Schmidt (2002). A summary of their results is given in Table 7.3. Again, these results point to very different search behaviour across the European countries. For each welfare regime type, the table shows the number of country/year combinations in which a given explanatory variable has a positive or negative significant relationship, or is not significantly related, to search propensity among the unemployed.

The age profile indicates that search propensity tends to increase up to a certain age, and decrease thereafter. In several countries, men are more likely to be actively searching for work than women, though the opposite is true in Greece (results not shown in the table). Marital status and educational levels (results not shown in the table) appear not to be significantly related to the likelihood of actively searching for work in most countries.

Attitudinal indicators are significantly related to the probability of active job search. A higher degree of optimism about one's job prospects is associated with higher search rates in the great majority of countries, while being satisfied with one's status as unemployed is (not surprisingly) related in most countries to a lower probability of searching for work.[2]

Search activity and re-employment

The obvious individual motive for job search is to get a job if one is unemployed, and a better job if one is already in employment. It is natural, then, to analyse job search in relation to the actual transitions occurring in labour markets, with special emphasis on exits from unemployment to a job.

Table 7.3   *Effects on search propensity for unemployed people (number of member countries with significant coefficients)*

Factor	Social-democratic			Liberal			Corporatist			Residual		
	+	−	n/s	+	−	n/s	+	−	n/s	+	−	n/s
Age	3	0	7	3	0	4	9	0	5	6	0	10
Age squared	0	4	6	0	4	3	0	10	4	0	11	5
Optimistic about finding a job	9	0	0	6	0	1	13	0	1	10	0	5
Satisfied with jobless situation	0	5	5	3	2	2	0	16	0	0	13	3

Note: Figures relate to results of probit regressions estimated for each country separately, and show the number of country/year combinations within each welfare-regime group, for which a significant relationship (+ or −) was found between the variable shown and the probability of actively searching for a job. 'n/s' indicates cases where no significant relationship was found.

Source: ECHP (1994–98), adapted from Pedersen and Schmidt (2002).

Pedersen and Schmidt (2002) analyse the relationship between job search and re-employment for a number of European countries. Their estimates compare the probability of an individual making the transition from unemployment to employment, or of remaining unemployed, with the probability of the unemployed person withdrawing from the labour market.

Table 7.4 summarises these results, showing the number of countries where the transitions in question are positively, negatively, or insignificantly related to a subset of variables.

Some factors have a similar impact on unemployed people's transitions across all welfare state regime types. The age profile indicates that the probability of both finding a job and remaining unemployed increases up to a certain age, and decreases thereafter. Men have typically higher transition rates into jobs than women, but they also tend to have a higher probability of remaining in unemployment (remember that both transitions are measured relative to an exit from the labour force). Both of these effects are common across all regime types.

Social Europe: living standards and welfare states

Table 7.4   *Factors influencing the probability of unemployed people moving into employment or remaining unemployed (number of member countries with significant coefficients)*

Factor	Social-democratic			Liberal			Corporatist			Residual		
	+	−	ns	+	−	ns	+	−	ns	+	−	ns
Unemployed–Employed												
Age	2	0	1	1	0	1	3	0	0	4	0	0
Age squared	0	2	1	0	1	1	0	2	1	0	4	0
Male	2	0	1	2	0	0	2	0	1	4	0	0
Optimistic about finding a job	2	0	1	1	0	1	1	0	2	4	0	0
Engaged in active search	3	0	0	0	0	2	1	0	2	3	0	1
Unemployed–Unemployed												
Age	3	0	0	1	0	1	1	0	2	4	0	0
Age squared	0	3	0	0	2	0	0	1	2	0	4	0
Male	1	0	2	2	0	0	2	0	1	3	0	1
Optimistic about finding a job	0	0	3	0	0	2	0	0	3	1	0	3
Engaged in active search	3	0	0	0	0	2	0	0	3	1	0	3

Notes: Results not available for Sweden, Austria or Luxembourg.
Figures relate to multinomial logit regressions, with moving out of the labour force as reference category, and show the number of countries within each welfare-regime group, for which a significant relationship (+ or −) was found between the variable shown and the likelihood of finding a job or remaining unemployed. 'n/s' indicates cases where no significant relationship was found.
Source: ECHP (1997), adapted from Pedersen and Schmidt (2002).

Being married tends to have a (surprising) negative impact on a transition to a job in the residual-type welfare states (which might capture a gender effect, since the coefficient on the 'male' variable is significant in these countries, and female participation rates are on average the lowest in the residual-type welfare state).

Three variables not summarised in the table – education,[3] health status and whether the individual is a homeowner – have little relationship with transition rates. However, there is a major relationship between expecting to be able to find a new job and actually finding one, particularly in the residual-type welfare states.

The central variable – active search – is significantly and positively related to getting a new job in seven of the 12 countries. In four countries (three of them social-democratic) active search is also positively associated with remaining in unemployment. This is not surprising, as both probabilities are measured relative to an exit from the labour market. Furthermore, the labour market states are measured at interviews in two successive years, and people observed to be unemployed at two points in time may of course have had spells of employment in between. Active search tends to have more significant effects in the social-democratic and the residual-type welfare states. In the social-democratic case this could reflect the effect of fairly strict monitoring of quite generous benefit systems, while it could also reflect the impact of economic incentives on unemployed people in the residual-type welfare states. The conclusion is that active search is associated with a lower probability of leaving the labour force, and a higher probability of getting a job conditional on remaining in the labour force.

On-the-job search
Search activity among people with jobs is related to allocational efficiency in the labour market, and also to income distribution, to marginalisation and poverty. Income mobility plays an important part in improving individuals' positions in the distribution of income and welfare over time. A person's income can obviously increase as a result of increasing tenure with one employer, with no on-the-job search being necessary. However, (upward) income mobility will in many cases demand a change of job, which usually requires search being undertaken while still in the former position.

At the same time, on-the-job search has a potential impact on the realised distribution of earnings over a person's lifetime. This is illustrated by Flinn (2002), who compares labour markets and inequality in Italy and the USA. High search activity in the US labour market results in a high frequency of movements between labour market states. The economic interpretation is that spells of employment in jobs with low wages in the USA, on average, are fairly short. Search activity thus becomes closely connected with the structure of realised earnings over time.

The more regulated labour markets in many continental European countries, with Italy used as a typical example in Flinn (2002), mean it is comparatively difficult to lay off existing staff ('insiders') in most continental labour markets. Partly as a reaction to this, deregulation has allowed firms to employ workers in short-term jobs on contracts that exclude them from the insider protection inherent in the job security rules. The outcome of this has been to create what Boeri (1999) terms an intermediate and transitory labour market state between employment and unemployment. Workers under these fixed, short-term contracts are under a strong obligation to engage in on-the-job search to avoid otherwise inevitable spells of unemployment and income losses. For this group of workers, the incentives for on-the-job search are expected to be clearly higher than for employed workers in a job with indefinite duration. At the same time, they compete for vacancies with unemployed workers: thus, the more short-term jobs there are in the economy, the greater the competition for job openings, and the greater are the incentives for unemployed workers to engage in job search. A comprehensive recent analysis of temporary jobs can be found in OECD (2002).

Figure 7.5   *Percentage of employed workers engaged in active job search: temporary workers, and all workers*

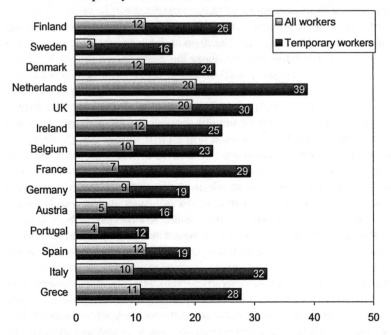

Source: ECHP (1994–97, and 1995–97 for temporary workers), adapted from Pedersen and Schmidt (2002).

Figure 7.5 shows how the proportion of workers engaged in on-the-job search varies across Europe, for all workers (lower bar) and temporary workers (upper bar). A comparison with Figure 7.4 shows that, as expected, job search propensities are much lower for employed (even temporarily employed) than for unemployed people.

In most countries, the proportion of all workers engaged in on-the-job search is around 10 per cent. It is higher in the Netherlands and UK, at around

20 per cent, and lower, at under 5 per cent, in Portugal and Sweden. Search propensity does not appear to be closely related to the proportion of workers in temporary jobs – for example, Spain has a fairly low search propensity and a high share of temporary jobs, see OECD (2002).

As expected, on-the-job search is much more common for temporary workers than for employed people as a whole. Countries where temporary workers are highly likely to search while still in work are France, the UK and Italy (around 30 per cent or higher) and particularly the Netherlands (39 per cent). Countries where temporary workers have a low propensity for on-the-job search are Portugal (12 per cent) and Austria and Sweden (16 per cent). In general, countries where search propensity is high for workers in general, it is also high for temporary workers.

Table 7.5 presents estimates of employed workers' probability of engaging in search activity. These use the same demographic variables as were used in the explanation of search activity among the unemployed (Table 7.4), plus two additional variables indicating job characteristics (job tenure, measured in the number of years the person reports having worked in his or her job; and a categorical variable indicating whether the job is temporary). Two further categorical variables indicating attitudes towards a worker's current income are also included (whether the person is at all dissatisfied with their earnings in their current job, and whether the household in which a person lives has any difficulty in making ends meet).

We would expect tenure to be negatively related to job search, since the probability of having realised a good match increases with increasing tenure. Having a temporary job, on the other hand, is expected to be positively related to search propensity. Finally, we expect that both the variables relating to dissatisfaction with income levels will be positively related to search propensity.

For those countries where a significant age effect is found, coefficients imply the probability of on-the-job search peaking at between 33 and 41 years of age. There does not appear to be any difference regarding gender, while being married tends to reduce on-the-job search, possibly reflecting the greater difficulties in taking up a new job (possibly implying a change of residence) where other family members are present. In contrast to unemployed search we find that having a higher education tends to increase active on-the-job search, most markedly in the social-democratic and residual groups.

Tenure has a consistent negative impact as expected, reflecting the fact that longer tenure reveals a higher probability of a good match having been found. At the same time it may reflect a positive relationship between earnings and tenure. We find the same consistent significant pattern in the impact of being in a temporary job.

Table 7.5   *Factors related to the probability of 'on-the-job' search*
               (number of member countries with significant coefficients)

Factor	Social-democratic			Liberal			Corporatist			Residual		
	+	−	ns	+	−	ns	+	−	ns	+	−	ns
Age	2	0	1	0	0	2	2	0	2	2	0	2
Age squared	0	3	0	0	2	0	0	2	2	0	2	2
Male	0	0	3	0	1	1	0	1	3	0	0	4
Married	0	3	0	0	2	0	0	2	2	0	1	3
High education	2	0	1	0	0	2	1	0	3	2	0	2
Job tenure	0	2	1	0	2	0	0	4	0	0	4	0
Temporary job	3	0	0	2	0	0	3	0	1	4	0	0
Dissatisfied with earnings	3	0	0	2	0	0	4	0	0	4	0	0
Difficulty making ends meet	2	0	1	1	0	1	2	0	2	2	0	2

Notes: Results not available for Sweden, or Luxembourg.
           Figures are based on probit regressions, and show the number of countries within
           each welfare-regime group, for which a significant relationship (+ or −) was found
           between the variable shown and the likelihood of engaging in on-the-job search.
           'n/s' indicates cases where no significant relationship was found.
Source: ECHP (1997), adapted from Pedersen and Schmidt (2002).

Finally, the role of economic incentives is clear. Dissatisfaction with earnings in the current job has a significant positive relationship with on-the-job search activity in every single country. Having difficulty making ends meet has the expected positive relationship with search propensity in all countries, though the relationship is not significant in all countries.

Unemployment and Income Inequality

One of the central assumptions in the discussion of economic policy is that high unemployment will increase income equality and poverty rates. This statement will obviously be true when one considers the distribution of market incomes, but as even the most generous welfare state does not cover 100 per cent of the income loss due to unemployment, one would also expect increased unemployment to lead to widening inequality of disposable incomes.

Figure 7.6 illustrates the close connection between unemployment and income inequality in the case of Denmark, for the core 25–59 age group. As expected, inequality in market incomes mirrors the unemployment rate quite closely. In the years with decreasing unemployment from 1983 to 1987, the Gini coefficient for market income decreases by about 5 percentage points. The subsequent long period of increasing unemployment from 1987 to 1994 is accompanied by an increasing inequality in the distribution of market incomes of about 15 points. Finally, the decline in unemployment after 1993 has been accompanied by a – fairly small – decline in inequality of market incomes.

Figure 7.6   Inequality of market incomes and disposable incomes in Denmark, 1983–97

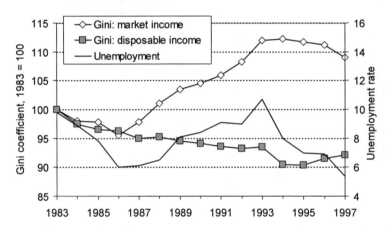

Note: Inequality measured by the Gini coefficient.
Source: Ministry of Finance (2000).

When disposable incomes are considered, the picture changes completely. The presumption is that despite the highly progressive taxation system in Denmark, an increase in unemployment would be associated with a more unequal distribution of disposable incomes. However, Figure 7.6 shows that there is no straightforward relationship between unemployment and the distribution of disposable incomes. The Gini coefficient for disposable income declines by about 10 per cent between 1983 and 1995, with no visible relationship to the cyclical changes in the economy. After 1995, inequality in disposable incomes appears to be increasing, despite falling unemployment in this period.[4]

The lack of a close relationship between changes in unemployment and inequality in disposable incomes is not a specifically Danish phenomenon.

This is illustrated in Figure 7.7, which plots the change in the Gini coefficients on disposable income against the change in unemployment rates between the mid-1980s and the mid-1990s for 16 OECD countries. The outlier on the right of Figure 7.7 is Finland with a dramatic 10 percentage-point increase in the unemployment rate accompanied by a 2 percentage-point increase in the Gini coefficient. In most other countries, inequality increased more modestly during this period. The correlation between the Gini coefficient and changes in unemployment is low, at +0.22, and it is obvious that no well-defined relationship exists between changes in unemployment and inequality of disposable incomes.

Figure 7.7   Relationship between changes in inequality of disposable incomes and changes in unemployment rates

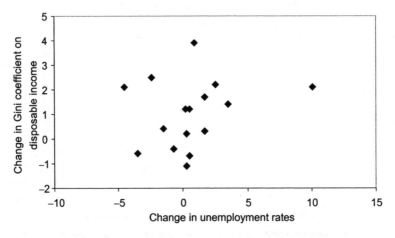

Note: Inequality is measured by the Gini coefficient, mid-1980s to mid-1990s.
Source: OECD Labour Force Statistics, and Förster and Pearson (2002).

In conclusion, the market income Gini coefficient relates straightforwardly to cyclical and trend factors in the labour market, while the disposable income Gini coefficient displays a puzzling 'over-robustness', or immunity to the large fluctuations in unemployment which many countries have experienced.

Unemployment benefits and income inequality
The well-known automatic stabilisers in the case of increasing unemployment are a reduction in tax payments and eligibility for a period of unemployment benefits for individuals who become unemployed. One of the main effects of these stabilisers is to dampen the impact of cyclical shocks on the distribution of disposable incomes compared to the distribution of market incomes: they

are part of the explanation of the 'robustness' discussed above. A study by Andersen and Schmidt (1999) illustrates cross-country differences in the extent of automatic stabilisation.

In this subsection we report on work by Deding and Schmidt (2002) which illustrates cross-country variability in a more specific way, using ECHP data to assess the influence of unemployment insurance benefits on the inequality of disposable incomes. The measured impacts will reflect differences between unemployment insurance systems, as well as the fact that the EU countries were in different stages of the economic cycle during the period of data collection (see Figures 7.1 and 7.2).

Figure 7.8   Average contribution to inequality from unemployment benefits, by average unemployment rate

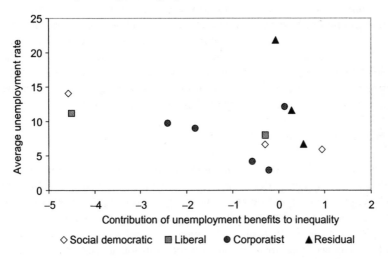

Note: Greece is omitted, as standardised OECD unemployment rates were not available –
            the contribution to inequality from unemployment benefits was small and positive at
            0.02.
Sources: Unemployment benefits' contribution to inequality (horizontal axis) from Deding and
            Schmidt (2002) using ECHP (1994–98). Unemployment rates (vertical axis) from
            OECD Outlook (2001).

The horizontal axis of Figure 7.8 shows the relative contribution of unemployment insurance benefits to overall income inequality in 12 of the EU countries, as a percentage of the Gini coefficient in each country. The four welfare-regime types are denoted by different symbols.

Cross-country differences in the cyclical position of the economy are illustrated on the vertical axis in Figure 7.8, as the average unemployment rate for the period 1994–98. The period is fairly short, but with that reservation in mind, there seem to be different patterns within different groups of countries. For the residual group, there appears to be very little relationship between the unemployment level and the distributional importance of unemployment benefits, while for the social-democratic group there is a strong relationship between unemployment and the distributional importance of benefits. The corporatist group falls somewhere between the two other groupings.

The tentative conclusion from Figure 7.8 is that there may be important differences in the way unemployment benefits influence inequality in different welfare regimes. However, more observations would be required to separate the impact from institutional factors from cyclical influences in a fully satisfactory way.

To sum up, the analyses discussed here suggest that the lack of a strong relationship between unemployment and the distribution of disposable income is fairly robust. This is well documented for Denmark and the other Nordic countries, and also seems to be the case in the other EU countries. The interpretation is that, at least in social-democratic welfare regimes, the welfare state has almost succeeded in eliminating the link between unemployment rates and inequality in disposable incomes.

Unemployment Traps

In this section we present empirical evidence on the magnitude and the importance of economic disincentives for low-paid workers, in the form of the 'unemployment trap', where an unemployed worker would be not much better off – or even worse off – after finding a low-waged job. The unemployment trap is the result of the interaction between a fairly low wage, fixed costs of working, income taxes and/or means-testing of benefits, and a fairly high degree of compensation from unemployment benefits for low-waged workers. The disincentives inherent in such a situation could reduce active job search, or for some groups could induce an exit from the labour market – either permanently into early retirement, or temporarily if a leave programme or support from other family members is available.

This section is based primarily on an illustrative Danish study – first because highly relevant data are available for this purpose in Denmark, and also because Denmark is one of the OECD countries with the largest labour supply disincentives for low-paid workers, as demonstrated by OECD (1996). Besides the results from the Danish study, we summarise results from studies using Belgian, Finnish and French data on unemployment traps.

The Danish study (Pedersen and Smith, 2002) is based on a panel sample survey, merged with data from administrative registers. This database enables us to construct very precise individual budget constraints, including information on the fixed costs of work in the form of commuting and childcare costs. Further, it is possible to combine this information with extensive information on labour supply, and on individual attitudes towards work. Individuals are observed over a period of three years from 1993 to 1996 and thus, one may test whether low-paid workers during this three-year period react to economic disincentives in terms of their search effort, labour supply, retirement, other transitions out of the labour force, and geographical mobility.

The results from this study indicate that economic incentives do affect behaviour significantly, despite the fact that a fairly large proportion of employed persons in Denmark work even though they might be better off unemployed. This last fact may be interpreted in different ways. First, although the strictness of the unemployment benefits system may be reduced during periods of high unemployment, collecting benefits is not a 'free choice'. Second, individuals consider the future as well as the present, and may realise that although claiming benefits may yield a higher income in the short run, it might imply losses in the long run due to depreciation of their human capital.

Finally, there are interesting and policy-relevant issues relating to the persistence of being in the unemployment trap. In the Danish data set, close to 20 per cent of those in such a trap at the initial interview were also in the same sort of trap at the second interview three years later.

Unemployment traps have been analysed for a number of European countries as well as Denmark. D'Addio et al. (2002) present results from a study using Belgian panel data for the years 1993–97. Estimating a sample selection model on these data, they calculate predicted wages for each unemployed individual, which are then compared with the unemployment benefits being collected. Unemployment traps are found to be important in Belgium, especially for long-term unemployed women – for whom entering a new job is often accompanied by a substantial decline in disposable income. Part of this decline is due to a depressing impact on the re-employment wages from long-term unemployment.

The same effect is found in a study on Finnish data by Holm et al. (1999), where the distribution of re-entry wages is significantly lower than the general wage distribution. In Finland, unemployment rose dramatically in the early 1990s, and a significant proportion of those covered by unemployment insurance were in a 'trapped' situation as measured by the private economic incentives they met.

Gurgand and Margolis (2002) present results from a study using a French data set, collected in 1998 and covering people who received the Guaranteed Minimum Income in 1996. For this selected group, they find a rather high proportion of people with no increase in disposable income from being employed. Data were not available on fixed costs of work which would increase this proportion even further.

This summary of results from these four European studies illustrates a general phenomenon of unemployment traps, where only the relative importance of different factors might shift, involving the benefit structure, the sensitivity of the wage offer distribution to individual unemployment, or the tax structure, as shown by the French case. Unemployment traps and policy discussions in relation to this problem are, however, not a specific European problem, as is shown by the detailed survey of the US situation in Gokhale et al. (2002). In the USA the Earned Income Tax Credit (EITC) has been a useful instrument for reducing problems in this area (see Scholz, 1996 and Hotz and Scholz, 2000). What makes the European situation more difficult is that the strongest impact from EITC-like instruments is found in environments characterised by a high variance in the earnings distribution, a relatively low minimum wage and fairly low income taxes at low wage rates. Roughly speaking, these conditions are much closer to being fulfilled in the USA than in most EU countries.

Summary and Concluding Remarks

In this chapter we have examined several issues relating to unemployment in Europe. The chapter opened with a brief survey of the development in average unemployment in the four welfare state regime types since the mid-1980s, showing that since the early/mid-1990s unemployment has been much lower in the social-democratic and liberal than in the corporate and residual regime types. It should be mentioned, however, that as far as unemployment is concerned, there are outliers within each welfare-regime type except the liberal.

Next, we addressed questions of the concept and measurement of unemployment. First, we presented evidence on the existence of a 'hidden labour force' in Europe, defined as a category of non-employed people between the formally unemployed and being out of the labour force. Analysis suggests that there does exist such a hidden labour force, made up of people who are not formally defined as unemployed, but who nevertheless retain some attachment to the labour force, and who behave differently from people who are outside the labour force for good. Empirically, people in the hidden labour force turn out in most countries to be much more similar to formally unemployed people than to those who are outside the labour force.

We then compared two different methods of measuring unemployment: the ILO criteria for classifying people as unemployed, versus classifying people as unemployed according to their own perception of their labour market status. We compared the probabilities of moving out of these two differently defined states of unemployment into either employment or inactivity in the subsequent year, and found that transition rates to employment are higher, but transition rates to inactivity are lower, using the ILO criteria.

We then analysed aspects of search activity, which is an important indicator of the functioning of the labour market – in the short run for matching people and jobs, and in the longer run for its impact on income distribution and poverty. First, we described and analysed search activity among the unemployed. Average search rates vary between countries in the range 40 to 80 per cent, without any systematic relationship with the different welfare-regime types. Next, we showed that search activity is significantly related to the expectation that job search may be successful, and also to an (implicit) measure of incentives.

The main purpose of search is to find a new job, so we then presented a summary of results from analyses of re-employment or remaining in unemployment measured against withdrawal from the labour force. Again, there is a strong relationship between an individual's expectations of job search success and the probability of re-employment. There is also a significant relationship between actively searching for work and an individual's chances of getting a new job. Active search seems to be more strongly related to finding a new job in the social-democratic and residual regime types than in the liberal and corporatist regime types.

We then proceeded to an examination of search activities among people who already have a job. As expected, the proportion of employed people engaged in on-the-job search is much smaller than the proportion of unemployed people searching for work. Again, there are big cross-country differences in the proportions engaged in on-the-job search, with a range between 5 and 20 per cent. A characteristic of current European labour markets is the widespread use of temporary workers to avoid some of the restrictions inherent in job security regulations. Temporary workers, as expected, search more than other workers, but there is no systematic relationship between the incidence of search and the relative importance of temporary jobs in the individual countries.

After the description of on-the-job search, we presented summaries of the results from statistical analyses of the propensity for this type of job search. Two job characteristics – job tenure and being employed in a temporary job – are significantly related to the probability of on-the-job search. Two variables measuring individuals' attitudes to their current income are also significantly related to the probability of search, indicating the importance of economic incentives for search behaviour.

We then turned to the relationship between unemployment levels and the distribution of income. It is evident that an increase in unemployment will result in a more unequal distribution of *market* income. However, the impact of unemployment on the distribution of *disposable* incomes is less clear. We started by looking at the Danish experience as an illustration of a period when increasing unemployment was accompanied by an increase in the inequality of market income, but at the same time by a decrease in the inequality of disposable income. Broadening the view to 16 OECD countries, we observed that inequality in the distribution of disposable income mostly increased between the mid-1980s and the mid-1990s, without having any clear relationship with unemployment. Next, we used ECHP data to evaluate the effect of unemployment benefits on inequality measured by the Gini coefficient. The dominant influence is, as expected, to reduce inequality. For the residual-type welfare state and for France, however, we found that unemployment benefits contribute to a greater, not a lesser, degree of inequality. Part of the cross-country variation in the relative effect of unemployment benefits on income distribution is due to countries being at different cyclical positions in the period over which ECHP data were collected. We concluded that at least the social-democratic welfare states have almost succeeded in eliminating the link between unemployment and the distribution of disposable income.

Finally, we took up a discussion of unemployment traps, where unemployed people have little or no economic incentive to find a job. A unique Danish data set combining a repeated panel with data from administrative registers makes it possible to identify people in an unemployment trap, and to follow their subsequent labour market profile. It turns out that economic incentives affect behaviour significantly, and the same is found in studies using Belgian, Finnish and French micro-data.

Overall, this chapter demonstrates that the ECHP, as a source of micro-level panel data collected in a consistent way across countries at different cyclical positions and having different institutional settings, provides an impressive resource for the analysis of a wide range of labour market behaviour. On many issues related to unemployment and job search, there are important differences between countries. However, in most cases the evidence suggests that these variations between countries do not fit neatly into the pattern of welfare state regime types.

Notes

1. Persons who are not able to start work within two weeks because they are awaiting recall from earlier job or have already agreed to start a job in the future are also considered to be unemployed.
2. For a detailed analysis of the relationship between job-satisfaction and different types of employment, see Kaiser (2002).
3. The lack of effect from education may be due to the three very rough categories of self-

reported education in the ECHP.
4. This effect is however dominated by the impact from low nominal interest rates on capital incomes, and thus not in any way related directly to changes in the labour market.

References

Andersen, T.M. and T.D. Schmidt (1999), 'The macroeconomics of the welfare state', in T.M. Andersen, S.E.H. Jensen and O. Risager (eds) *Macroeconomic Perspectives on the Danish Economy*, Basingstoke: Macmillan, 264–84.

Arulampalam, W., P. Gregg and M. Gregory (2001), 'Unemployment scarring', *The Economic Journal*, F577–F584.

Boeri, T. (1999), 'Enforcement of employment security regulations, on-the-job search and unemployment duration', *European Economic Review*, **43**, 65–89.

D'Addio, A.C., I. De Greef and M. Rosholm (2002), *Assessing Unemployment Traps in Belgium Using Panel Data Sample Selection Models*, IZA Discussion Paper no. 669.

*Deding, M. and T.D. Schmidt (2002), 'Differences in income inequality across Europe – market driven or ...?', *EPAG Working Papers*, **37**, Colchester: University of Essex.

Flinn, C.J. (2002), 'Labour market structure and inequality: a comparison of Italy and the U.S', *Review of Economic Studies*, **69** (3), 611–45.

Flinn, C.J. and J.J. Heckman (1982), 'Models for the analysis of labor force dynamics', in R. Basmann and G. Rhodes (eds), *Advances in Econometrics Vol. 1*, Greenwich, C: JAI, pp. 35–95.

Flinn, C.J. and J.J. Heckman (1983), 'Are unemployment and out of the labor force behaviorally distinct labor force states?', *Journal of Labor Economics*, **1**, 28–42.

Förster, M. and M. Pearson (2002), 'Income distribution and poverty in the OECD area: trends and driving forces', *OECD Economic Studies*, **34**, 1–39.

Gokhale, J., L.J. Kotlikoff and A. Sluchynsky (2002), 'Does it pay to work?', *NBER Working Papers*, **9096**.

Gregory, M. and R. Jukes (2001) 'Unemployment and subsequent earnings: estimating scarring among British men 1984–94', *The Economic Journal*, F607–F625.

Gurgand, M. and D.N. Margolis (2002), *Welfare and Labor Earnings: an Evaluation of the Financial Gains to Work*, IZA Discussion Paper no. 461.

Holm, P., T. Kyyrä and J. Rantala (1999), 'Household economic incentives, the unemployment trap and the probability of finding a job', *International Tax and Public Finance*, **6**, 361–78.

*Holst, E. and C.K. Spiess (2001), 'Labor market attachment of "Not economically active persons" – new aspects of hidden labour force in Europe', *EPAG Working Papers*, **24**, Colchester: University of Essex

*Holst, E. and C.K. Spiess (2002), 'Labour market attachment of people outside the labour force – an explorative analysis of the hidden labour force in Europe', *Schmollers Jahrbuch (Journal of Applied Social Sciences)*, **122**, 55–8.

Hotz, V.J. and J.K. Scholz (2000), 'Not perfect, but still pretty good: the EITC and other policies to support the U.S. low-wage labor market', *OECD Economic Studies*, **31**, 25–42.

*Kaiser, L.C. (2002), 'Job satisfaction: a comparison of standard, non-standard and self-employment across Europe with a special note to the gender/job satisfaction paradox', *EPAG Working Papers*, **27**, Colchester: University of Essex.

*Kaiser, L.C. and T. Siedler (2000), 'Exits from unemployment spells in Germany and the United Kingdom: a cross-national comparison (1990–96)', *EPAG Working Papers*, 7, Colchester: University of Essex.

McCall, J.J. (1970), 'Economics of information and job search', *Quarterly Journal of Economics*, **84**, 113–26.

Ministry of Finance (2000), *Finansredegørelse 2000 (Fiscal Report 2000)*, Copenhagen.

Mortensen, D. (1970), 'Job search, the duration of unemployment and the Phillips curve', *American Economic Review*, **60**, 847–62.

OECD (1996), *Employment Outlook*, Paris: OECD.

OECD (2001), *Employment Outlook*, Paris: OECD.

OECD (2002), *Employment outlook*, Paris: OECD.

*Pedersen, P.J. and T.D. Schmidt (2002), 'Search activity and re-employment – a European perspective', *EPAG Working Papers*, **34**, Colchester: University of Essex.

*Pedersen, P.J. and N. Smith (2002), 'Unemployment traps: do financial disincentives matter?', *European Sociological Review*, **18**, 271–88.

Scholz, J.K. (1996), 'In-work benefits in the United States: the earned Income Tax Credit', *Economic Journal*, **106**, 156–69.

* Direct output from EPAG's *DynSoc* research programme (see page 268).

8. Income and Patterns of Inequality

Ruud J.A. Muffels, Joachim Frick and Wilfred Uunk

Introduction and Background

Understanding the diversity of people's lives certainly involves the way economic resources such as income and wealth are distributed across persons and households at the national as well as the cross-national level. The ongoing process of European economic and social integration might be expected to lead to less diversity and more convergence of the distribution of economic resources across countries. On the other hand, the enlargement of the European Union (EU) might lead to a widening of existing disparities due to the access of relatively poor countries with a lower welfare, slower economic growth and perhaps wider income inequalities.

The globalisation of production and consumption, the increased demand for highly skilled labour in the 'knowledge economy' and the resulting greater labour mobility within and across national borders, as well as the quest for a more flexible labour market to adapt quickly to changing market demands, have led to greater instability of employment careers. People face more intermittent periods of non-employment and more insecurity in income and work during the various stages of life. Against the background of these trends and the broader topic of our research on the dynamics of social change, it appeared obvious to research the income distribution and inequality in a variety of European welfare states. If under the influence of these major societal changes, households experience more rapid and adverse shocks in terms of income streaming and employment changes over time, the question of their likely effect on income inequality and mobility patterns across countries and welfare regimes seems a relevant and valuable one.

Outline of the chapter
As set out in the introduction, the main focus of this chapter is on the impact of welfare-regime types on explaining country variations in income inequality and income mobility. But instead of presenting a comprehensive picture of the income distribution and income mobility patterns, the studies

conducted in this domain were aimed at tackling some particular conceptual or policy-relevant issues. Particular case studies are introduced (on, for example, regional incomes, on the contribution of 'imputed rent' to total income, on the economic position of immigrants and on the consequences of divorce) to illustrate the potential contribution of highly focused income studies to our understanding of economic welfare.

After a brief summary of the data and the concepts of income and of inequality used in the analysis, the chapter has been structured according to three main topics:

- variations in household income across countries and regions;
- the distribution of income by its components; and
- changes in personal and household income over time.

In the final section we report on the results of two case studies on the income position of immigrants and on income changes after divorce. Both case studies illustrate how the income position of particular vulnerable groups in society might change due to the operation of country- or regime-type-specific taxes and social security policies.

The chapter is concerned with the whole of the income distribution – from rich to poor – in each country. The next chapter focuses specifically on the issue of poverty, defined in terms of households on low incomes. The next chapter after that examines the consequences of low income in terms of deprivation.

Defining Income and Measuring Inequality

International comparisons of income are usually based on the national accounts, which add up the components of income for each country as a whole. On a European scale, it is comparisons such as GDP per head that enable us to know, for example, how much richer northern and western are than southern and eastern countries. But the national accounts provide no information about the range of incomes between households within countries, so it is impossible to assess the impact of country effects in the overall distribution of income, or to identify poor or rich households. Many countries have undertaken substantial household income surveys, and the collation of broadly comparable data sets by the Luxembourg Income Study (LIS) has been one of the major developments in comparative research in recent years (Berthoud and Iacovou, 2003). But it is based on cross-sectional data only. As such, it does not allow analysis of changes in incomes within households over time as a result of changes in the socio-economic positions of individual household members and of changes in household composition itself.

The European Community Household Panel (ECHP) was originally set up to create a European data set on income and has provided us with a unique source of information on the income distribution and especially on the income movements over time within and across various types of households, countries and welfare regimes. The empirical analyses presented in this chapter make use of ECHP as well as of some national European panel studies, namely the British Household Panel Survey (BHPS) for the UK, the German Socio-Economic Panel (GSOEP), and the Dutch Socio-Economic Panel (ISEP).

Definition of income

Before we discuss the findings of our research on income it is helpful to define what we mean by income. The panel surveys used here clearly have some limitations and impose a definition of income that captures only part of the economic resources an individual or household possesses. Most surveys, including the ECHP, permit us to study net cash income on a personal and household basis but not in-kind income (employment services, home production), nor wealth (the value of assets such as an owner-occupied house). Hence we take net cash personal and household income as the starting point for the analysis. This income concept includes market income (labour and capital income) as well as welfare state income (benefits, transfers). Looking at the role of welfare regimes we consider the variation in welfare state income and how it affects income inequality on a cross-sectional basis and over time. However, welfare states impact the income distribution not only by their transfer policies, but also, and maybe even more so, by their tax policies. For this reason, an attempt is made to look particularly at the role of taxes in reducing gross inequality. The outcomes have to be interpreted with caution since the data on taxes and gross income contain a lot of caveats and problems for some countries, which makes it troublesome, in some cases, to arrive at reliable and robust estimates. Nevertheless, the patterns we observe for most of the countries under scrutiny seem plausible and corroborate the findings of other research using different data sets.

To be more precise about the sort of information at our disposal for the income analyses, in Table 8.1 we present information on the components included in our definition of household income, using the ECHP as our reference database. It can be seen that the ECHP provides us with much detail about the various components of income. Total income is calculated as the sum of these amounts, across all members of the household, over the previous year – January to December. The income data collected in any survey year (for example, 1999) therefore relate to the previous calendar year (for example, 1998).

Much effort has been expended both by national data agencies and by

Eurostat to make the definitions of the income sources as consistent as possible. Nevertheless, comparisons across countries always have to take account of the possibility that inconsistencies may have arisen. This issue might be especially important for the Belgian data.[1] When figures for that country are far out of line with other members of the continental/corporatist group, it may be appropriate to attribute the variation to measurement problems.

Table 8.1   Income sources derived from the ECHP

	Components included
Income from labour	Wages and salaries
	Self-employment earnings
Income from capital	Interest and dividends on investments
	Property/rental income (imputed rent is not included except for two case studies)
Income from transfers	Private transfers received
	Unemployment-related benefits
	Old-age/survivors' benefits (public + private pensions combined)
	Family-related allowances
	Sickness/invalidity benefits
	Study grants
	Any other public benefits
	Social assistance
	Housing allowances
Other (private) income	Alimony, inheritance, private intra-family transfers

Source: ECHP (1994–98), adapted from Deding and Schmidt (2002).

Comparing incomes between households and between countries
If we want to compare incomes of different households within countries, we need to standardise household incomes to correct for differences in needs, which are related to household size and household composition. In the literature, a variety of equivalence scales has been developed to correct for these differences in needs across households. The one applied here is the one used in much research for the European Commission and is called the modified OECD scale. It assigns a weight of 1 to the head of the household, 0.5 to each other adult household member and 0.3 to each child. So it assumes that a couple needs 50 per cent more income to be at the same level

of economic welfare as a single adult person. For each additional child, a household needs 30 per cent more income than a single adult to arrive at the same welfare level.

For comparing incomes across countries we need also to correct for differences in purchasing power or price levels between countries. The purchasing power parities, as calculated and published by Eurostat, have been used to correct the national income amounts expressed in units of purchasing power. The unit of account is 'purchasing power standards' (pps) but can be thought of as roughly equivalent to the current Euro.

Measuring income inequality
Apart from measuring income, we are confronted with the issue of measuring the inequality of income. There is abundant literature on the sort of inequality measures that might be applied (see, for example, Atkinson and Bourguignon, 2000). They differ in how sensitive they are for transfers at the higher or the lower ends of the distribution. In using different measures being sensitive to different parts of the distribution, we want to avoid the bias resulting from the choice of a particular coefficient. It goes beyond the scope of this chapter to go into further detail here (see, for example, Shorrocks, 1982).

The indices used here are the Gini coefficient, the mean logarithmic deviation (Theil zero), the coefficient of variation (CV) and the ratio of the richest to the poorest incomes (99th to 1st percentile). The Gini coefficient is widely used and simple in its logic and understanding. It is also not very sensitive to transfers at either end of the distribution. While the CV is more sensitive to transfers at the upper end, the mean logarithmic deviation is more sensitive to the bottom end transfers; its main value in this analysis is that the overall range of inequality can be decomposed additively into between-area and within-area components.

The Distribution of Annual Income by Country, Regime Type and Region

Variation in incomes by country and regime type
One of our starting points was that the level of prosperity might vary substantially across countries, particularly between northern and southern Europe. It was contended in Chapter 1 that family income and inequality might vary substantially not only across countries, but also across the four types of welfare regime. The 'residual' welfare-regime type distinguishes itself with its familial characteristics and its immature and selective social security system granting poor benefits and, in some cases, lacking a guaranteed minimum benefit system. The level of economic development in this regime generally lags behind the one of the welfare capitalist regimes in

continental and northern Europe, which is shown by lower levels of per capita income, less economic growth, less employment and more unemployment (see also Muffels et al., 2002). We also expect the level of equivalent income to be lower in residual regimes because of the larger family size (see Chapter 2). We further suspect the income dispersion to be highest in the least 'decommodified' regimes where the share of market incomes in total income is highest and the income dispersion is more strongly driven by market forces such as in liberal regimes.

Table 8.2 shows the distribution of net equivalent household income between countries and regime types, and the level of income inequality according to various inequality measures (see also Nolan and Maître, 1999).

The general pattern observed here seems to fit in with the picture derived from the national accounts, as far as it concerns the ranking of countries' average incomes. Looking at incomes adjusted for purchasing power parities, we observe relatively high equivalent income levels in liberal regimes and rather low levels in the residual regimes, corroborating our conjectures made earlier. Ireland, however, does not seem to fit particularly well in the liberal type given its relatively low mean and median equivalent income. In some respect, Ireland appears to be more like the representatives of the residual welfare-regime type with which it also has in common highly accentuated Catholicism. The social-democratic and corporatist regimes are in between the two extremes.

The ordering of countries according to the inequality figures follows a similar pattern. Inequality appears highest for either the liberal or the residual regime. This corroborates our conjectures made beforehand. The social-democratic regime seems most equalised. However the Netherlands does not seem to fit very well in the social-democratic regime. The Netherlands, contrary to what we believed beforehand, has a quite high level of inequality that is set on an even par with the levels for corporatist countries like Germany or France. The inequality results for Belgium look awkwardly high which raise doubts about the quality of the Belgian income data, though the median income figure looks more plausible. Among the residual regimes, Portugal is shown to have the highest income inequality according to all measures followed by Greece, Spain and Italy. Portugal is also one of the countries with the highest poverty rates (see next chapter).

Regional variations in income
Much of the discussion of comparative analysis in Chapter 1 was concerned with the role of country and regime as a potential explanation for variations in people's experiences across Europe. Inequality measured by the ratio of the richest and the poorest household incomes at the EU level is 100:1, ranging from just 300 pps a year up to 30 000 pps a year and upwards.[2] If every

household were assumed to have the average income of the country in which they lived, the ratio of the best-off and worst-off countries would drop to 2.5:1, indicating that the country effect is relatively unimportant. Differences *between* countries account for only 5.5 per cent of overall inequality in household incomes in the EU, leaving the other 94.5 per cent as inequality between households *within* countries (Berthoud, 2004).

Table 8.2   Level of net household equivalent income and income inequality according to various measures

Regime/Country	Median income	Mean income	Inequality between households		
			Gini coefficient	Coeff. of variation	Mean log deviation
Social-democratic	*12.36*	*13.98*	*0.276*	*0.665*	*0.106*
Finland	10.67	11.81	0.232	0.484	0.092
Sweden	11.37	12.32	0.236	0.498	0.103
Denmark	14.07	15.21	0.217	0.444	0.082
Netherlands	13.34	15.16	0.274	0.652	0.137
Liberal	*13.44*	*15.50*	*0.333*	*0.824*	*0.200*
UK	13.64	15.70	0.328	0.737	0.195
Ireland	10.35	12.47	0.314	0.746	0.165
Corporatist	*13.13*	*14.82*	*0.290*	*0.679*	*0.147*
Belgium	13.95	16.98	0.338	0.963	0.208
France	12.50	14.08	0.285	0.553	0.141
Germany	13.36	15.07	0.278	0.628	0.138
Austria	13.64	14.84	0.250	0.519	0.112
Residual	*8.56*	*10.15*	*0.336*	*0.684*	*0.224*
Portugal	6.69	8.54	0.375	0.820	0.247
Spain	8.12	9.90	0.339	0.684	0.207
Italy	9.38	10.78	0.309	0.626	0.177
Greece	7.51	9.22	0.356	0.797	0.224
EU	11.74	13.39	0.317	0.693	0.183

Notes: Incomes are measured in 1000s of Euros pps, with equivalent incomes below 300 pps and above 250 000 pps removed from the sample.
Because the Gini and CV measures (unlike the mean log deviation) are not decomposable into within- and between-group components, inequality figures for regime type are not a weighted average of the figures for the countries belonging to that particular type.

Source: ECHP (1998) except for Finland, where 1996 data are used; authors' own calculations.

Figure 8.1   Median regional net household equivalent incomes

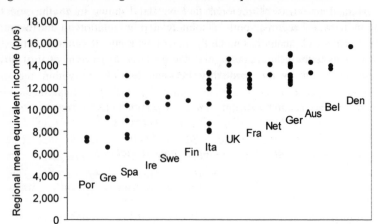

Note: Countries are ordered by their national median income, but spaced equally along the
             horizontal axis.
Source: ECHP (1999), adapted from Berthoud (2004).

An alternative view is that country or regime is not the best way of presenting geographical variation but that we should consider more disaggregated levels such as region or communities. The ECHP allowed us to disaggregate by region (Figure 8.1).[3]

Greece and France are not the poorest and richest countries, and the fact that they contain the poorest (mainland Greece: median income 6568 pps) and richest regions (Ile de France: 16 694) illustrates the importance of variations between regions within countries.[4] The two regions of Greece are much more widely spaced than any of the other two-region countries. Among the large countries, France is characterised by having a single relatively rich region, with all other regions closely grouped at a lower level. The UK is similar, except that there are two rich regions, followed by a group of less prosperous ones. Spain's and Italy's regions are widely spaced; Germany's are quite tightly grouped (Berthoud, 2004).

The regional map suggests that the economic boundaries of southern Europe should be drawn to include Greece and Portugal, two-thirds of Spain and one-third of Italy. The unclear position of Spain and Italy in country-level analysis could be explained by the fact that each of them is, in a sense, 'two nations'. This clearly suggests that regional variations are significant, relaxing the view that country variations are likely to be the most important factor (Berthoud and Iacovou, 2003).

Table 8.3 summarises the patterns of regional inequality in the five large countries, each with at least eight regions. The UK and Spain have similar ranges of overall inequality, but in Spain twice as much of that variation can be explained in terms of regional factors. Italy shows much the widest variation between regions, both absolutely and in relation to the overall national picture; Germany has much the narrowest range of variation between regions – one-sixth of the Italian figure. But the largest part of inequality must still be attributed to the inequality between households within regions (Berthoud, 2004). For the whole EU, only 7 per cent of total inequality between households can be attributed to the variation between regions.

Table 8.3   *Measures of inequality within and between regions: the five large countries (mean logarithmic deviation)*

Measure	UK	France	Germany	Spain	Italy
Index of inequality across all households in the country	0.209	0.164	0.142	0.208	0.173
Index of inequality across households *within* regions	0.202	0.154	0.139	0.194	0.155
Index of inequality *between* regions	0.007	0.010	0.003	0.014	0.018
Between-region inequality as a percentage of overall inequality	3.4%	6.2%	2.2%	6.6%	10.3%

Source: ECHP (1999), adapted from Berthoud (2004).

The Components of Income and the Impact on Inequality

The scale of taxes and of transfers

If regime types matter, one might suspect that the income variations across regimes will be particularly signalled by variations in the level and distribution of social transfer income through which governments try to achieve their social policy goals. Disaggregating net, after tax income into market income and transfer income, might therefore provide a much more detailed insight into the role of policies in explaining cross-country variations in income (see Figure 8.2).

A complication, though, is that the ECHP classifies all pensions as social transfers, without distinguishing between public and private sector providers. In Figure 8.2 the shares of market income (labour + capital income), transfer income and taxes as ratio to total net income are given for the various countries, listed in order of regime type.

*Figure 8.2   Ratio of direct taxes, transfers and market incomes to average
net household income (mean log deviation)*

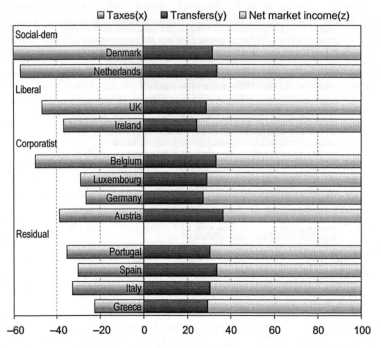

Note: The graph shows that for every €100 of net household income, an additional x has
already been retained by government, y consists of transfers from governments and
from pension schemes and z is market income after tax.

Source: ECHP (1994–98), adapted from Deding and Schmidt (2002).

There is some evidence that the tax levels and the share of transfer
incomes are indeed lower in residual countries but the findings for the other
types of regimes are not as clear-cut as we might have expected. The UK, as a
liberal country, has a low share of transfer income but a rather high tax level.

The components of income inequality

The gross/net factor calculated by Eurostat for the ECHP has been used to
calculate the average tax rate on gross income, including income tax and
social security contributions. The inequality of gross income measured by the
Gini coefficient has been used to decompose inequality into a part that may
be attributed to the dispersion in taxes and a remaining part reflecting the
dispersion in after tax, net income. The extent to which taxes reduce total
gross inequality is summarised in Figure 8.3.

Figure 8.3 Percentage of total inequality of gross income absorbed by taxes

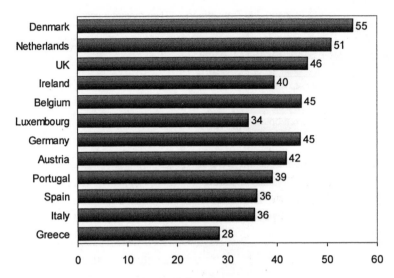

Note: Inequality measured by the Gini coefficient.
Source: ECHP (1994–98), adapted from Deding and Schmidt (2002).

The higher the proportion of overall inequality captured by taxes, the more progressive taxation appears to be and the higher the level of redistribution of gross income by taxes. Denmark and the Netherlands, both belonging to the social-democratic cluster, have taxes absorbing more than 50 per cent of overall inequality. We find also for the corporatist countries, Germany, Belgium and Austria, proportions of inequality captured by taxes of 40 to 50 per cent. Levels of 30 to 40 per cent are found in the residual southern countries and Luxembourg. These findings are reasonably robust when different measures of inequality are tested. Further evidence also shows that countries with higher average tax rates also have more progressive tax rates, except for Germany. We could conclude from this that the more 'decommodified' welfare regimes are, the higher the tax rate and the higher the impact of the government on redistributing pre-government or market income. About 80 per cent of the remaining inequality of net incomes may be attributed to the dispersion of labour income (see Deding and Schmidt, 2002).

The variation in the proportion of inequality captured by labour income across the various countries is apparently very small, Belgium being an outlier. However, there is some reason to believe that this outcome for Belgium has to be taken with caution as an artefact of the data. Considering the results for capital income, the distribution across the countries also looks

Figure 8.4   Percentage of overall inequality attributable to the dispersion of transfer income

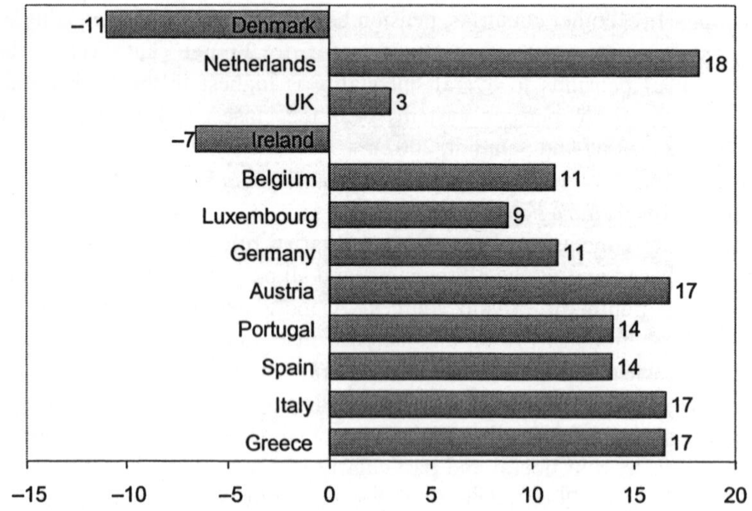

Note: Inequality measured by the Gini coefficient.

very similar. On average about 5 to 10 per cent of overall inequality can be attributed to the within-country dispersion of capital income.

The overall level of inequality in the Netherlands is 20 per cent *higher* after transfers have been taken into account than if income was calculated on the basis of net market income (see Figure 8.4). Also in the residual countries Portugal, Italy, Spain and Greece, transfer income *increases* inequality by about 10 to 20 per cent. The extent to which transfer income affects overall inequality varies considerably more across countries than was the case for labour or capital income. It is counter-intuitive to find that for most of the countries under scrutiny, except for Denmark and Ireland, transfer incomes seem to increase inequality rather than to reduce it. The reason is that in many cases, income transfers are not flat-rated but linked to the level of previous earnings.

Disaggregating transfer income by the type of transfer income may unravel the underlying mechanism (see Figure 8.4).

The main regressive effect of transfers is derived from pension income. Remember that 'pensions' includes both public and private schemes. Generally, public pensions offer rather uniform benefits whereas occupational and private pensions, which are capital-funded, show much more variation and closer linkage to lifetime earnings. In principle, pensions *reduce* inequality between elderly people (as a group) and the rest of the population, but *create* inequality within the retired population. Denmark is the only country where the net effect of pension incomes is to reduce the inequality of net incomes. In all other countries, pension benefits contribute to inequality of net incomes in the order of magnitude of 5 to 20 per cent. Again, the contribution of pensions to overall inequality is highest in the Netherlands and Germany, whose pension systems bear the closest linkage to lifetime earnings (see Deding and Schmidt, 2002).

Who gains from welfare benefits?
This surprising conclusion about the inegalitarian roles of transfers, and of pensions, is based on treating all transfers, and all pensions, together, whether derived from public or private sources. A more detailed analysis of the relative contributions of market and state incomes focuses on households of working age, where pension income does not play an important role.

Evidence in the next chapter shows that the impact of transfer income in moving people out of poverty is highest in social-democratic and corporatist regimes and lowest in liberal and particularly low in residual regimes in the south (Maître et al., 2002). This finding suggests that the mitigating role of the state in reducing inequality in net, after tax, income is particularly due to raising the lowest pre-government or market incomes at the bottom end of the distribution, particularly in social-democratic regimes. Evidence for the question who receives most government transfers is found in Table 8.4 where we depict the mean share of welfare state income as a percentage of total net income by income groups, country and welfare regimes.

Ordering the population by income quintile (20 per cent income groups of equal size), we find the highest share of welfare state income transferred to the bottom income group in liberal regimes, next highest in social-democratic regimes and lowest in residual regimes. This result for the liberal regimes seems odd, but notice also that liberal regimes show by far the highest bottom-to-top quintile ratio.

This indicates that liberal regimes set up their welfare state income according to Beveridgian principles, that is they tend to target benefits to the worst-off and render few benefits to the better-off. Much lower ratios are found in social-democratic and corporatist regimes reflecting the continental Bismarckian systems in which benefits are meant to stabilise incomes over time, for which reason they are closely linked to previous earnings up to certain income ceilings. They are therefore distributed over a much wider range of the income distribution. Residual regimes also show a typical pattern; an immature welfare system granting low benefits distributed over a wide range of the income distribution. For this reason the 'bottom-to-top' ratio is lowest in the residual regimes.

Table 8.4   Mean welfare state income for households whose head is aged 25–54, by income quintile

Regime/Country	Bottom (1)	(2)	(3)	(4)	Top (5)	Ratio (1)/(5)
Social-democratic	52.6	29.0	17.6	11.8	8.2	6.4
Denmark	44.0	27.2	19.7	15.0	8.3	5.3
Finland	61.7	38.6	23.0	17.6	11.1	5.6
Netherlands	50.2	22.2	19.7	5.5	6.0	8.4
Liberal	67.1	32.5	11.1	5.7	2.7	25.3
UK	63.3	28.8	10.0	6.1	3.2	19.8
Ireland	71.5	36.9	12.5	5.2	2.1	34.0
Corporatist	40.5	19.3	11.9	9.4	6.1	6.6
Belgium	57.0	24.3	12.6	8.6	9.7	5.9
Luxembourg	31.7	16.5	16.4	9.5	3.4	9.3
Germany	35.1	14.8	8.2	6.6	3.1	11.3
Austria	35.3	21.3	14.6	13.7	7.5	4.7
Residual	24.5	14.3	11.0	9.4	6.1	4.0
Portugal	31.3	15.8	9.5	8.3	5.0	6.3
Spain	35.1	23.0	17.1	15.4	7.6	4.6
Italy	15.4	7.2	11.0	9.4	6.1	4.0
Greece	14.8	9.7	8.6	6.5	6.5	2.3

Source: ECHP (1996), adapted from Maître et al. (2002).

Further multivariate analyses show that welfare state benefits are particularly targeted on households whose head is unemployed or inactive, on lone-parent households and on households with lower-educated heads (Maître et al., 2002; see also Deding and Schmidt, 2002). Although manual workers appear at first sight to be high recipients of benefits, it turns out that this is largely explained by the other characteristics considered. In fact, rural small holders are the only occupational group whose income from this source is significantly higher than average. The unemployment effect is strongest in liberal and social-democratic regimes and weakest in residual regimes (see Table 8.5). The lone-parent effect is also strongest in liberal and social-democratic regimes and again weakest in residual regimes. But also in the typical corporatist Germany, the lone-parent effect is rather strong (a coefficient of 21.9, not shown in Table 8.5). The general conclusion might therefore be that welfare states, be it liberal, social-democratic, or even corporatist, are generally aimed at targeting benefits to the worst-off in terms

Table 8.5   *Selected characteristics affecting the share of welfare state*
            income in total income by regime type: households whose head
            is aged 25–54 (regression coefficients)

Regime	Unemployed/ Inactive	Lone parents	Less than secondary education	Small holder occupation
Social-democratic	56.8***	21.4***	8.2***	7.5***
Liberal	61.1***	24.1***	6.8***	5.1**
Corporatist	39.5***	15.1***	6.8***	24.6***
Residual	37.9***	12.2***	1.2*	9.4***

Notes: Coefficients from an ordinary least squares regression equation.
            Asterisks denote significance of coefficients: *** 1%, ** 5%, * 10%.
Source: ECHP (1996), adapted from Maître et al. (2002).

of low income, weak employment status, low education levels, low social
class and unfavourable household conditions.

The impact of transfer policies on mitigating inequality between social
groups might therefore be rather high. That their effect is likely to be smaller
in liberal regimes than in social-democratic or corporatist regimes might be
deduced from the fact that liberal regimes tend to have less generous benefits
for a smaller portion of the population. Liberal regimes are shown to be
target-*efficient,* but the findings on poverty presented elsewhere in this book
reveal that they are not very *effective* in preventing or combating economic
hardship or poverty.

In-kind income: the impact of imputed rent on inequality
The ECHP defines income in cash terms and does not account for non-
monetary or in-kind income. However, non-monetary resources are becoming
increasingly important, particularly for the purpose of assessing the level of
inequality in a particular country. One example of in-kind income is 'imputed
rent' from owner-occupied housing. The benefit stems first from not needing
to pay rents and second from obtaining a return on private investment in real
estate. In order to test how sensitive inequality analyses are to this issue, we
analysed the relationship between imputed rent and cash income in two
countries where more detailed surveys are available – (West) Germany
(GSOEP) and the UK (BHPS) (Frick and Grabka, 2002).[5]

There are various methods of calculating imputed rent, two of which are
used in the panel data sets underlying our analysis.

The *opportunity cost* approach used in the German panel starts with the gross rent actually paid by renters, including costs for water and electricity and other items. Regressing this rent measure on type, age, size and quality of the dwelling, applying this information to otherwise comparable owner-occupiers and finally deducting owner-related costs yield a measure of net imputed rent.

The *capital market* approach used in the UK panel has its starting point in the alternative use of investing the capital tied up in the house. The value of imputed rent is given by the current net equity times the implicit interest rate, which is assumed to be a nominal 6 per cent.

The calculations of imputed rent show large dissimilarities between the two countries, from 9 per cent of total income in the UK to only 3 to 4 per cent for West Germany. This is due to the lower share of homeowners in Germany (47 per cent) than in the UK (72 per cent). The effects for households who are outright owners and do not pay mortgages any more (particularly older people) are much higher, about 16 to 24 per cent in the UK and about 12 to 15 per cent in West Germany. The inclusion of imputed rent for Germany and the UK yields either a small decrease in overall inequality, which is in line with most of the results from the literature, or a small increase in the level of inequality in 1998 (especially in the UK), dependent on the sort of inequality measure used.

Recall that inequality is highest in the liberal nations, including the UK, and lower in corporatist Germany. We would have expected a larger negative effect on inequality in the liberal UK, but the high UK tax levels seem to reverse the outcomes. The levelling effect of imputed rent on inequality is largest for outright owners (20 to 30 per cent in both countries in 1997/98) and by definition absent for renters. The between-group inequality for owners and renters is raised by taking imputed rent into account but the within-group inequality, particularly among owners, has been strongly reduced. The effect of imputed rent on income inequality is particularly due to the levelling impact on the within-group inequality of elderly people. Their well-being is, however, considerably increased, so investment in one's own home might be seen as a successful means of private old-age provision.

These findings suggest that, though the within-group inequality of the elderly is significantly affected by imputed rent, the level of overall inequality in a country may be less sensitive to this issue.

Income Change and Income Mobility

Medium- and long-term incomes
The information on inequality presented in Table 8.2 was based on single-year estimates and the ranking of countries and regimes might, to some

extent, be affected by the different stage each economy might be at in the business cycle. It is, in any case, interesting to view the results over a longer time horizon. Over time, people experience incidental shocks in their income stream which might be evened out in the longer term and which have an exaggerated effect on the annual picture. The changes in incomes over time might result from behavioural responses of family members to adverse income shocks by changing household working patterns, by family formation events (children and adults moving in or out), or by positional changes in the welfare system (changes in income transfers). Over a longer time frame, we might expect the likelihood of income changes to become larger because people moving into different stages of their life-cycle might be more likely to experience all sorts of life events like marriage or divorce, the birth of a child, the ageing of children, children leaving home or the death of the spouse. But the occurrence of life events may also be related to changes in the employment situation, to the gain or loss of work or working hours of the head, the partner and of co-residing children. Eventually, the income situation might change due to the intervention of governments through their transfer and tax policies (changes in the level or duration of the benefits or in the entitlement conditions). The longitudinal information required for examining income change over time is exactly the sort of information only panel surveys can provide.[6]

First, we view the level of equivalent income and income inequality over a five-year period of time. In Table 8.6 we present the regime type effects using the panel data for a five-year period of time and consider the welfare-regime pattern again.

By and large, the results on the level of equivalent incomes and income inequality look very similar to the annual ones presented in Table 8.2. Over five years the level of equivalent income is about equal to the annual figures. The corporatist and liberal regime have again the highest level of median equivalent income and the residual regime the lowest. The residual regime, together with the liberal regime, show the highest inequality according to all measures. The level of long-term inequality is shown to be generally lower than annual inequality (compare the first and last columns of Table 8.6), particularly for the liberal and social-democratic regimes.

This seems to suggest that these regimes are more successful in reducing income fluctuations over time. For the liberal regime, this inequality-reducing effect operates either through the family or the market whereas for the social- democratic regime it is accomplished through social security policies guaranteeing a minimum income and providing high levels of replacement income in case of earnings losses due to unemployment or disability.

Table 8.6 *Level of net household equivalent income and income inequality averaged over five years, by welfare-regime type*

Regime	Median income	Gini co-efficient	Coeff of variation	Mean log deviation	Median income over one year	Gini coefficient over one year
Social-democratic	12.68	0.229	0.473	0.086	*12.36*	*0.276*
Liberal	13.14	0.287	0.583	0.136	*13.44*	*0.333*
Corporatist	13.25	0.259	0.559	0.113	*13.13*	*0.290*
Residual	8.83	0.298	0.590	0.149	*8.56*	*0.336*
EU	11.87	0.286	0.592	0.140	*11.74*	*0.317*

Notes: Median income measured in 1000s of Euros, pps.
Figures in last two columns from Table 8.2.
Data for 1995–98 for Austria, and 1996–98 for Finland. Sweden not included.
See also notes to Table 8.2.

Source: ECHP (1994–98), authors' own calculations.

Second, we focus on the role of the market and the government in reducing inequality, over a much longer time period. For this purpose we use the longer-running national panel studies of the Netherlands, Great Britain and West Germany and examine whether the long-term performance of governments in reducing inequality is different from the short-term outcomes. The three countries at the same time represent different regime types: the Netherlands representing the social-democratic regime, Great Britain the liberal regime, and West Germany the corporatist regime (see also Goodin et al., 1999; Headey et al., 2000).

The focus here is particularly on the impact of governments on the reduction of inequality through their social security policies. Results are presented in Table 8.7 for pre- and post-government figures to examine the presumed egalitarian effect of taxes and state transfers for the short, medium and long term.

It is apparent that pre-government as well as post-government income inequality is lower in the medium term than in the short term for all countries, and lower again in the long term than in the medium term. It turns out that the market and the government are equally responsible for reducing income inequality over time. The social-democratic government of the Netherlands apparently did a better job in reducing inequality over time than the corporatist West German or liberal UK governments.

Table 8.7   *Inequalities in short- and long-term equivalent incomes and redistributive effect, for three countries*

Period	Netherlands			West Germany			UK		
	Pre-govt	Post-govt	Redistribu-tion [b]	Pre-govt	Post-govt	Redistribu-tion [b]	Pre-govt	Post-govt	Redistribu-tion [b]
Short-term									
1987	0.40	0.28	32%	–	–	–	0.42	0.26	40%
1993	0.43	0.31	28%	0.52	0.31	39%	0.45	0.28	39%
Medium-term									
1985–89	0.35	0.22	37%	–	–	–	0.38	0.22	42%
1990(1)–94(5) [a]	0.39	0.25	36%	0.48	0.28	42%	0.41	0.24	40%
Long-term									
1985–94	0.35	0.21	40%	–	–	–	0.36	0.21	41%

Notes: a: data for 1990–94 for the Netherlands and 1991–95 for the UK and West Germany.
b: Redistribution effect is given by [(Gini(pre)-Gini(post)) / Gini(pre)].
Source: National panel studies for the Netherlands (SEP), West Germany (SOEP) and the UK (BHPS), adapted from Muffels et al. (1999).

Income mobility

But how stable or mobile are individuals' and households' incomes over time? There is a wide range of mobility measures but the one most commonly used is the change in the quintile ranks of income units between time periods (that is, between t_1 and t_2). This measure of relative mobility in society is generally based on a mobility matrix in which the year-on-year change in the distribution of household income is represented by the proportion of income earners in each equal income group (for example, 20 per cent of all incomes) either staying in the same income group or moving into a higher or lower income group (see also Headey and Muffels, 2003). We use the second instead of the first ECHP wave as the start year to depict mobility over time since there is some evidence of poor quality in the income data in the first wave. Comparing individuals' incomes in the second and the fifth waves, we present in Table 8.8 the stability as well as the four-wave mobility rate across the various quintiles (20 per cent income groups).[7]

Table 8.8   Four-year income mobility across quintiles (percentage of households)

Regime/Country	On diagonal (stability)	One cell off diagonal	Two or more cells off diagonal	Upward mobility	Down-ward mobility
Social-democratic	47	36	17	40	14
Denmark	41	40	19	43	16
Netherlands	49	35	16	39	12
Liberal	42	38	20	34	23
UK	42	38	20	35	24
Ireland	50	38	13	33	18
Corporatist	53	34	13	30	18
Belgium	45	32	23	36	19
France	53	37	11	29	18
Germany	54	33	14	29	17
Austria	46	37	17	31	24
Residual	48	38	15	15	37
Portugal	55	31	13	13	31
Spain	48	39	13	16	36
Italy	46	38	16	17	37
Greece	35	41	25	7	58

Source: ECHP (1994–98), authors' own calculations.

Stability in income positions is reflected in the percentage of households staying on the diagonal of the four-year mobility matrix. The literature suggests a number of mobility measures (such as the cross-product ratio) to depict the extent of mobility, but for the purpose of this book we simply use the movements on and off the diagonals of the matrix and whether the mobility is upwards into a higher quintile or downwards into a lower quintile. The movement off the diagonal upwards or downwards and by one cell or by two or more cells (that is, by one quintile or by two or more quintile positions) represents the extent of relative income mobility over the four-year period.

There appears to be quite some mobility even over this short period. Mobility is highest in the liberal UK and in the residual countries Italy and Greece. Portugal shows a rather high level of income stability over the four-year period. However, Portugal also resembles the other residual countries in showing a high level of downward mobility. Highest stability and hence lowest mobility is attained in the corporatist countries of France and Germany.

The evidence in Table 8.8 also shows that on average the level of upward mobility is higher than the level of downward mobility except for the residual regime. One would expect in a stable income distribution that moves up are offset by moves down. This might not be true for various reasons. First, the income distribution is not stable while only people were included staying in the panel for the entire period. For that reason, during the panel period people's incomes may rise due to life-cycle changes (such as ageing) for which reason upward moves may outbalance downward moves. Second, in a growing economy and the more equal society is, the more lower-income people share the economic gains of the flourishing economy and the more likely they are to experience an upward move. Recall that during the panel period most countries were in an upward phase of their economy. Table 8.8 indeed shows that in a more equal society (the social-democratic countries), there are more upward and less downward moves than in a more unequal society (liberal countries). Finally, it might be true that many small gains (losses) are indeed offset by few large losses (gains). Whatever the reasons, our interest goes less to the size of the mobility flows than to the differences in mobility across the various regime types. These differences appear large. The findings show that upward mobility is lowest and downward mobility highest in all residual regimes, but particularly in Greece. It is not easy to become rich in the residual countries but when one has become rich it is hard to stay rich. Our expectation that upward mobility is highest in the liberal regime appeared untrue. Upward mobility shows to be substantially higher in the social-democratic regime and downward mobility much lower compared to the liberal regime.

Although the variation across regime types is quite wide and in the expected direction, the table also reveals clearly the rather large variation in income mobility patterns within regime type. To describe mobility patterns is easier than to understand them. To explain income mobility we have to identify the processes initiating mobility and to see whether these processes differ across countries and regimes.

Household Incomes: Two Case Studies

There is a huge range of specific issues concerning the incomes and dynamics of particular population groups. In this final section, we present two case studies to illustrate how cross-national surveys can shed light on complex questions. The first case study deals with the incomes of the immigrants and the role of governments in improving their situation. The other follows the changing incomes of women who experience divorce. These case studies illustrate how particular known vulnerable social groups in society fare over time in terms of their relative income position and socio-economic fate. Again, we examine the differential outcomes across regime type.

The incomes of immigrants

The twin processes of European integration and wider globalisation highlight the importance of migration as an issue. The increasing inflows of immigrants in many Western societies are likely to affect the overall income distribution, while the position of the immigrant population in the income distribution is rather different from the native-born population. The evidence from the literature suggests that immigration has a small negative effect on average market incomes (particularly on gross wages) and leads to a small increase in inequality.

Table 8.9   *Relative incomes of immigrants compared to the native-born population (native-born population = 100)*

Regime/Country	Pre-government income			Non-market income	Taxes and contri-butions	Total post-govern-ment income
	Total	Labour	Non-labour			
Social-democratic						
Denmark	47	47	47	274	46	*85*
Liberal						
UK	107	106	138	91	110	*104*
Ireland	117	117	106	102	131	*110*
Corporatist						
Luxembourg	103	103	102	75	111	*97*
Germany	71	74	36	121	68	*78*
Austria	97	98	63	89	96	*95*
Residual						
Spain	107	104	202	87	104	*105*
Italy	105	105	93	76	108	*100*

Note: Sample of households with prime-aged heads.
Source: ECHP (1994–98); data for the UK and West Germany derived directly from BHPS and GSOEP; adapted from Büchel and Frick (forthcoming).

In Table 8.9 we present some information on the relative incomes of the immigrant population compared to the native-born population in selected European countries (Büchel and Frick, forthcoming).[8] Concentrating the analyses on the population in households with prime-aged heads (20 to 60 years of age), marked cross-country variation was found. First, in most countries immigrants' pre-government or market income situation is not worse but sometimes even better than that of the native-born population – the exceptions are Denmark, West Germany and Austria. Denmark seems to be a special case since the immigrants' market income is only 47 per cent of what native-born people earn.

The share of non-market or transfer income appears extraordinarily high in Denmark (60 per cent of post-government income against 20 per cent for households with native-born heads). For that reason, the share of transfer income is almost three times as high as for the native-born population. The underlying reason for the exceptional position of Denmark seems to be the relatively high proportion of low-skilled people coming from non-EU countries. The figures for post-government income show that the redistribution policies of the Danish government substantially improve their income position. Immigrants appear to pay low taxes in Denmark and receive strong income support.

West Germany also presents itself as a special case since the immigrants' income position before and after government intervention was much worse than that of their native-born counterparts. Nevertheless, immigrants pay lower taxes but receive more income support than their native-born co-citizens. On balance, the West German government seemed to do little in terms of redistribution policies to improve immigrants' post-government income situation.

Most governments have no need to improve the income situation of the immigrants, because immigrants by and large seem to be capable of managing their household incomes themselves. The Irish, Luxembourg and also the UK governments even worsen the immigrants' relative income position a bit through their taxes and social security policies. The relatively high level of market income of immigrants in Ireland must be attributed to the high skill level of the immigrant population, mainly from the UK and the USA.

Using multivariate techniques controlling for various socio-economic characteristics, Büchel and Frick (forthcoming) further examined the effect of country of origin and the extent of integration on the immigrants' economic position over the five-year period. A distinction was made between immigrants from EU countries and from non-EU countries. A household was assumed more integrated if at least one adult household member was native-born, referred to as a 'mixed' household. Büchel and Frick found some evidence that mixed households are doing much better than non-mixed immigrant households in terms of their pre- and post-government income; the former often show no significant difference from their native-born counterparts. Mixing alone appears not to be sufficient for economic performance, though, since in Denmark and West Germany mixed immigrants from non-EU countries had lower market incomes than the indigenous population, which is likely to be due to their lower human capital as well. However, it turns out that the Danish and West German governments did a lot to improve the income situation of mixed and non-mixed non-EU immigrants through their tax and social security policies. The non-mixed immigrant population fare worse in general but in some countries their post-government incomes are improved through the redistribution process, as seemed to be particularly the case in West Germany.

The main conclusion is that the marked cross-country differences in the pre- and post-government incomes of immigrants persist even after controlling for variations in country of origin and the level of integration into the host society.[9] This clearly suggests that institutional differences at the national level in the treatment of immigrants in the labour market and in the social security system account for much of the variation in immigrants' economic performance. Social and socio-economic policies seem to matter a lot in shaping a nation in which native-born people and immigrants can perform with equal success.

Income changes after divorce

The second case study focuses on the effects of divorce. There is ample evidence that marital splits and separations of cohabiting relationships have lasting effects on the ex-partners' income streams in the following years. Women, in particular, seem to suffer from income losses due to separation or divorce, while men undergo very small income losses or even experience gains in equivalent income. It also appears that the income loss is larger when women have children to take care of and when they have invested little in their human capital during the period preceding marriage.

Uunk (2003) has used the ECHP data to study the economic consequences of divorce in 12 countries over the period 1994–98. Although the number of divorces at the national level appears to be too low to make sound cross-country comparisons, the data enable us to compare clusters of countries such as the welfare-regime classification. We contend that welfare regimes differ in the institutions affecting women's economic position after divorce. They particularly differ in (a) the levels of social security and welfare support, and (b) the extent to which they encourage female employment. Given the regime-type characteristics, we expect women in social-democratic welfare states to suffer the least, economically, from separation. State support is rather generous and the social-democratic regimes promote female employment, during marriage as well as after. Women in corporatist welfare states are expected to be worst off. Poorer welfare support, and the dominance of the male-breadwinner model will cause women to experience more serious economic strain when they divorce. Women in liberal countries and residual countries from southern Europe are expected to take an intermediate position. Welfare state support is generally much less generous than in corporatist and social-democratic regimes, for which reason women in liberal and residual regimes need to work to earn a decent living.

Yet, not all of the differences among welfare states in the economic consequences of divorce necessarily result from the institutional set-up. Part of the differences may result from differential composition — with respect to work patterns, education profiles and family life – of the population of divorced women. To investigate institutional effects, these compositional differences have to be taken into account.

The data analyses were performed on a subsample of 667 women who were between 18 and 65 years in the first wave and who experienced a divorce or (non-)marital separation at any point of time during the panel period. Income changes were assessed by comparing disposable household income in the years before and after divorce. Table 8.10 summarises the average change in mean household income after divorce (including separations) by regime type. Note that household composition necessarily changes over the comparison period, but the figures have been expressed in terms of equivalent income which takes this into account.

The table clearly documents the substantial decline in women's household income after divorce, which for the 12 European countries examined here amounts to 15 per cent of the pre-divorce figure. The largest drop in income, from 15 000 to 12 000 pps a year (a change of 20 per cent), is observed for the corporatist regimes. The lowest income decline is observed in the liberal regimes, at 10 per cent. Divorced women in social-democratic and residual regimes saw their income fall by 13 per cent, which is in between the percentages for the other regimes.

That institutions matter might be seen from the figures for the corporatist and social-democratic regimes because the income before divorce is nearly the same, but after divorce the income is 13 per cent higher in social-democratic than in corporatist regimes. This is most likely to be due to more generous income support to divorced women in the social-democratic regimes. In residual and liberal regimes, however, the drop in income due to divorce is smaller, partly because the level of pre-divorce income is already lower. These regimes seem to have a minimum floor of income support, below which the income of these divorced women cannot fall.

Table 8.10   *Changes in mean net household equivalent income after divorce, by regime type*

	Before divorce (pps)	After divorce (pps)	% change
Social-democratic	15 895	13 852	−13
Corporatist	15 304	12 249	−20
Liberal	12 619	11 307	−10
Residual	9 826	8 589	−13
All	14 023	11 851	−15

Source: ECHP (1994–98), adapted from Uunk (2003).

The importance of institutional arrangements in reducing negative economic consequences of divorce is substantiated by decomposition of these income changes by income source. The decomposition analysis shows that in social-democratic and liberal regimes, the share of social transfers in pre- and post-divorce income is much higher than in the corporatist and residual countries. In addition, social-democratic and liberal regimes redistribute income much more strongly by their income support systems (transfer income increases by 20 per cent between the pre- and post-divorce periods) than the other regime types. The rise in income support benefits in liberal regimes indicates that they tend to target benefits on the lowest incomes. Lone-parent households in liberal regimes certainly belong to the lowest income stratum.

The question addressed earlier, whether regime-type effects will disappear once we have included compositional factors, has been dealt with by means of multivariate analysis. The dependent variable is the log of post-divorce equivalent income regressed against pre-divorce equivalent income and a number of work- and family-related characteristics before and after divorce. Demographic variables (age at divorce and previous marital status) seem to contribute little to the explanation, but human capital and work-related factors prior to divorce contribute a lot. A higher education and more work hours before divorce lower the income loss after divorce.

The analyses show that when these compositional factors are controlled for, regime-type differences become stronger instead of weaker. Women in corporatist regimes experience an even greater income loss after divorce when they had the same background characteristics as other European women. More detailed analyses show that the actual income loss of divorced women in corporatist regimes is weakened due to their relatively high level of education, the high pre-divorce labour supply and the low number of children before divorce. The role of these characteristics look surprising for women in corporatist regimes but they are likely to be due to selective divorce. Divorce in corporatist regimes is rather uncommon and more easily attainable for women with a high socio-economic position.

The evidence presented here shows that there exists a wide variation in the economic consequences of divorce across welfare regimes in the EU. The main substantive lessons to be learned from the findings are that income mobility patterns associated with divorce are ruled by policies and social and economic processes in the domains of human capital-building, household formation and career patterns. Panel data seem undoubtedly the source of information we need to unravel these complex societal processes, and to define innovative policy routes for tackling the issues at stake.

Conclusions

The main issue addressed in this chapter is about the role of welfare regimes in explaining differences in prosperity levels across countries, differences in levels of income inequality disaggregated by source of income and by social groups and differences in income mobility patterns. The ECHP and national panel studies have been used to tackle the issue at hand. We used an amended version of Esping-Andersen's typology (Esping-Andersen, 1990) and distinguished a fourth 'residual' model. We found evidence in favour of the regime-type classification but also evidence contradicting it dependent on the particular issues covered in the research.

The distribution of total equivalent household incomes seems to support the regime hypothesis (although specific countries like Ireland do not fit very well in the classification categories), but when we refine our analyses and examine the distribution of the numerous income components the picture blurs. Liberal regimes, for example, have low levels of transfers but high tax levels. The findings indeed show that liberal and southern regimes have the suspected highest inequality, and the social-democratic regimes the lowest, but the results are not as robust as we predicted beforehand. The results, however, seem robust if we move from annual figures to a longer time horizon.

But the question of whether country or regime is the best way of presenting geographical variation needs a richer account of cross-country variations and requires disaggregation by regions and even communities. Then we find that regional variations are significant, but they still account for only 7 per cent of the total variance in equivalent household incomes across households.

Looking at the effects of different sources of cash income, it is clear that market incomes are largely responsible for inequality, but transfer incomes may also contribute to inequality because they are linked to previous earnings. Regime-type effects are generally confirmed but if we disaggregate our analysis further and look at the various components of market and transfer income the picture changes. Pension systems, for example, differ considerably and affect inequality at the national level. It is not so much regime-type effects being important for explaining differences in inequality of pension incomes but more the distinction between pay-as-you-go systems and capital-funded systems.

It appears that the various welfare regimes are more consistent in terms of the distribution of state transfers. All regimes tend to target their welfare benefits to the low-educated, lone-parent families and the (long-term) unemployed.

Many of our results are affected by the definition of income used. Our data measure only cash income, leaving wealth and in-kind income components out of sight. Looking at the effects of one in-kind component, imputed rent from homeownership, it turns out that the effect on overall inequality is not very high but that it has a substantial effect on within-group inequality, particularly among the elderly.

Then we considered income mobility patterns across countries and regime types. Many of the hypotheses concerning regime-type differences in the redistributive impact of the taxes and benefits seem to be confirmed, although the differences between countries are smaller than expected and less clear-cut. It also turned out that income mobility rates do not necessarily follow the picture derived from the regime-type classification. Germany has much less stability and more mobility than we expected for a corporatist country, and Portugal also has much less mobility than we expected for a residual regime.

The same type of conclusion can be drawn from the two case studies we performed in the final part of the chapter. With respect to immigrants, much of the differences across countries seems little to do with the regime-type from which classification but appears more closely connected with the part of the world immigrants originally came (EU or non-EU countries), the level of integration in society ('mixing' with the native-born population) and institutional differences in the treatment of immigrants. These differences go back to cultural and historical factors rooted in the evolution of society over time.

Comparing income changes one year before and after divorce showed that regime-type effects are important in their own right to explain levels of post-separation income. They become even more important when controlling for compositional differences across regimes. This underlines the importance of regime effects, but on the other hand, some findings were a bit odd in light of the regime hypothesis. After divorce women in liberal regimes tend to suffer less than expected and women in corporatist regimes more than expected.

Therefore, we should be careful not to use the regime-type classification without testing its relevance and appropriateness in light of the issue under study. Including institutional differences in a more detailed and sophisticated way might be a better strategy to follow in order to assess whether regime-type variables remain significant after inclusion of the appropriate institutional variables. Much of the research carried out so far needs improvement in the richness and time-horizon of the data to arrive at more final and robust conclusions. The results so far using these panel surveys are intriguing and promising. These data sources offer ample opportunities to enrich our understanding of performance and functioning of our societies and the role of social policies in a European and comparative perspective.

Notes

1. For the ECHP database issued in February 2000, Eurostat mentioned problems with the Belgian income data in Data Alert number 3. The data used here were issued at a later date, but we suspect that these problems had still not been resolved in this later version.
2. ECHP data for 1999. The 'richest' is defined here as the 99th percentile of the all-EU distribution; the 'poorest' as the 1st percentile.
3. For the definition of region Eurostat's regional classification system known as the Nomenclature of Territorial Units for Statistics (NUTS) has been used. The analysis here uses the broadest regional classification available in each country (NUTS1) as its starting point. But even here, smaller countries naturally tend to divide their populations into relatively small regions, and it is necessary to re-group regions so that the units in each country are of broadly comparable size. For more details about this regrouping see Berthoud (2004).
4. The calculated incomes by region are adjusted for ppp differences at the national level, that is, price differences at the regional level are assumed to be negligible.
5. The source paper also includes analysis of imputed rent in the USA (based on the PSID) but the US results are not included in this summary.
6. Households form, split and change composition over time, so it does not make sense to calculate an income trajectory for a whole household over several years. Instead, the analysis follows *individuals* from year to year, noting the equivalent incomes of the households they are a member of in each year.
7. The sample contains all persons being a panel member for the entire period 1995–98 (known as the longitudinal population). Quintiles are defined on each year's income distribution meaning that the measure of relative mobility used in the analysis reflects the change in the quintile ranking between t_1 and t_2.
8. Note that the analysis is based on household surveys and will not cover immigrants who are not resident in households, or who are unwilling or unable to take part in interviews. Since those omitted from the data may also be excluded from other aspects of the nation's core social and economic activities, the household-based analysis might over-estimate the level of integration of immigrants. This will be an especially important consideration in countries with a significant level of illegal immigration in the early and mid-1990s.
9. See Büchel and Frick (2004) for a more detailed analysis of the large heterogeneity among immigrants' economic performance (capacity) in Germany and the UK when using information on race/ethnicity and detailed country of origin, which is available from the national panels SOEP and BHPS, respectively. This detailed approach also shows that the positive effect of redistribution found for non-EU migrants to Germany comes, to a large extent, from the somewhat preferential treatment of ethnic Germans (*Aussiedler*) from Eastern Europe.

References

Atkinson, A.B. and F. Bourguignon (2000), *Handbook of Income Distribution*, Amsterdam: Elsevier.

*Berthoud, R. (2004), *Patterns of Poverty across Europe*, Bristol: Policy Press.

*Berthoud, R. and M. Iacovou (2003), *Diverse Europe: Mapping Patterns of Social Change Across the EU*, Swindon: ESRC.

*Büchel, F. and J.R. Frick (forthcoming), 'Immigrants' economic performance across Europe – does immigration policy matter?', *Population Research and Policy Review* (*EPAG Working Papers*, 42).

*Büchel, F. and J.R. Frick (2004), 'Immigrants in the UK and in West-Germany – relative income positions, income portfolio, and redistribution effects', *Journal of Population Economics* (forthcoming).

*Deding, M.C. and T.D. Schmidt (2002), 'Differences in income inequality across Europe – market driven or ...?', *EPAG Working Papers*, 37, Colchester: University of Essex.

Esping-Andersen, G. (1990), *The Three Worlds of Welfare Capitalism*, Cambridge: Polity Press.

*Frick, J.R. and M.M. Grabka (2002), 'Imputed rent and income inequality: a decomposition analysis for the UK, West-Germany and the USA', *EPAG Working Papers*, 29, Colchester: University of Essex.

Goodin, R., B. Headey, R. Muffels and H.-J. Dirven (1999), *The Real Worlds of Welfare Capitalism*, Cambridge: Cambridge University Press.

Headey, B. and R. Muffels (2003), 'Policy Goals and Outcomes in "Three Worlds of Welfare Capitalism"', *Journal of Applied Social Science Studies* (Schmollers Jahrbuch), 123, 127–42.

Headey, B., R. Muffels, B. Goodin and H.-J. Dirven (2000), 'Is there a trade-off between economic efficiency and a generous welfare state? A comparison of best cases of "The Three Worlds of Welfare Capitalism"', *Journal of Social Indicators Research*, 50 (2), 115–57.

*Maître, B. and B. Nolan (2000), 'Income mobility in the European Community Household Panel Survey', *EPAG Working Papers*, 4, Colchester: University of Essex.

*Maître, B., C.T. Whelan and B. Nolan (2002), 'Household income packaging in the European Union: welfare state income and welfare regime', *EPAG Working Papers*, 35, Colchester: University of Essex.

*Muffels, R., D. Fouarge and R. Dekker (1999), 'Longitudinal poverty and income inequality: a comparative panel study for the Netherlands, Germany and the UK', *EPAG Working Papers*, 1, Colchester: University of Essex.

Muffels, R., P. Tsakloglou and D. Mayes (eds) (2002), *Social Exclusion in European Welfare States*, Cheltenham, UK and Northampton, MA, USA: Edward Elgar.

*Nolan, B. and B. Maître (1999), 'The distribution of income and relative income poverty in the ECHP', *EPAG Working Papers*, 3, Colchester: University of Essex.

Shorrocks, A.F. (1982), 'Inequality decomposition by factor components', *Econometrica*, 50, 193–211.

*Uunk, W. (2003), 'Welfare state regimes and the economic consequences of separation – evidence from the European Household Panel Survey, 1994–98', *EPAG Working Papers*, **40**, Colchester: University of Essex.

* Direct output from EPAG's *DynSoc* research programme (see page 268).

9.   The Dynamics of Income Poverty

Richard Layte and Didier Fouarge

Introduction

As earlier chapters in this book have shown, there is a great deal of diversity across European Union (EU) countries in the distribution of employment and unemployment, the structure of households and crucially, in the manner in which the state intervenes in the nexus between the household and the labour market through the tax and welfare structure. The last chapter described how these differences influence the distribution of income in these societies and showed that states differ widely in terms of their levels of income inequality. In this chapter we extend this analysis by examining the distribution of poverty within EU states, but drawing upon the longitudinal analyses of the European Panel Analysis Group (Muffels et al., 1999; Fouarge and Muffels, 2000; Layte et al., 2000a 2000b; Whelan et al., 2001, 2003; Layte and Whelan, 2003), we also investigate the important issue of low-income dynamics.

Poverty research has shown that simply observing which individuals or households have a low income at a single point in time is seriously inadequate as a measure of their economic status, and can actually obscure the nature and causes of long-term disadvantage. Although economists have differentiated between current and longer-term or 'permanent' income for over half a century, research on poverty dynamics has only become possible in recent decades with the availability of panel surveys. Until the 1990s panel surveys were still only available for a small group of countries, but the collection of the European Community Household Panel Survey (ECHP) has now made the study of poverty dynamics possible for far more countries.

Although poverty dynamics must be seen as an essential element of analysis, this is not to underplay the importance of a great deal of cross-sectional poverty research which has given us a clear picture of the extent of and trends in income poverty across nations (Atkinson et al., 1995; Gottschalk and Smeeding, 1997). In this chapter, we present an examination of work which has taken a longitudinal perspective on poverty. We touch upon the issue of the persistence of poverty in the second section. The third and fourth sections focus on income changes and poverty dynamics. The long-term redistribution through welfare state transfers is briefly dealt with in the fifth section, whereas the sixth section concentrates on the duration of poverty spells. Before we can do either of these things however, we first need to tackle the difficult issue of how to measure poverty; this is the focus of the first section.

Measuring Poverty

Although at first glance the definition and measurement of poverty would seem simple (we all like to believe that we recognise poverty when we see it), in reality it has been the focus of a great deal of debate. In everyday use, poverty in developed countries is often seen as an inability to attain a 'decent' or 'adequate' standard of living. Since what is seen as adequate is likely to change over time and across societies, this means that the definition is essentially relative. Some researchers have argued for a more absolute notion of poverty, but relative definitions have become dominant in both academic and policy circles, a view expressed well by Piachaud (1987: 148): 'Close to subsistence level there is indeed some absolute minimum necessary for survival but apart from this, any poverty standard must reflect prevailing social standards: it must be a relative standard.' The relative poverty concept was adopted by the Council of the European Commission in their decision of 19th of December 1984: '[T]he poor shall be taken to mean persons, families and groups of persons whose resources (material, cultural and social) are so limited as to exclude them from the minimum acceptable way of life in the member state in which they live.'

Of course any such definition still needs to be operationalised and a number of different approaches have been put forward for the measurement of poverty. These approaches divide broadly along two axis: those that use objective as opposed to subjective definitions[1] and those that measure poverty either as deprivation or expenditure as opposed to using income (see Chapter 10). Different approaches have their merits, but the work upon which this chapter is based is an objective/indirect approach using income as the yardstick upon which resources are measured and a poverty line set at some fraction (usually 50, 60 or 70 per cent) of median income. This is also the approach taken by a number of EU Commission or EUROSTAT studies (see also Atkinson et al., 2002), although mean income was also used in some instances (Institute of Social Studies Advisory Service (ISSAS), 1990; O'Higgins and Jenkins, 1990; Hagenaars et al., 1994; Eurostat, 1999). The next chapter uses alternative measures of poverty in the form of deprivation indices and shows how these are related to the income poverty measures used in this chapter.

Needs and resources

At its simplest, a household's living standard can be said to be the result of the balance between the *resources* of the household and the *needs* of the household across time. The level of resources is a fairly simple concept to understand and most commonly operationalised, though not always,[2] as money income from different sources. The 'needs' of a household on the other hand can be more varied. The simplest example of the way that the needs of a household can vary is with the number of household members. The more people living in the household, the greater the level of resources that will be required to sustain it. But the needs of a household can also be affected by a broad range of characteristics such as the age, sex or health status of the individuals in the household to name just a few. For example, children will require a different level of resources compared to adults and older adults may need fewer resources than younger adults. Poverty then is the outcome of a longitudinal process of accumulation and erosion as the flow of resources into the household and the level of needs fluctuate. As we will go on to see in the third section, changes in poverty status over a given period may thus be the result of a change in either resources (the numerator) or demographic composition and needs (the denominator).

If we 'unpack' this simple picture further, it is quickly apparent that we also need to understand the context within which households and individuals live if we are to explain their risk of poverty. Though we can identify the characteristics of the individuals in the household that determine the level of resources available at any one point in time, these will vary depending on the context, most obviously between countries where different socio-economic structures and welfare regimes may well 'decommodify' individuals to varying degrees and smooth income flows (Esping-Andersen, 1990; Gallie and Paugam, 2000). Thus the extent to which a particular socio-economic status not only provides information about current demands or resources, but also serves as a proxy for longer-term imbalances between obligations and economic capacity, will be crucially influenced by the degree to which mechanisms that buffer the cash nexus are in place. Evidence of this effect can be found in recent research which shows that the relationship between current lifestyle deprivation and socio-economic factors influencing the level of resources available to households varies systematically across countries in a manner that is broadly consistent with welfare-regime theory (Layte et al., 2001). Moreover, the relationship between current income and lifestyle deprivation (as we will see in more detail in the next chapter) also varies in the same manner being weak in northern European countries such as Denmark, the Netherlands and Germany, moderate in Liberal welfare regimes such as the UK and Ireland and strongly related in the residual regimes of the southern European countries (see Muffels and Fouarge, 2003).

Having gained a better conceptual grasp of what shapes poverty risk, we can now go on to examine the distribution of poverty in EU states. In this section, we will be using data from the ECHP which allows us to compare poverty rates for different countries using fully harmonised data (see Chapter 1). The latest wave of the ECHP available at the time of the analysis was the fifth wave carried out in 1998 (using 158560 individuals across 13 countries)[3] and this is employed here using a relative income poverty line set at 60 per cent of national median equivalised household income. Later on in the text, poverty lines set at 50 and 70 per cent of median income will also be used. The equivalisation undertaken here is to take account of the differing size of households since the same level of income would lead to a lower standard of living in a household with a greater number of individuals. The 'equivalence scale' which we use here is commonly referred to as the modified Organization for Economic Co-operation and Development (OECD) scale where the first adult is given a value of 1 and all subsequent adults a value of 0.5 and all children (aged less than 14) are given a value of 0.3.

The last chapter examined the distribution of income and income inequality in EU countries and showed that levels of inequality varied widely between countries. As we are using a relative income poverty line in this section, this is also a function of the level of income inequality in a society (though in a more limited form), thus we would expect to see considerable variation between countries in poverty rates. As has already been suggested, the level of inequality within a country is strongly influenced by the welfare regime with more social-democratic welfare regimes (see Chapter 1 for an outline of the Esping-Andersen welfare-regime typology) and corporatist regimes having higher levels of taxation and greater income redistribution than both liberal and residual regimes. Given this we would expect to see higher levels of income poverty in those countries with liberal and residual regimes such as Ireland, the UK, Italy, Greece, Spain and Portugal.

Figure 9.1 shows that we do indeed see an ordering of countries in terms of poverty rates which is highly suggestive of the welfare-regime pattern outlined above. Using the typology set out in Chapter 1 we can see that both the social-democratic countries which we have data for in 1998 are at the top of the figure with the lowest income poverty rates whilst the southern European countries and particularly the UK can be found at the bottom. This ordering of countries changes little over time, even during economic cycles and does suggest that the welfare regimes in these countries contribute substantially to the extent of poverty.

Research has shown that poverty is not spread evenly across population groups. For example, it is usually found that, other things being equal, factors such as unemployment, where income from the market is lost, and single parenthood, which restricts one's ability to work, would lead to a higher risk of income poverty (see, for example, Eurostat, 2001).

Figure 9.1 National poverty rates

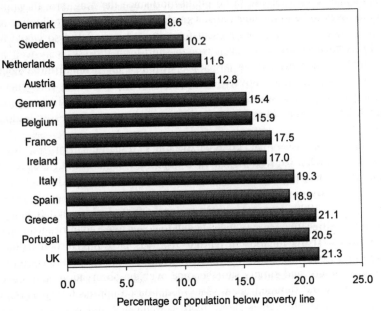

Percentage of population below poverty line

Note: Poverty line defined as 60 per cent of median income.
Source: ECHP (1998), authors' own calculations.

The Persistence of Poverty

Cross-sectional poverty analysis is an effective way of examining the overall risk of poverty and the particular risk faced by specific groups. It cannot however tell us anything about the risk of experiencing persistent or long-term poverty, or recurrent poverty where an individual would move in and out of poverty repeatedly over time. Although few would welcome the experience of short-term poverty, the temporary experience of low income is much less likely than repeated or long-term exposure to low income to damage life chances and lead to serious deprivation. In this sense, it is important from both an academic and social policy perspective to understand the extent to which poverty is persistent and which groups are more likely to experience it since the extent of persistent poverty could indicate inflexibilities in the welfare system and labour market.

Although cross-sectional poverty studies reveal the groups who are at risk of experiencing poverty, they can also be misleading. Bane and Ellwood (1986) use the example of a hospital: a survey of the patients in the hospital at one moment would produce different conclusions on who was ill than a survey over a longer period as the former would be biased towards those illnesses that caused long-term hospitalisation since the long-term ill would be more likely to be in the hospital at a single point in time. Short illnesses on the other hand would only be present for a limited period and so would be less likely to be seen. This, even though short-term illnesses may well be more frequent and make up a larger proportion of the hospital throughout. Similarly, cross-sectional poverty analysis also only points to the general characteristics of those who are poor and cannot easily unravel the processes which led to poverty, or perhaps more importantly, those processes leading from it.

In the short history of poverty dynamics research, most has been undertaken in the USA, but this situation began to change in the 1990s when income panel data became available more widely in Europe. Although first confined to analyses of Dutch, German and British data (Heady et al., 1994; Goodin et al., 1999; Fouarge, 2002; Jenkins, 2000; Jenkins and Schluter, 2003) poverty dynamics research has begun to cover more countries using the data of the ECHP. There are four types of methods used in poverty dynamics research: the N-year income to needs ratio method is based on the notion of permanent income and simply sums income over the observation period and divides this by the summed needs. The model-based approach to persistent poverty on the other hand is rather more complicated and is based on the decomposition of the income to needs ratio into permanent and transitory components allowing an estimate to be made of the level of persistent poverty (Lillard and Willis, 1978; Duncan and Rodgers, 1991; Fouarge and Muffels, 2000). The fraction of N-years in poverty approach simply counts the number of years below the poverty line over a set observation window and chooses a cut-off above which persistent poverty is said to have occurred, or creates a poverty profile combining both the length and number of poverty years (Coe, 1978; Duncan, 1984; Muffels et al., 1999; Whelan et al., 2003). Lastly, the spell-based approach uses duration models to estimate the hazard of leaving a poverty spell at given durations and for different characteristics and from this estimates the mean duration of a spell (Bane and Ellwood, 1986; Stevens, 1995; Fouarge and Layte, 2003). Note that for the purpose of such longitudinal studies, individuals are followed over time though they are assigned the income level and poverty status of the household to which they belong at each point in time.

Using panel data, research has begun to examine a number of crucial questions about the nature of longitudinal poverty: first, is poverty more common when viewed longitudinally rather than cross-sectionally? Second, can we identify a tendency towards poverty persistence and recurrent poverty and does this vary in its extent across countries? Third and lastly, what types of events are more likely to lead to entry into and exit from poverty and does the importance of these events differ between countries and regimes?

Table 9.1   Poverty rates over one year and over four years

Country	Mean annual poverty rate A	Proportion experiencing poverty in any of four years B	Ratio A/B
Denmark	9.4	20.1	2.14
Netherlands	11.1	20.7	1.86
UK	21.1	36.6	1.74
Ireland	19.1	36.4	1.91
Belgium	16.6	33.2	2.00
France	17.0	28.3	1.67
Germany	15.4	23.0	1.49
Portugal	22.6	38.7	1.72
Spain	19.5	36.0	1.85
Italy	19.2	35.0	1.82
Greece	21.6	38.2	1.77

Note: 60 per cent median income poverty line.
Source: ECHP (1994–97), adapted from Layte and Whelan (2003).

Looking at the first of these questions, Layte and Whelan (2003), using the ECHP, compared mean cross-sectional poverty rates to the proportions experiencing poverty over a four-year period (1994–97) and found that poverty was indeed more common when viewed longitudinally. Their results are shown in Table 9.1. The table shows that the proportion of persons that *ever* experienced poverty between 1994 and 1997 is roughly twice the size of the cross-sectional estimate. Interestingly, although the country ordering of longitudinal poverty is similar to that of cross-sectional poverty, the country order of the ratio of the two is more variable. For example, though a far smaller proportion of Danes experience poverty in any one year, the ratio of this to those having ever experienced poverty over the four years is actually the highest of all countries. The reason for this is, as we will go on to see in subsequent analyses, that the burden of poverty is spread far more widely in Danish society (in other words a greater proportion of people experience a spell of poverty), but fewer people experience persistent poverty.

If poverty is more common longitudinally than cross-sectionally, can we also identify a tendency towards poverty persistence and recurrent poverty and does this vary in its extent across countries? Layte and Whelan (2003) also investigated this question using the fraction of N-years in poverty methodology (that is, counting the number of years poor over their four-year observation period) and found that persistent poverty varied greatly across countries. Using an extension of this methodology, Fouarge and Layte (2003) examined the extent to which poverty was recurrent as well as persistent. Rather than simply counting the number of years that individuals were below the poverty line, Fouarge and Layte used this information, plus the number of discrete 'spells' of poverty to compute a poverty typology, or profile, defined as follows:

- the persistent non-poor: never poor during the accounting period;
- the transient poor: poor only once during the accounting period;
- the recurrent poor: poor more than once, but never longer than two consecutive years; and
- the persistent poor: poor for a consecutive period of at least three consecutive years.

The profile approach makes it possible to distinguish between short single spells of poverty and recurrent poverty, as well as looking at persistent poverty of three or more years. Using five waves of the ECHP, Fouarge and Layte (2003) found that the majority of people in all countries avoid poverty completely over the five-year period, but the proportion varied considerably across countries (see Table 9.2).[4] More interestingly however, if persistent poverty was defined as experiencing three or more years in poverty,[5] it ranged widely from 3.5 per cent in Denmark to over 18 per cent in Portugal. The data further show that the pattern of recurrent poverty was very similar to that found for persistent poverty with the social-democratic countries having lower levels than the corporatist states, which themselves performed better than the liberal and residualist states. For example, whereas Denmark and the Netherlands had recurrent poverty rates of around 6 per cent, France and Germany had rates of around 8 per cent. The liberal states of Ireland and the UK had higher rates of around 11 per cent whereas the residualist states of Greece, Spain and Italy had rates of between 12 and 15 per cent. Only Portugal failed to fit the regime typology with recurrent poverty rates of around 10 per cent. Table 9.3 also underlines the fact that the social-democratic and corporatist regimes spread the risk of poverty more widely across society compared to the liberal and residualist with relatively high proportions experiencing transitory poverty. The comparative level of persistent poverty between countries appears to be fairly robust using different income poverty lines and different techniques – Fouarge and Muffels (2000) found that persistent poverty was higher in the UK compared to Germany and the Netherlands using the model-based estimates of persistent poverty methodology outlined earlier.

Table 9.2   Poverty profiles in Europe (row percentages)

Country	Never poor	Transient poor	Recurrent poor	Persistent poor
Denmark	77.4	13.2	6.0	3.5
Netherlands	77.9	9.6	6.1	6.4
UK	61.4	13.4	11.1	14.1
Ireland	63.8	10.7	10.6	14.9
Belgium	63.9	13.4	10.8	11.9
France	68.4	10.4	7.9	13.3
Germany	73.4	11.1	7.7	7.8
Portugal	58.8	13.7	9.5	18.1
Spain	60.0	13.5	15.1	11.4
Italy	62.1	12.6	12.3	13.2
Greece	58.5	13.9	12.4	15.2
Europe	66.2	12.0	10.1	11.7

Note: 60 per cent median poverty line.
Source: ECHP (1994–98), reproduced from Fouarge and Layte (2003).

In an attempt to quantify this tendency to persistence, Layte and Whelan (2003) compared the proportions experiencing different numbers of years poor to the proportions that would be expected *if* the experience of poverty in any one year, based on the cross-sectional average over the same period, was independent in each year. The approach thus asks whether – net of the average level of poverty across the period – the experience of poverty is more concentrated on some individuals rather than others. Their results show that on the basis of independence, we would expect a far lower proportion of people in every country to avoid poverty than we actually observed in Table 9.1, around 50 per cent lower in most countries with figures ranging from around 30 per cent in Denmark to 48 per cent in Ireland, Greece and Portugal. The corollary of this difference is that far fewer people experience one or more years of poverty than would be expected. However, it is the difference in the actual persistent poverty experienced when compared to that expected that is striking. Across the countries the expected proportion experiencing three or more years of poverty is never more than 34 per cent of the actual proportion and in Denmark this drops to just 17 per cent. Their results show that far fewer people experience any poverty and far more experience persistent poverty than we would expect given cross-sectional poverty rates. This suggests that there is some 'inertia' to the experience of poverty that tends to lead to multiple, rather than single years in poverty.

Table 9.3   Influences on the risk of being persistently poor: households of working age (ordered logit regression coefficients)

Number of children	0.252
Single parent	0.831
No-one employed	1.087
Low education	0.658
Head of the household loses job	0.257
Head of the household finds job	−0.359

Notes: Selected coefficients from an ordered logit model.
           All coefficients are significant at the 1 per cent level.
           A positive (negative) coefficient indicates an increased (decreased) risk of persistent poverty.
Source: ECHP (1994–98), adapted from Fouarge and Layte (2003).

Explaining the persistence of poverty
So far, we have seen that welfare-regime types are important in determining the degree of both persistent and recurrent poverty in a country and that both vary widely between regime types. For example, Ireland, the UK and the southern European countries show high rates of persistent poverty, particularly when compared to countries such as Denmark, the Netherlands and Germany. But what individual and household characteristics are more likely to lead to persistent poverty? To examine this question Fouarge and Layte (2003) applied multivariate analysis to estimate the effect of different covariates on the probability of being in each of the poverty profile groups described above. The approach used recognises that there is an order to the categories with recurrent poverty being a worse outcome than transient poverty, and persistent poverty a worse outcome than recurrent poverty.

Four types of variables were included in the model which were likely to be important factors characterising the different profiles: personal and household characteristics (age, sex, marital status, household composition, number of children, marital status); socio-economic characteristics (education level, labour market participation at the household level, health situation); household formation events (divorce or separation) and lastly, labour market events (increase or decrease in the number of employed adults in the household or in the number of hours worked). The variables were measured at the beginning of the observation period, and thus did not change across time (apart from those variables measuring change in status across the period).

In order to gain a better understanding of the labour market events associated with poverty spells, the analysis was limited to individuals living in a household where both the head and the partner – if any – were of working age (aged 16 to 64).

These models showed that a number of factors are predictive of longer and more frequent spells of poverty. In terms of personal and household characteristics, being a single parent and having a larger number of adults and children in the household were both predictive of longer and more frequent poverty, as we would expect given our previous analyses in this chapter. The employment status of the household members was found to be an important predictor of the long-term poverty risk. This is also true for the education level: lower levels of education for the head of household is associated with a larger probability of experiencing long-term poverty, even after correction for employment status. Single people who were unemployed were particularly at risk of experiencing frequent or persistent poverty spells. The importance of the variables was underlined by the addition of variables expressing change in the employment status of household members which showed that the head of the household losing a job contributed significantly to an increase in the risk of recurrent and persistent poverty (and vice versa).

Changes in Needs and Changes in Income

So far we have addressed the first two of the questions outlined at the beginning of this chapter and now have a reasonably clear picture of the way that persistent poverty rates differ from cross-sectional poverty rates and how this varies by the measure used and country observed. The national context and individual and household characteristics are, as we have already seen, of undoubted importance in shaping the experience of poverty, but the two are likely to interact in complex ways since different regimes treat individuals and households in very different manners depending on their circumstances and history. In this section we adopt an 'incidence'-based approach to see which factors explain poverty transitions, how this varies by country and what this tells us about the interaction between welfare regimes and individual characteristics. In doing this, we seek to answer the third of the questions set out in the second section: what type of events are more likely to lead to entry into and exit from poverty and does the impact of these events differ between different countries?

In answering this question we need to move away from the analysis of individuals to the analysis of transitions – of which a particular individual may have several[6] – so that we can understand what factors are more likely to lead to poverty transitions. Thus, rather than following a single individual for the observation period we need to look at the characteristics of a person or household the year before and after a poverty transition as this will tell us which factors are implicated in poverty transitions.

In doing this however, it is necessary to think more deeply about how different 'events' can lead to poverty transitions.[7] For example, we know that certain characteristics make a person more likely to experience poverty such as having a low education or having a larger than average number of children, but these are general risk factors and not the 'triggering' event that leads to poverty. Instead we need to look at the specific changes in a person's life, or in their household that leads them into poverty. This sounds simple enough, but such events may themselves actually be highly complex and difficult to analyse. For example, a person may become poor because the income of their household fell and this in turn occurred because the number employed in the household fell. Yet the separation or divorce of the married partners in the household and the exit of one employed adult may have triggered this train of events.

In attempting to clarify some of this complexity, we can follow Layte and Whelan (2003) in dividing transition events into those associated with changes in the resources numerator and those more associated with the needs, or demographic denominator of poverty status. Change in either of these factors could lead to a poverty transition. Remember that for the purpose of longitudinal research, individuals are assigned the equivalised income of the household to which they belong at the time of interview. So a change in this measurement can be caused either by a change of income or a change in household composition affecting the needs of the household. Layte and Whelan examined whether resources or needs were the primary reason for poverty transitions by cross-tabulating the two variables after they had been grouped into decreasing, increasing or unaltered categories. Change in the level of resources in the household was measured as change in the household's net income,[8] whereas change in 'needs' was measured as any change in the household equivaliser itself, that is, the number of adults and children in the household weighted by the 'modified OECD' equivalence scale.

Rather than show all the possible categories of this cross-classification, Table 9.4 gives the results of those that cover the overwhelming majority of transitions for the 11 countries of the ECHP database for transitions into 70 per cent median income poverty between 1994 and 1997. What is immediately clear is that the majority of transitions occur because of decreases in income rather than increases in the level of needs, varying between 54 per cent in Ireland and 77 per cent in Denmark and Spain. The impact of changes in the level of needs only becomes important when accompanied by income decreases, this category making up between 9 per cent of transitions in Denmark and 24 per cent in Ireland.

Table 9.4   Transitions into poverty by changes in income and needs (row percentages)

Country	Income < and needs same	Income < and needs >	Both same	Income same and needs >	Other
Denmark	76.9	9.4	12.5	0.3	1.0
Netherlands	56.7	16.9	20.9	4.1	1.4
UK	62.9	22.7	10.5	1.1	2.8
Ireland	53.9	23.7	12.5	4.2	5.7
Belgium	72.0	16.3	8.7	1.0	2.0
France	68.1	15.0	11.3	2.4	3.2
Germany	75.8	12.8	9.5	1.1	0.9
Portugal	70.0	14.0	8.6	2.8	4.7
Spain	76.7	13.4	6.4	1.2	2.3
Italy	75.3	14.5	6.4	1.3	2.4
Greece	71.2	16.3	7.8	2.0	2.8

Note: 70 per cent median poverty line.
Source: ECHP (1994–97), from Layte and Whelan (2003).

Is the same pattern true of movements out of poverty? Table 9.5 shows a comparable table to Table 9.4, except that this time we examine transitions out of 70 per cent income poverty. If anything, the dominance of changes in income is clearer here than in Table 9.4 with between 54 per cent of Danish exits and 80 per cent of Greek exits stemming from income changes alone. In fact, in Denmark over 23 per cent of transitions from poverty occur where income increases, but the level of needs is increasing as well.

Table 9.5   *Transitions out of poverty by changes in income and needs (row percentages)*

Country	Income > and needs >	Income > and needs same	Income > and needs <	Both same	Other
Denmark	23.3	54.1	16.1	6.5	0.0
Netherlands	6.6	79.0	13.3	1.1	0.0
UK	7.9	73.5	17.5	1.1	0.0
Ireland	17.1	60.1	21.2	1.3	0.3
Belgium	10.6	75.0	10.4	3.7	0.3
France	6.4	71.3	19.1	2.9	0.3
Germany	4.1	75.5	14.1	6.0	0.3
Portugal	6.4	74.3	16.7	2.4	0.2
Spain	8.2	75.7	13.2	2.4	0.5
Italy	8.4	77.5	10.4	3.0	0.7
Greece	6.5	80.0	12.7	0.7	0.1

Note: 70 per cent median poverty line.
Source: ECHP (1994–97), from Layte and Whelan (2003).

Income Changes and Exits from Poverty

If transitions both into and from poverty tend to be more strongly associated with changes in income rather than demographic changes, are different sources of income of greater importance across countries and if so what does this tell us about the effects of welfare regimes? Layte and Whelan (2003: 90) outlined three hypotheses on these issues:

Hypothesis 1: Different welfare regimes influence the bundle of incomes, 'the income package' that individuals and households receive. Given the more generous and greater provision of transfers in social-democratic and employment-centred regimes we would expect that a smaller proportion of transitions will be due to changes in state transfers in subprotective and liberal regimes as compared to employment-centred and particularly social-democratic regimes.

Hypothesis 2: On the other hand, the order of regimes will be reversed in terms of the importance of earnings in poverty transitions with earnings being of greatest importance in subprotective regimes since a greater proportion of households' income packages in these states is made up of earnings.

Hypothesis 3: The third hypothesis centres on the importance of different types of individuals in households and how this may vary across states given greater 'familialism' in residualist welfare states combined with high employment protection for 'insider' groups who tend to be older males. Given this, we hypothesised that changes in the incomes of the main earner in the household will be more important in the residualist states of southern Europe compared to all other types with liberal and employment-centred regimes being moderate in this respect.

We can examine evidence on the first two of these hypotheses in Figure 9.2. Because of space limitations, rather than show data for both entry into poverty and exit from poverty, here we focus solely on exits as the patternings in terms of the hypotheses at issue are very similar across entry and exits. As such, Figure 9.2 shows the proportion of transitions from poverty made up by changes in different types of household incomes (only transitions where income is changing). There is a clear differentiation between the countries, and, more importantly, the groups of countries in terms of the importance of social welfare transfers and incomes from earnings. Whereas in Denmark 20 per cent of transitions from poverty are as a result of increases in social welfare payments, this type of income is implicated in only 8 per cent of transitions in Greece, 4 per cent in Spain and 2 per cent in Portugal. The Netherlands, Belgium, France, Ireland and the UK making up an intermediate group. With Denmark our representative of the social-democratic regime and the southern European states the subprotective, this patterning clearly supports Hypothesis 1, although the usual definition of Italy as a subprotective state could be questioned given the importance of social welfare in poverty exits.

When we turn to the importance of earnings across states we see almost the opposite picture with earnings increases making up around 40 per cent of all transitions out of poverty in Spain and Portugal, whereas earnings are implicated in only 17 per cent of Danish exits. On the other hand, earnings are of more importance in the Netherlands at almost 26 per cent of transitions out of poverty, a higher figure than France and Belgium and Ireland.

The differential importance of earnings across the countries for exits from poverty is less clear than for social welfare, though earnings play a smaller role in Denmark and Belgium and an important part in Spain and Portugal, both as we might expect. Against expectations, earnings increases have a larger role in the Netherlands and the UK, particularly when combined with some form of social transfer.

The third of the hypotheses from Layte and Whelan (2003) stated above centred on the importance of different types of individuals in households and how this may vary across states. Given greater 'familialism' in residualist welfare states combined with high employment protection for 'insider' groups – who tend to be older males – we hypothesised that changes in the incomes of the main earner in the household will be more important in the residualist states of southern Europe compared to all other types with liberal and employment-centred regimes being moderate in this respect.

Figure 9.2   Transitions out of poverty by type of increase in income

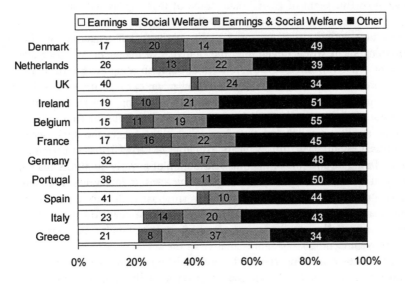

Note   Poverty line defined as 70 per cent of median income.
Source: ECHP (1994–97), adapted from Layte and Whelan (2003).

Looking at entry and exit patterns across countries, the patterns indeed seem to support the hypothesis that the household head's earnings will have a greater role in the subprotective states. The household head's earnings making the largest contribution are Greece, Italy and Spain, though Ireland follows close behind, whilst the lowest proportion is found in Belgium and Germany.

The Duration of Poverty Spells

In the previous section, we changed the focus of analysis from descriptions of years in poverty to one based on transitions to look at the processes leading to and from poverty. What this perspective could not do, however, was examine the extent to which the probability of exit changed over the duration of the poverty spell. One of the central concerns of both researchers and policy makers is the speed at which people leave poverty, since longer spells of poverty are likely to be far more damaging in terms of deprivation and economic strain experienced. One method of looking at poverty durations is through exit probabilities, but to do this we need to move to a 'spell-centred' mode of analysis. Whereas in the last section we simply examined transitions from poverty, regardless of the duration in poverty, here duration is our prime interest. However, because we can only observe spells of poverty through the window of five years of ECHP data, some of these spells will already have begun before ('left-censored'), or still be ongoing at the end of the observation period ('right-censored'). We avoided 'left-censoring' by only examining spells which began after the first year of the panel. We controlled for right-censoring and derived estimates of duration using the transition rate. These are calculated by dividing the number of exits or transitions from poverty in each year by the population at risk of exiting, that is, the number still poor. This means that sample sizes are quite large for the first year, but become steadily smaller and thus less reliable the longer the spell period. Unfortunately, the short run of years available in the ECHP data prevent us from offering an analysis of the true distribution of poverty durations since no spell can be more than three years long if completed, or four years if censored (using currently available data). However, it is useful to compare the durations derived from the exit probabilities between countries. Note that in Chapter 7 similar methods are applied to the study of exit from unemployment.

Table 9.6 from Fouarge and Layte (2003) shows the overall exit probabilities for the ECHP sample of poverty spells at each year of their duration. The figures show that the overall exit probability for all EU countries included in the table (first row) falls quickly between the first and second years of poverty from 46 per cent to 31 per cent, but then the rate of decrease slows so the exit rate is 24 per cent by the third year (remember there are no transitions after the third year to calculate exit probabilities from).

Cumulating these results we can see that 72 per cent of the people just beginning a spell of poverty will have left after three years. Interestingly, these results are very close to those found by Bane and Ellwood (1986), who found that the exit probabilities in their US sample were 45 per cent in the first year, 29 per cent in the second and 25 per cent in the third. Luckily they had access to the Panel Study of Income Dynamics (PSID) panel survey which has 12 years of usable poverty data and so they were also able to estimate long-run transition rates. Using this data they found that exit probabilities carried on decreasing after the third year reaching just over 7 per cent by the eighth year. Given the similarity in exit rates between these European findings and the US results found by Bane and Ellwood (1986), we could use their extrapolations of a mean poverty spell duration of 2.7 years. Later work by Stevens (1995: 18) has adjusted this estimate using multiple rather than single spells of poverty for the same person and found that the average poverty spell over a 15-year observation window is four years.

It is likely that exit probabilities also differ between countries in the EU and applying the same welfare-regime theory employed throughout this chapter, we could envisage seeing a particular pattern. Fouarge and Layte (2003) offered this hypothesis:

Hypothesis 4: The social-democratic countries will have higher initial exit rates, but lower levels of incentives will lead to sharply falling exit rates from poverty as duration increases. In liberal and southern regimes on the other hand, low initial exit rates compared to corporatist and social-democratic countries will be maintained leading to roughly similar poverty durations across different regimes.

Table 9.6 *Exit rates from 60 per cent median income poverty by spell duration 1994–98 (percentages)*

Country	Spell length		
	1 year	2 years	3 years
Europe	46.0	31.3	23.7
Denmark	55.2	37.0	19.2
Netherlands	47.7	23.3	24.6
UK	41.7	27.2	34.5
Ireland	47.2	28.2	25.4
Belgium	47.9	25.9	17.9
France	42.8	32.8	14.0
Germany	47.6	33.0	15.7
Portugal	40.5	29.9	32.7
Spain	49.7	32.5	22.0
Italy	48.6	37.2	16.9
Greece	24.1	29.7	25.9

Source: ECHP (1994–98), adapted from Fouarge and Layte (2003).

Table 9.6 also shows the country-specific exit probabilities. Although there are differences in the exit rates in the table, the overall spread of rates is actually quite small with only 15 per cent separating the highest and lowest rates and seven of the countries being within 8 per cent of each other (though the Danish rate in the first year is clearly higher than in the other countries). After one year of poverty, the Danish exit rate of 55 per cent is 6 percentage points higher than the next highest rate in Spain. At the other end of the scale Portugal, the UK and Greece have the lowest exit rates – the Portuguese rate being less than three-quarters of the Danish rate. However, as the duration of poverty lengthens, the country order changes quite substantially with the Dutch rate falling by 51 per cent, the Belgian rate by 46 per cent and the Irish rate by 40 per cent between the first and second years. Similarly, between the second and third years, the French rate drops by over 55 per cent so that whereas in Denmark approximately 77 per cent of those entering poverty will have left by the third year, in the Netherlands this rate is 70 per cent, in Belgium 68 per cent and lowest in France at 67 per cent. Interestingly, the slower decrease in the exit probability in Portugal means that after three years, 72 per cent of those who entered a spell of poverty will have left, the fourth highest rate. What implications do the results from this section have for our hypotheses in this chapter?

In many respects the results from this descriptive analysis are congruent with our fourth hypothesis. It is clear that Denmark, our prime social-democratic country, has the highest initial exit rate, although the Netherlands, the other representative of the social-democratic regime, has a more average transition rate around the same range as the corporatist countries of France, Germany and Belgium. Greece, Portugal and the UK have low initial exit rates, but Italy, Ireland and Spain all have rates close or greater than the corporatist countries. However, as hypothesised, we do see large decreases in the exit rates of the social-democratic and corporatist countries after the first year with the Dutch, Belgian and French rates dropping quickly whilst the liberal and southern regime rates tend to be maintained. These patterns mean that after three years, the proportions who have left poverty are very close across countries with only 10 per cent separating the highest and lowest rates and nine countries being with 7 per cent of each other.

Conclusions

This chapter has drawn on the work of the European Panel Analysis Group to offer an examination of the dynamics of income poverty across EU states. Poverty analysis is now well developed, but until comparatively recently, poverty research tended to be cross-sectional in nature, even though poverty itself is far from a static phenomenon. Until the mid-1990s, the analysis of poverty dynamics was restricted to Germany, the Netherlands, Great Britain and the USA because these were the only countries with suitable survey data. However, the recent availability of five waves of the ECHP data set makes it possible for the first time to examine poverty dynamics processes across a number of countries. This chapter has asked three basic questions: first, to what extent is poverty a more common experience when viewed longitudinally rather than cross-sectionally? Second, can we identify a tendency towards poverty persistence and does this vary in its extent across countries? Third and lastly, what type of events are more likely to lead to entry into and exit from poverty and does the impact of these events differ between different countries?

In terms of the first question, we saw that poverty is experienced by a far higher number of individuals when viewed longitudinally rather than cross-sectionally. Thus, using 60 per cent of median income poverty, the ratio between the longitudinal and cross-sectional numbers was between 1.5 and 2.1. However, though more people experience poverty than when compared to cross-sectional figures, if we extrapolate from the mean cross-sectional poverty line to an *expected* experience of poverty on the basis of independence between years in poverty, what we actually see are far fewer people experiencing poverty and a polarisation of persistent poverty. This is important since it suggests an 'inertia' to the experience of poverty that can 'trap' individuals and households, but the effect varies between countries with those from more social-democratic and employment-centred regimes being less polarised and closer to expectations based solely on probability theory.

The difference in the polarisation of poverty across countries was just one confirmation in the chapter of the welfare-regime typology set out in Chapter 1. Not only did liberal and residual regimes tend to increase the risk of persistent poverty, they also increased the risk of recurrent, or repeated poverty as shown by the analysis of the poverty profiles set out in Fouarge and Layte (2003). The analysis of the poverty profiles also showed that individual and household characteristics too were very important in determining the risk of persistent and recurrent poverty with demographic characteristics such as being a single parent, or being in a household with larger numbers of adults and children all contributing to an increased risk. However, the greatest increase in risk came from socio-economic variables such as the employment status and level of education of the individuals in the household. These analyses described the factors leading to persistent and repeated poverty, but did not uncover the factors implicated in transitions into and from poverty. By disaggregating transitions into and from poverty in the fourth section by the 'events' leading to transition we found that changes in the level of income were of vital and prime importance. However, we hypothesised that the sources of income and the person responsible in the household would differ dramatically across countries given different regime characteristics and these hypotheses were confirmed by analysis. Similarly, when we turned to the interaction of individual and household characteristics with regime type in the last section we found that changes in both the ability of the household to generate resources and the level of need led to transitions into and from poverty, though the patterning by regime was clearer for factors affecting resources.

We also used transition rates to examine how country context and poverty duration impacted on exit from poverty. Applying welfare-regime theory once again we found that the social-democratic states such as Denmark had higher exit rates than liberal or residual states, but this patterning was not as strong as in previous sections. From the point of view of income redistribution, it has been shown that notwithstanding the success of the liberal regime reducing medium-term poverty, both pre- and post-transfer poverty rates are found to be highest there. However, it is generally true that welfare state policies are more egalitarian in the longer term.

The availability of truly comparative longitudinal income information opens up areas of analysis that were unimaginable before, and allow us to begin to disentangle the role of different factors in producing disadvantage and particularly the role of the institutions and regulations of state. Across the EU there are a variety of different types of welfare arrangements which influence the life chances and standard of living of citizens in different ways and which often effect citizens in different ways depending on their characteristics.

A major lesson drawn from the research by the European Panel Analysis Group relates to the great added value of longitudinal data at the micro level. Whereas cross-sectional poverty studies can only tell us who is in poverty at a single point in time, longitudinal data on income allows us to study and explain movements in and out of poverty over time and to see to what extent poverty is a long-term and persistent experience rather than a temporary situation. Being able to understand what factors influence the probability of experiencing a longer spell of poverty is crucial not only for an academic understanding of how different individual and household characteristics interact with varying socio-economic systems and institutions, but also for the development of more effective social policy interventions.

Notes

1. 'Objective' definitions use information about the population in question whereas 'subjective' definitions make use of the opinions of the population.
2. Though income consumption measures and 'direct' measures of household resources are also used (Whelan et al., 2001).
3. The version of the ECHP used does not include data for Luxembourg and Finland for 1998.
4. The table includes only the 11 ECHP countries for which income information is available for all five waves.
5. The European Commission has accepted a definition of persistent poverty based upon being currently poor and being poor in two of the previous three years (though not necessarily the

last). This is very much a cross-sectional definition of persistent poverty and thus we do not adopt it here.

6. Unfortunately it is not possible to control for censoring using this approach, thus, as in the first section of the analyses in this chapter, here we use a balanced panel of those in the ECHP database from 1994 to 1997 weighted appropriately.

7. As we are using relative income poverty lines it is also possible that a person could enter or leave poverty without any form of change if median income and thus the poverty line moves around them. Income measures are also prone to random fluctuation that can also lead to poverty transitions.

8. To minimise the influence of random error in income change, Layte and Whelan (2003) took only changes of 10 per cent or more in income as indicative of change.

References

Atkinson, A.B., L. Rainwater and T. Smeeding (1995), *Income Distribution in OECD Countries: Evidence from the Luxembourg Income Study*, Paris: OECD.

Atkinson, A., B. Cantillon, E. Marlier and B. Nolan (2002), *Social Indicators: the EU and Social Inclusion*, Oxford: Oxford University Press.

Bane, M.J. and D.T. Ellwood (1986), 'Slipping into and out of poverty: the dynamics of spells', *Journal of Human Resources*, **21**, 1–23.

Coe, R.D. (1978), 'Dependency and poverty in the short and long run', in G.J. Duncan and J.N. Morgan (eds), *5000 American Families: Patterns of Economic Progress Vol. 6*, Ann Arbor, MI: Institute for Social Research, University of Michigan, MI, pp. 273–96.

Duncan, G. (1984), *Years of Poverty, Years of Plenty*, Ann Arbor, MI: Institute for Social Research, University of Michigan.

Duncan, G. and W. Rodgers (1991), 'Has children's poverty become more persistent?', *American Sociological Review*, **56**, 538–49.

Esping-Andersen, G. (1990), *The Three Worlds of Welfare Capitalism*, Cambridge: Polity Press.

Eurostat (1999), *European Community Household Panel (ECHP): Selected Indicators from the 1995 Wave*, Luxembourg: OOPEC.

Eurostat (2001), *The Social Situation of the European Union 2001*, Luxembourg: OOPEC.

Fouarge, D. (2002), *Minimum Protection and Poverty in Europe: an Economic Analysis of the Subsidiarity Principle within EU Social Policy*, Amsterdam: Thela Thesis.

*Fouarge D. and R. Layte (2003), 'Duration of poverty spells in Europe', *EPAG Working Papers*, **47**, Colchester: University of Essex.

*Fouarge, D. and R. Muffels (2000), 'Persistent poverty in the Netherlands, Germany and the UK: a model based approach using panel data for the 1990s', *EPAG Working Papers*, **15**, Colchester: University of Essex.

Gallie, D. and S. Paugam (2000), *Welfare Regimes and the Experience of Unemployment in Europe*, ESRI Books and Monographs Series 157, Oxford: Oxford University Press.

Goodin, R.E., B. Heady, R. Muffels and H.J. Dirven (1999), *The Real Worlds of Welfare Capitalism*, Cambridge: Cambridge University Press.

Gottschalk, P. and T. Smeeding (1997), 'Cross-national comparisons of earnings and income inequality', *Journal of Economic Literature*, **35**, 633–87.

Hagenaars, A., K. de Vos and M.A. Zaidi (1994), *Poverty Statistics in the Late 1980s: Research Based on Micro-data*, Luxembourg: OOPEC.

Heady, B., P. Krause and R. Habich (1994), 'Long and short term poverty? Is Germany a two-thirds society', *Social Indicators Research*, **31**, 1–25.

Institute of Social Studies Advisory Service (ISSAS) (1990), *Poverty in Figures, Europe in the Early 1980s*, Luxembourg: Eurostat.

Jenkins, S. (2000). 'Modeling household income dynamics', *Journal of Population Economics*, **13** (4), 529–67.

Jenkins, S. and C. Schluter (2003), 'Why are child poverty rates higher in Britain than in Germany? A longitudinal perspective', *The Journal of Human Resources*, **38** (2), 441–65.

*Layte, R. and Whelan, C.T. (2003), 'Moving in and out of poverty: the impact of welfare regimes on poverty dynamics in the EU', *European Societies*, **5** (2), 167–91.

*Layte, R., B. Maître, B. Nolan and C.T. Whelan (2000a), 'Poverty dynamics: an analysis of the 1994 and 1995 waves of the European Community Household Panel Study', *EPAG Working Papers*, **10**, Colchester: University of Essex.

*Layte, R., B. Maître, B. Nolan and C.T. Whelan (2000b), 'Persistent and consistent poverty: an analysis of the 1994 and 1995 waves of the European Community Household Panel Study', *EPAG Working Papers*, **11**, Colchester: University of Essex.

*Layte, R., B. Maître, B. Nolan and C.T. Whelan (2001), 'Explaining deprivation in the European Union', *Acta Sociologica*, **44** (2), 105–22.

Lillard, L. and R. Willis (1978), 'Dynamics aspects of earnings mobility', *Econometrica*, **46**, 985–1012.

*Muffels, R. and D. Fouarge (2003), 'The role of European welfare states in explaining resources deprivation', *EPAG Working Papers*, **41**, Colchester: University of Essex.

*Muffels, R., D. Fouarge and R. Dekker (1999), 'Longitudinal poverty and income inequality: a comparative panel study for the Netherlands, Germany and the UK', *EPAG Working Papers*, **1**, Colchester: University of Essex.

O'Higgins, M. and S.P. Jenkins (1990), 'Poverty in the EC: estimates for 1975, 1980 and 1985', in R. Teekens and B. Van Praag (eds), *Analysing Poverty in the European Community*, Luxembourg: Eurostat.

Piachaud, D. (1987), 'Problems in the definition and measurement of poverty', *Journal of Social Policy*, **16** (2), 147–64.

Stevens, A.H. (1995), *Climbing Out of Poverty, Falling Back In: Measuring the Persistence of Poverty over Multiple Spells*, Cambridge MA: National Bureau of Economic Research.

*Whelan, C.T., R. Layte, B. Maître and B. Nolan (2001), 'Income, deprivation and economic strain: an analysis of the European Community Household Panel', *European Sociological Review*, **17** (4), 357–72.

*Whelan, C.T., R. Layte, B. Maître and B. Nolan (2003), 'Persistent income poverty and deprivation in the European Union: an analysis of the first three waves of the European Community Household Panel', *Journal of Social Policy*, **32** (1), 1–32.

* Direct output from EPAG's *DynSoc* research programme (see page 268).

10. Deprivation and Social Exclusion

Christopher T. Whelan, Richard Layte and Bertrand Maître

Introduction

Earlier chapters have considered a range of issues relating to the conventional relative income line approach to the measurement of poverty. In this chapter, we proceed to consider how alternative approaches involving the direct measurement of lifestyle deprivation have developed largely in response to accumulating evidence that challenges the validity of income-based measures as sufficient indicators of broader command over resources. In so doing, we shall seek to shed some light on the validity of critiques of the income approach to poverty that have been associated with the emergence of the social exclusion perspective. In developing our thesis, we shall argue in favour of multidimensional and dynamic perspectives, in the sense of combining information on income and lifestyle deprivation and measuring such phenomena over time. However, we shall argue that this must be done within an appropriate conceptual framework and with sufficient attention being paid to measurement issues. In particular, we shall seek to draw attention to the fact that the degree of correlation between different forms of deprivation is often a great deal weaker than is imagined and shall stress the need to empirically establish, rather than assume, the scale and significance of multiple deprivation.

Viewed in a broad perspective, the notion of social exclusion is not an entirely new one. Thus Townsend (1979) in his seminal work considered poverty to involve *exclusion* through lack of *resources*. His emphasis on participation versus exclusion serves to make explicit the relative nature of the concept and has been widely adopted in recent discourse in developed countries. Falling below a relative income line is an indirect measure of exclusion from a minimum acceptable standard of living. The general rationale is that those falling more than a certain 'distance' below the average are excluded from the minimally acceptable way of life of the society in which they live because of a lack of resources. In relying on income poverty lines to make statements about poverty defined in this way, it is necessary to assume that those falling below the specified income poverty line are experiencing unacceptable levels of deprivation. The problem that must be confronted though is that, as has been recognised for some time by Ringen (1987, 1988), low income turns out to be a quite unreliable indicator of poverty in this sense, because it fails to identify households experiencing distinctive levels of deprivation. Various studies of different industrialised countries have indeed found a substantial proportion of those on low incomes not to be suffering from deprivation while some households above income poverty lines do experience such deprivation.[1] Even where a variety of deprivation dimensions are distinguished, and one focuses on those that might be expected to relate most closely to current income, major discrepancies between income and deprivation are still found (Muffels, 1993; Nolan and Whelan, 1996a, 1996b). Furthermore, as one goes from less stringent to more stringent definitions of income poverty, as in moving from 60 per cent of mean income to 40 per cent of mean income, there is no evidence that one is more successful in identifying progressively more deprived groups (Whelan et al., 2001).

In arguing the case for going beyond income, we recognise that many would continue to wish to reserve the term poverty for low income relative to a particular level of needs and view other forms of deprivation as, in large part, a consequence of such 'poverty'. From this perspective the main value of deprivation measures is to assist in calibrating income thresholds (Gordon et al., 2000). In principle, we have considerable sympathy with such an approach and the clear distinction between resources and outcomes that it involves. However, we continue to have reservations about the success of the method in practice. Nonetheless, as will become clear, we continue to attach marked significance to income measurement. Yet, in the absence of sufficient information on longer-term erosion and accumulation of resources, defining poverty solely in terms of income exposes us to the danger of failing to identify those groups most at risk of exclusion from customary life-standards and increases the likelihood that we may seriously misunderstand the processes that lead to such exclusion.

The social exclusion perspective offers a somewhat wider critique of the relative income approach than that associated with debates in the poverty literature. Some suspicion exists that the emergence of the term to centre stage may reflect the hostility of some governments to the language of poverty and the attraction of substituting a 'less accusing' expression (Berghman, 1995; Room, 1995). Nonetheless substantive claims have been made for the merits of conceptualising issues in terms of social exclusion rather than poverty, and it is worthwhile trying to tease out the issues and arguments. A number of authors associated with the London School of Economics' Centre for the Analysis of Social Exclusion have stressed five aspects of the notion – relativity, multidimensionality, agency, dynamics, and multi-layering (Atkinson, 1998; Hills, 1999). Kleinman (1998) concludes that the term is being employed to denote multiply deprived groups, trapped in cycles of fatalism, concentrated in the worst housing states and at risk of transmitting their fate across generations. As he observes, one consequence of this manner of defining social exclusion is that it defines the key social cleavage as between a comfortable majority and an excluded minority.

Much of the treatment of social exclusion overstates both the novelty of emphasising multiple disadvantage and the limitations of traditional poverty and social class analysis. If one seeks to evaluate the utility of the social exclusion perspective, it would seem necessary to avoid the caricature that sees poverty research as having adopted a static unidimensional perspective. As the previous chapter has shown, poverty research, driven by the availability of panel data, has led the way in highlighting income and poverty dynamics (Bane and Ellwood, 1994). Even in the absence of such data, many studies of poverty from the Joseph Rowntree Foundation onwards have taken the description of the poor as the starting point for an analysis of processes.

Attempts to grapple with the changing nature of social stratification have thus provoked increased reference to the emergence of forms of multiple disadvantage, which are qualitatively different from that formerly associated with working-class disadvantage or with exposure to income poverty. The shift from a unidimensional to a multidimensional perspective, from static to dynamic analyses and to an emphasis on social relations, has become a defining characteristic of the social exclusion perspective. Yet the volume of research documenting the nature and extent of multiple disadvantage has been rather modest and has focused largely on the effects of unemployment and employment precarity on social isolation (Paugam, 1996a, 1996b; Paugam and Russell, 2000).

In this chapter, by taking into account both income poverty and deprivation and their persistence over time, we shall seek to address issues relating, in particular, to multidimensionality, multiple deprivation and dynamics. In so doing, we shall argue that the development of a satisfactory framework requires that, while continuing to acknowledge the central importance of income, we must move beyond a focus on income poverty at a point in time to a much broader concern with the accumulation and erosion of resources over time.

In this chapter, we shall endeavour to present our evidence in as non-technical a fashion as possible. Our findings should therefore be taken as illustrative and we will refer readers to a number of sources where these issues have been dealt with more comprehensively. Our discussion will proceed broadly as follows. In the next section we will address the issue of multidimensional deprivation by identifying a number of distinct dimensions of deprivation and examining their relationship to income poverty. In the following section we will focus on the scale of, and risk of exposure to, multiple disadvantage in the sense of simultaneous experience of different forms of deprivation. A shift of perspective is then involved as we move from a consideration of a set of within-country relationships to an attempt to account for cross-national differences in levels of deprivation. In particular, we seek to develop an understanding of the role that welfare regimes play in accounting for such differences. Returning to a relative perspective, we then extend our analysis to take into account a temporal dimension for both income poverty and lifestyle deprivation. While our analyses up to this point involve straightforward comparisons of levels of deprivation within and between countries, it now becomes necessary to treat deprivation items differently in each country. This is because we want to construct deprivation thresholds in each country that correspond in conceptual terms to relative income poverty lines. Thus unless one wished to construct a deprivation threshold that corresponded to a European relative income line, it does not make sense to treat individual deprivation items as having equivalent significance or impact across countries. Having adopted an appropriate weighting procedure that addresses this issue, we then proceed to explore the relationship of persistent poverty to persistent deprivation and the way in which both types of disadvantage contribute to our understanding of the manner in which respondents experience their economic circumstances.

Multidimensional Deprivation

While, as Matasganis and Tsakloglou (2001) note, the popularity of the term 'social exclusion' is probably not unrelated to its vagueness, most recent attempts to clarify the concept involve reference to dynamics and multidimensionality (Atkinson, 1998; Hills, 1999; Sen, 2000). In following this lead we wish to distinguish between *cumulative disadvantage* and *multiple deprivation*. We will use the former term to refer to the dynamic process involved in the accumulation of disadvantages of social position over time. In the context of this chapter, such disadvantage will be represented by persistence of poverty or deprivation over a number of years and by variables that serve as proxies for longer-term command over resources such as experience of unemployment and social class.[2] In employing the latter term we wish to focus on multidimensionality at a point in time and the notion that social exclusion involves not just low income but simultaneous exposure to a range of deprivations.[3]

In attempting to address these issues on an empirical basis, we take advantage of the availability within the European Community Household Panel (ECHP) of information over time and across dimensions at each point in time. Whelan et al. (2001) identified 23 household items in the first wave conducted in 1994 that could serve as indicators of lifestyle deprivation. The format of the items varied but in each case they sought to produce measures that can be taken to represent enforced absence of widely desired items. One way to proceed would be to construct a summary index of deprivation employing all 23 items. However, a study based on Irish data suggests not only that distinct dimensions of deprivation exist but that these are differentially related to income (Nolan and Whelan, 1996a). The fact that relatively little attention has been paid to the manner in which items hang together, and whether it is appropriate to combine them in a single index, is unfortunate, because ignoring such dimensionality may lead to misleading conclusions regarding the determinants of deprivation. The first stage in an analysis of lifestyle deprivation is thus to examine systematically the range of deprivation items to see whether the items cluster into distinct groups.

A factor analysis conducted across the 12 countries included in the first wave of the ECHP identified five dimensions that were cross-nationally uniform. The dimensions identified were as follows:

- basic lifestyle deprivation – comprising items such as food and clothing, a holiday at least once a year, replacing worn-out furniture and the experience of arrears for scheduled payments;
- secondary lifestyle deprivation – comprising items that are less likely to be considered essential such as a car, a phone, a colour television, a video, a microwave and a dishwasher;
- housing facilities – housing services such as the availability of a bath or shower, an indoor flushing toilet and running waters likely to be seen as essential;
- housing deterioration – the existence of problems such as a leaking roof, dampness and rotting in window frames and floors; and
- environmental problems – problems relating to noise, pollution, vandalism and inadequate space and light.

These dimensions, and more particularly the basic and secondary dimensions, will be central to our analysis. However, we will also make use of indicators relating to specific elements of social exclusion relating to neighbourhood problems and social isolation.

In Figure 10.1 we address the question of the extent to which the persons in poverty are differentiated from others in terms of the deprivation dimensions. In order to do so for each dimension we take the simple, but fortunately effective indicator of the percentage lacking at least one item and calculate the percentage difference between those below 60 per cent of median income and all others. Thus for the basic dimension we find that the largest difference between those below 60 per cent of median income and all others is in France, the UK and the Netherlands, where over 40 per cent more of the former lack a basic item. Eight other countries are found in the range 25 to 38 per cent. The lowest differences are found in Portugal and Greece where of course the overall levels of deprivation are highest. Overall, the basic items prove to be remarkably consistent discriminators between those in and out of income poverty across the countries of the European Union (EU).

Figure 10.1   Difference between poor and non-poor in the percentage lacking at least one item in each deprivation dimension

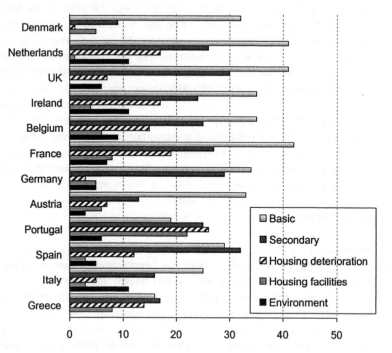

Note: Poverty line defined as 60 per cent of median income.
Source: ECHP (1996), adapted from Giorgi and Verma (2003).

When we turn to the secondary dimension we find that while these items also consistently discriminate between those in income poverty and those not, the extent of the observed difference is less in most cases and the magnitude of the difference is somewhat more variable. The largest difference of 32 per cent is observed for Spain followed by the UK with 30 per cent. We find a group of six countries comprising Germany, France, the Netherlands, Portugal, Ireland and Belgium, in the range 24 to 29 per cent. In Austria, Italy and Greece, the difference ranges between 13 and 17 per cent. Finally the items are least discriminatory in Denmark where the difference falls to 9 per cent. Although the secondary items are less powerful than the basic ones they do consistently discriminate between those in income poverty and those not.

The same is not true for the housing deterioration items. In Denmark, Germany and Italy the percentage difference between those in and out of income poverty does not exceed 5 per cent. In Austria and the UK the difference is less than 10 per cent and for five other countries the figure falls between 14 and 19 per cent. Only in Portugal does it exceed 20 per cent. For the facilities items the picture is clearer. Only in the case of Portugal do they prove to be effective discriminators. For the remaining countries the percentage difference does not exceed 8 per cent. The environmental items also fail to provide consistent discrimination. For the Netherlands, Ireland and Italy differences in the range of 11 per cent are observed. However, in Denmark and Greece the observed differences are actually negative, indicating that those not facing income poverty are actually more likely to experience such problems, although the differences are marginal. For the remaining countries the differences are positive but modest. Thus the basic and secondary items prove to be substantially more effective cross-national discriminators between respondents in income poverty and others than the housing and environmental items.

Multiple Deprivation

The process by which people come to be exposed to multiple deprivation and a progressive rupturing of social relations has been a central concern of the social exclusion literature. Berghman (1995) views social exclusion as involving a social process in which the creation and reinforcement of inequalities leads to a state of deprivation and hardship from which it is difficult to escape. Thus, Paugam (1996a) focuses on the process leading from precarity to social exclusion, or as Paugam (1996b) labels it the 'spiral of precariousness'. The need to move from a static definition of poverty based solely on income to a dynamic and multidimensional perspective was stressed. Kleinman (1998) notes that one consequence of employing the term 'social exclusion' to denote multiply deprived groups is that it defines the key social cleavage as between a comfortable majority and an excluded socially isolated minority. This tendency is also stressed in Room's (1999: 171) discussion of notions of continuity and catastrophe in the social exclusion literature.

Attempts to grapple with the changing nature of social stratification have thus provoked increased reference to the emergence of multiple disadvantage, which is qualitatively different from that formerly associated with working-class disadvantage or with the exposure to poverty. Yet, at the same time as the shift from a unidimensional to a multidimensional perspective, from static to dynamic analyses and to an emphasis on relations have become defining characteristics of the social exclusion perspective, the volume of research documenting the nature and extent of multiple disadvantage has been rather modest. Efforts have largely focused on the effects of unemployment and employment precarity on social isolation (Paugam, 1996a, 1996b; Paugam and Russell, 2000).

In view of this, it is regrettable that much of the treatment of social exclusion overstates both the novelty of emphasising multiple disadvantage and the limitations of traditional poverty analysis. In relation to the first issue, our earlier analysis has shown the danger of assuming, rather than establishing, multiple disadvantage by demonstrating that the relationship between income poverty and deprivation varies systematically across dimensions. Furthermore, as Heath (1981) stresses, if we wish to document the existence of multiple deprivation, we have to go beyond the degree of association between variables for the population as a whole and demonstrate the scale of overlap at the extremes. Significant inter-correlation among variables does not in itself guarantee that any substantial proportion of the population experiences multiple disadvantage. With regard to the second issue, it is necessary to point out that panel analysis of income data has led the way in highlighting poverty dynamics and persistence and in offering an opportunity to assess the consequences of sustained exposure to poverty (Duncan, 1984; Bane and Ellwood, 1986). The availability of such information in the ECHP data now offers the opportunity to connect questions of income poverty persistence to those relating to multiple, or overlapping, disadvantage and in turn, assess the extent to which notions of spirals of precariousness are useful or appropriate.

Thus, in the analysis that follows, we seek to establish the extent to which those persistently in income poverty in the sense of falling below 60 per cent of median income are exposed to multiple deprivation. Those who face income poverty over time constitute prime candidates for exposure to multiple disadvantage. In order to make our analysis as accessible as possible, we operate with very simple indicators of multiple deprivation. In Figure 10.2 we show the percentage of persons living in households exposed to persistent income poverty that are experiencing the enforced absence of an item on at least three of the five dimensions identified earlier. It should be stressed that this is an extremely minimalist definition of multiple deprivation. It does not, for example, require that respondents be found among the most deprived quartile or decile on any dimension. However, these simple indicators will serve our current purposes as long as it is kept in mind that more stringent definitions would lead us to observe significantly lower levels of multiple deprivation, particularly in the less affluent southern European countries.

Figure 10.2   Multiple deprivation by number of years in income poverty

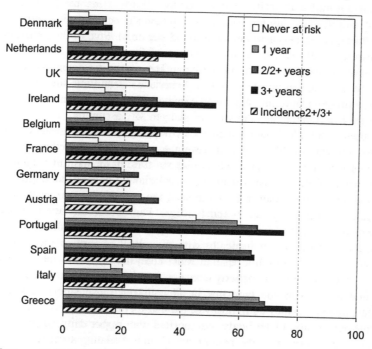

Notes: Multiple deprivation is defined as lacking an item in at least three out of five
dimensions of deprivation.
Poverty line defined as 60 per cent of median income.
Source: ECHP (1994–97), adapted from Giorgi and Verma (2003).

The results of this analysis show that, among those never in income poverty, multiple disadvantage is a rare phenomenon. Only in the less affluent countries does the relevant figure exceed one in six and only in Greece and Portugal is it close to one in two. In the latter countries, the pervasiveness of multiple deprivation is shown by the fact that 58 and 45 per cent respectively of those who are never in income poverty during the four-year period still experience enforced absence of an item on at least three of the dimensions. With a few minor exceptions, the experience of multiple disadvantage increases, the greater the experience of income poverty over time. Ireland provides a good example. For those who succeed entirely in avoiding income poverty, the rate of experiencing multiple disadvantage is 13 per cent. This figure rises to 19 per cent for those who were in income poverty in one year and to 31 per cent for those income poor on two occasions. Finally, for those who were in a state of poverty in at least three out of four years, it peaks at 51 per cent. Belgium illustrates a very similar trajectory, with the figure going from 8 to 13 to 23 per cent and finally to 46 per cent. Overall a majority of those facing persistent income poverty are multiply deprived in only four countries – Ireland (51 per cent), Spain (65 per cent), Portugal (75 per cent) and Greece (78 per cent). Five of the remaining countries, the Netherlands, Belgium, Italy, the UK and France, are found in the range running from 40 to 49 per cent. The remaining countries, where even those facing persistent poverty experience relatively low risks of multiple disadvantage, are Austria, Germany, Luxembourg and Denmark, which are found in the range running from 15 to 32 per cent.

Shifting from a risk to an incidence perspective, we can identify three clusters of countries. The first comprises those countries where those facing persistent income poverty make up around one-third of the multiply deprived. These include Belgium, the Netherlands and Ireland. For the second group of countries the figure is closer to one in four; these comprise France, the UK, Germany, Austria, Italy, Spain and Portugal. For Greece the figure falls to one in five, and for Denmark to one in twelve. Thus while the risk of multiple deprivation increases systematically with the extent of exposure to income poverty, it still remains true that in most countries the majority of those facing persistent income poverty are not multiply deprived. Even more emphatically we can conclude that in all countries those facing persistent income poverty constitute a minority of the multiply deprived.[4]

Thus, while persistent poverty is associated with higher deprivation across the range of dimensions, the magnitude of such differences varies sharply across the dimensions. Multiple but modest association does not translate into multiple overlapping disadvantages. Thus, although it is beyond the scope of this chapter to provide a comprehensive analysis of the determinants of each dimension, it is clear that rather different sorts of factors are involved in each case. Many who experience basic deprivation do not experience housing deprivation and *vice versa*. As a consequence, accounts of multiple disadvantage based on the assumption of high levels of correlation between different types of deprivation will be seriously misleading. Where correlations between types of deprivation are modest, the numbers exposed to multiple deprivation are inevitably a great deal less than those affected by any particular deprivation.

Figure 10.3   Percentage of persistently poor reporting crime or vandalism in their neighbourhood

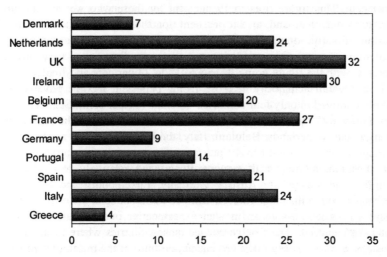

Note: Poverty line defined as 70 per cent of median income.
Source: ECHP (1994–97), adapted from Whelan (2002a).

Before proceeding further, we provide a couple of further illustrations of this point. A great deal of recent discussion of poverty and social exclusion has concentrated attention on the spatial concentration of disadvantage in areas or neighbourhoods and the manner in which isolation from mainstream values leads to behaviour and orientations which contribute to a vicious circle of deprivation.[5] The ECHP data show no systematic relationship between persistent poverty and the probability that one considers one's area to suffer from problems relating to vandalism and crime. Furthermore, as is clear from Figure 10.3, the vast majority of the persistently poor do not report such problems in their area. Given the weakness of the observed association, variation across countries in the extent to which the persistently poor experience vandalism and crime largely reflects cross-national variations in the overall level of the latter problems. Thus the persistently poor experience problems of vandalism or crime on a scale that reflects societal problems rather than any specific difficulties with persistent poverty as such. This, of course, does not preclude the existence of 'black spots' characterised by persistent poverty and chronic neighbourhood problems relating to crime and vandalism, but it does imply that only a rather small minority of the persistently poor will be found in such areas.

Whelan et al. (2001) also concluded that persistent poverty contributes little to indicators of social isolation. This observation is in line with Paugam and Russell (2000: 269) and Gallie et al. (2003) who conclude, on the basis of a consideration of the impact of unemployment and labour market precarity, that sociability in societies has its 'own distinctive dynamics with longer-term historical roots in very different paths of economic and cultural development'. This does not exclude the possibility that those exposed to persistent poverty may suffer disadvantage in the quality of their networks in relation to factors such as access to employment opportunities, although this should be established rather than assumed. However, our evidence does provide a warning against any type of general argument linking multiple disadvantage with social isolation and should make us wary of vicious-circle type arguments in which such isolation is a key mechanism.

Explaining Cross-national Differences in Deprivation[6]

Thus far we have concentrated on a comparison of the impact of persistent poverty within countries. In this section, taking as our starting point the finding that the relationship between income and lifestyle deprivation varied across countries, we seek to develop our understanding of the determinants of deprivation by attempting to explain variation in levels of such deprivation between EU countries. The measure of deprivation we employ combines the basic and secondary deprivation dimensions employed earlier. We refer to this measure as current lifestyle deprivation (CLSD). Whelan et al. (2001) show that the relationship between income and deprivation is subject to a great deal of cross-country variation. Thus the current lifestyle deprivation measure employed in this chapter is found to be weakly related to income in northern European countries such as Denmark, the Netherlands and Germany which are characterised by social-democratic or corporatist welfare regimes, moderately related in countries with liberal welfare regimes such as Ireland and the UK and strongly related in southern European countries with residualist welfare regimes. This pattern is clearly consistent with the hypothesis that different types of welfare state regimes involve different degrees of 'decommodification' and smooth income flows to differing degrees (Esping-Andersen, 1990; Gallie and Paugam, 2000). However, trying to test this hypothesis using either regime dummies or macro-level variables presents real difficulties because of the small number of countries available for comparison (Goldthorpe, 1997).

Recently Goodin et al. (1999) have sought to overcome some of these difficulties through an in-depth study of varying outcomes associated with membership of countries which typify three of the main types of welfare regimes. The approach we adopt here involves yet another strategy that takes advantage of the comparative database provided by the ECHP and in particular the first wave of that survey. It starts from a recognition that the impact of low income on deprivation depends on the length of time low income persists, the presence of other resources such as savings or assets, and the availability of monetary or non-cash transfers from family or social networks and the state. This emphasises the fact that resources are accumulated and eroded over time and this will not necessarily be captured by income measures. Households get to their present position by numerous paths and via different experiences. For example, we would expect that those who have experienced intermittent and insecure employment in the past, but are now employed, would have higher levels of deprivation than those who have had stable employment. Furthermore, we expect that critical life events such as divorce, separation or lone parenthood will distinguish in deprivation terms between those currently at similar levels of current income, because of what they imply about the relative balance between resources and obligations.

Viewed in this context, we hypothesise that variability in the relationship between income and deprivation across countries may reflect corresponding variability in the extent to which current income serves as a satisfactory indicator of command over resources. This is much more likely to be so in societies dominated by the cash nexus than in societies with developed welfare state arrangements, supportive social networks and employment relationships based on long-term commitment and trust rather than short-term contractual arrangements. This line of reasoning suggests that cross-national differences in deprivation may arise, not only from variation in levels of affluence, resulting from long-term trends in development, but from the extent to which potential disadvantage associated with factors such as class position are given free rein. The former will be captured, to some extent, by variation in the distribution between countries of different household and individual characteristics that are associated with disadvantage. Such variation will also be influenced by a variety of other factors such as type of welfare regime and long-term socio-demographic developments, the explanation of which will be primarily of a historical kind. Of greater sociological interest is the fact that such characteristics may also vary in their influence across different countries. Thus the extent to which a particular socio-economic status not only provides information about current demands or resources, but also serves as a proxy for longer-term imbalances between obligations and economic capacity, will be crucially influenced by the degree to which mechanisms are in place that buffer the cash nexus.

Our analysis involves an assessment of the extent to which country differences in levels of deprivation can be explained by corresponding variation in the distribution and impact of resource- and need-related factors and in their consequences. We attempt to substitute the names of variables for those of countries or indeed welfare regimes. Of course the results of any such analysis are then open to interpretation in terms of macro-typologies. However, an understanding of which specific variables contribute to an explanation of cross-country differences in deprivation would constitute a significant advance. We operate with two broad categories of variables tapping, respectively, needs and resources. The key resource variables on which we focus (apart from income) are employment status, social class and education. The crucial need factors (in addition to the needs adjustment implicit in the standard equivalence scale) are household type and marital status.

*Figure 10.4   Bivariate effects of particular disadvantages on current life-
            style deprivation, ECHP 1994 (regression coefficients)*

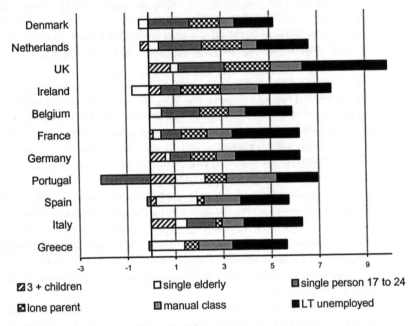

Notes: Coefficients are from an ordinary least squares regression equation, also controlling
            for equivalent income.
            Characteristics based on the household reference person.
Source: ECHP (1994), adapted from Layte et al. (2001).

The socio-demographic profiles of the countries included in our analysis differ in a largely predictable manner. People in southern countries are more likely to have low levels of educational qualification, or to be in manual work, farming or self-employment. On the other hand households in northern Europe are more likely to have a household reference person who is single, divorced or female. Other factors are more country-specific. Thus Ireland and Spain have high long-term unemployment rates and the former has a high number of households with three or more children.

Variation in such factors could account for some portion of cross-national differences in deprivation even if the impact of each factor was constant across countries. However, socio-demographic factors are likely to have greater explanatory power where there is evidence that their effect varies across countries. In Figure 10.4 we provide a straightforward analysis of the extent to which such variation exists. It must be remembered in interpreting these effects that we are not controlling for any characteristics other than those shown, and that the coefficients are deviations from the national mean.

- Starting first with the impact of being a single elderly person, the effects are basically at two levels with the southern European countries having considerably larger effects than the northern ones. In the case of Ireland and Denmark, the elderly are shown to experience less deprivation than the rest of the population.

- On the other hand if we look at the effect for being a young person living alone (aged 17 to 24) we find the opposite pattern with the southern European states, except Italy, having negative estimates. This may well be because it is rare in these countries for the young to live independently (see Chapters 2 and 3), thus those that do are usually fairly affluent. In the northern European states on the other hand, single young people have higher deprivation scores.

- Turning to the effect of being a lone parent, there is a substantial degree of variation across the countries, although this characteristic has a positive effect on deprivation across all countries. Lone parents face the least tariff in the southern European states followed by France, Germany, Denmark and the Benelux countries. The UK and Ireland stand apart as countries with a high level of deprivation associated with being a single parent.

- Having a larger number of children (3+) does tend to lead to higher levels of deprivation, but the effect is rather small when compared to the other variables, the largest being in Italy and the UK.

- The effect of the reference person being long-term unemployed is high and positive across all of the countries and underlines the impact of such a characteristic on living standards across the EU. Nonetheless there is variation with the effect being least in Denmark, Portugal and Belgium and greatest in the UK and Ireland.

- Finally, we come to the effect of the head of household being in the manual working class. Once again we see a north/south divide in this effect with the southern European countries having higher estimates, although this easy demarcation is complicated by the inclusion of the UK and Ireland among the high-effect countries. Portugal turns out to have by far the largest effect here, followed by Ireland and Spain. At the other end of the scale, being manual working class in Denmark exerts less than half the effect of being in the same position in the UK.

In order to allow an assessment of the impact of specific variables on cross-national differences in deprivation, in Figure 10.5 we show the variations between countries as one controls for needs, resources, resources plus needs, the variable impact of resources and needs across countries and finally income. The results show that cross-national differences cannot be accounted for by household structure. On the other hand, taking into account resource variables significantly reduces country differences and allowing for variable impact of long-term unemployment and manual class produces a further significant reduction. At this point the outstanding country differences are between the southern European countries and all others. Although both sets of factors contribute independently to our ability to predict deprivation, it is the resource factors that are crucial in explaining country effects. While this set of variables has effects that are substantial across countries, significant country interactions exist for long-term unemployment and manual class, which conform to our expectations from welfare-regime theory.

Figure 10.5   Country effects on current lifestyle deprivation

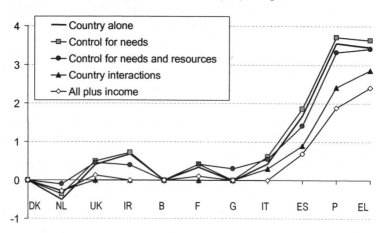

Note: Estimates controlling for other factors as well as those shown in legend.
Source: ECHP (1994–97), adapted from Layte et al. (2001).

Persistent Poverty and Persistent Deprivation[7]

Up to this point, our analysis of deprivation has deliberately been kept simple in that we have dealt with indices built on straightforward counts of such items. This approach has the value of being extremely transparent and at the same time both gives a concrete picture of what is involved in being multiply deprived and allows straightforward comparisons across countries. However, giving each of the lifestyle deprivation items an equal weight implies a rather different rationale to that involved in constructing relative income poverty lines. Effectively a common standard is being applied across countries, rather than a relative standard that takes the average level of living in the country in question into account. As a consequence, there will be much wider gaps between countries than will be the case with relative income poverty lines. If we sought to construct a deprivation measure corresponding to a relative income measure, we would not wish to assume that the enforced absence of a video recorder involved the same level of deprivation in each country. We would rather want to take into account societal norms. Furthermore, we would like to be able to locate each individual relative to the average level of deprivation in the society.

In order to fulfil these conditions we construct a weighted version of the CLSD measure in which the lack of each individual item is weighted by the proportion of households possessing that item in each country. As a consequence, inability to afford an item such as a video recorder will be counted as a more substantial deprivation in Denmark than in Greece. The weighted CLSD measure makes it possible to identify for each country a deprivation threshold above which the proportion of respondents matches as closely as possible that found below a specified income line. This allows, in principle, for the mismatch between poverty defined in income and deprivation terms to vary from 0 to one 100 per cent.

We can see from Figure 10.6 that our ability to predict being above the threshold is substantially improved by taking the persistence of income poverty into account. For all countries, there is a clear increase in the percentage deprived as exposure to income poverty increases. In Italy, for example, the percentage above the deprivation threshold rises from 10 per cent for those who entirely avoid income poverty, to 19 per cent for those poor on one occasion, to 27 per cent for those poor on two occasions, and to 52 per cent for those poor in at least three out of four years. Similarly, in the UK the figure rises from 8 per cent for those avoiding income poverty, to 27 per cent for those poor in one year and to 45 per cent for those poor in two out of three years. Overall, among those never falling below the income poverty line, the percentage above the deprivation threshold is equal to or exceeds 10 per cent in only five countries and reaches a maximum of 13 per cent in Greece. Among those poor on one occasion, a minimum of one in ten are above the threshold in seven of the 12 countries and the maximum value is 32 per cent (in Portugal). For those in income poverty on two out of four occasions the relevant figure exceeds 30 per cent in seven of the nine countries, with the maximum value in Spain (51 per cent). Among those persistently poor the percentage who are deprived falls below 40 per cent in only three countries, and in nine countries a minimum of approximately half of individuals are above the threshold. There is a clear and systematic relationship between the degree of persistence of income poverty and relative lifestyle deprivation.

Figure 10.6   Percentage of people above deprivation threshold, by number of years in poverty

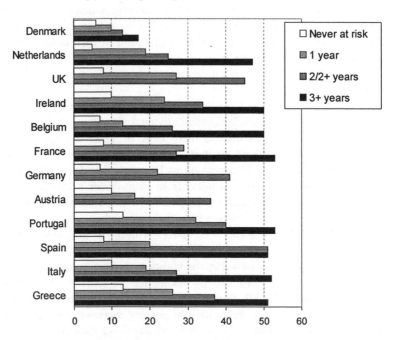

Note: Poverty line defined as 60 per cent of median income.
Source: ECHP (1994–97), adapted from Giorgi and Verma (2003).

The analysis reported above shows that persistent poverty measures do bear a significantly closer relationship to deprivation than their cross-sectional alternatives and come much closer to displaying the properties we require of a poverty measure. However, to date most of the concern with issues of dynamics has focused on income poverty and very little on measures of deprivation. This may to some extent be due to an implicit assumption that deprivation is more stable than low income. In what follows, we extend our analysis of income-deprivation consistency to take into account the relationship between *persistent* income poverty and *persistent* deprivation. As in the case of income poverty, once again persistence has been defined as fulfilling the appropriate condition in three out of the four years, including the last year as a necessary constraint. However, in Germany, the UK and Austria, data availability requires that this condition be amended to meet the criteria in two out of three years.

Contrary to expectations, analysis of the ECHP shows that over a four-year period, movement into and out of the higher ranges of the deprivation continuum was just as frequent as movement above and below the 60 per cent median income poverty line. Furthermore, while there is a clear and systematic relationship between persistent poverty and persistent deprivation, the degree of overlap is far from perfect.

If we examine cross-national variation in the percentage of those below the 60 per cent income line who are also found above the corresponding deprivation threshold, we find that Denmark once again represents a complete outlier with only 5 per cent of those who are persistently in income poverty being persistently above the deprivation threshold. Apart from Denmark, the level of consistency varies from 22 per cent in Austria to 44 per cent in the UK. Eight of the twelve countries are found in the range running from 30 to 40 per cent. This pattern is very similar to that observed at the cross-sectional level. Thus, while knowledge of the extent and persistence of income poverty helps to predict point-in-time deprivation, switching to persistent measures for income and deprivation does not increase the degree of consistency observed. Clearly factors other than persistent income poverty are important in determining persistent deprivation. It is to these factors that we now turn our attention.

Multivariate analysis shows that persistent income poverty has a substantial effect on exposure to persistent deprivation even when we control for a range of socio-demographic influences. However, it is equally true that both resource and need factors are predictive of persistent deprivation, even when we control for persistent income poverty. This is particularly true of the resource variables. Poor education, working-class status and labour market disadvantage all serve as important paths to persistent disadvantage even where persistent income poverty is not a significant mediating factor. The same is true of 'need' type variables, although the effects are more modest and are more clearly apparent in northern European countries. It is clear from the results that the modest overlap between both types of disadvantage should not be confused with a weak structuring of persistent deprivation.

Figure 10.7   Extent of economic strain by persistent deprivation among those persistently poor

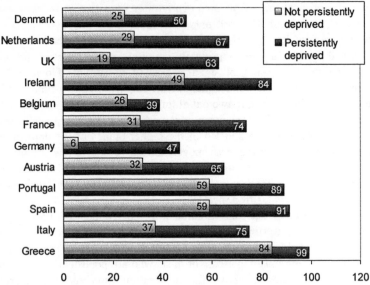

Source: ECHP (1994–97), adapted from Giorgi and Verma (2003).

The question remains as to why we should pay particular attention to persistent deprivation over and above its relationship to persistent income poverty. In order to answer this question, we proceed to examine the relationship of both types of persistence to perceptions of economic strain. Our indicator of economic strain relates to whether the respondent's household was reported to be experiencing difficulty in 'making ends meet'. Given our interest in the consequences of the extremes of income poverty and deprivation, we distinguish between those experiencing extreme difficulty and all others. Economic strain is measured on the basis of the information given in the third wave of the ECHP relating to the situation in 1996. In all countries, rates of economic strain are higher among the persistently deprived than among those persistently in income poverty, in many cases substantially so. An extreme example of this is Denmark, where about one in four of those in income poverty are in households experiencing economic strain, compared to three out of four in deprived households. The respective figures for the Netherlands are 39 and 68 per cent, for the UK 39 and 67 per cent, and for Ireland 61 and 75 per cent. These differences are substantially less pronounced in the southern European countries. As a consequence, if we leave these countries aside, the level of economic strain among those persistently in income poverty ranges from 22 per cent in Germany to 61 per cent in Ireland whereas among the persistently deprived it runs from 37 per cent in Germany to 75 per cent in Ireland. In 11 of the 12 countries more than half of the persistently deprived households are experiencing economic strain compared to less than half in the case of persistent income poverty.

Further proof of the independent impact of persistent deprivation is provided in Figure 10.7, which focuses on the subset of persons that are persistently poor. In every case, those who are persistently deprived experience a great deal more economic strain. Thus in the case of Ireland, the respective percentages are 49 and 74 per cent, in the UK 19 and 63 per cent, in Belgium 26 and 39 per cent and in Italy 37 and 75 per cent. If we exclude the extreme values for the less affluent southern European countries, for those persistently in income poverty but not persistently deprived, the range of economic strain runs from 6 per cent in Germany to 49 per cent in Ireland. For those who experience both forms of persistence problems, the range runs from 47 per cent in Germany to 84 per cent in Ireland. In 10 of the 12 countries more than one in two of such respondents resides in households experiencing economic strain.

Conclusions

The social exclusion perspective has focused attention on the processes leading to exposure to multiple disadvantage and social isolation. Despite the influence the perspective has had on both academic and policy discussions, conceptual analysis has remained imprecise, and empirical evidence modest. Furthermore long-standing methodological issues relating to the analysis of multiple disadvantage have largely been ignored.

Advocates of the social exclusion perspective have frequently criticised poverty analysis for being static and unidimensional. However, these are by no means necessary features of poverty analysis and in this chapter we have made use of the ECHP in order to examine the extent to which persistent income poverty results in multiple deprivation and social isolation. The persistently poor individuals clearly constitute prime candidates for exposure to multiple disadvantage and a spiral of precariousness. However, our analysis showed that even in the case of lifestyle deprivation, where we might expect relationships to be most straightforward, the observed pattern does not conform to one of systematic multiple disadvantage. This is perhaps most vividly illustrated by the fact that, in general, the persistently poor are not a great deal more likely than others to consider that they live in areas affected by vandalism or crime, and the vast majority of the poor do not live in such areas. Thus, even by applying a somewhat more restricted definition of multiple deprivation than that which features in the social exclusion literature, only a rather modest proportion of the persistently poor fulfil the requirements. Furthermore, we find no evidence that such deprivation has distinctive consequences for the persistently poor.

When we focus on social isolation we are led to similar conclusions. It appears to be influenced a good deal more by cross-national cultural variations than by persistent income poverty. Pictures of those exposed to continuous poverty as socially isolated appear to be seriously misleading. This does not exclude the possibility that they suffer additional disadvantages related to the quality of their social networks but this is rather different from social isolation or a rupturing of social networks. These findings may seem less surprising when we note the recent observation by Portes (2000: 5) that the problem in poor inner city areas in the USA 'is not that people do not know each other or help each other, but the resources to do so are so meagre and the social ties so insulated as to yield meagre returns'.

Persistent poverty is systematically related to a number of dimensions of deprivation, although this varies across dimensions. By moving beyond current income we are able to make significant progress in resolving some of the issues associated with the fact that the relationship between current income and deprivation often appears to be remarkably low. However, the fact that persistent poverty exerts multiple influences does not necessarily result in extremes of multiple disadvantage on any substantial scale. The relationships we observe are probabilistic and, as is true in the social sciences as a whole, even what we consider to be strong relationships often involve modest levels of correlation. It is clear that a great many factors, other than persistent income poverty, play a role in determining deprivation, and that these factors will vary across dimensions. Furthermore, movement in and out of deprivation appears to be no less frequent than movement in and out of income poverty and persistent deprivation exerts a substantial independent effect on experience of economic strain.

Understanding deprivation cannot simply involve a focus on a cleavage between a multiply deprived and excluded minority and a comfortable majority. A more accurate picture is likely to be that painted by Heath (1981: 128) who sees 'deprivation as a vicissitude (sometimes transitory), which strikes broadly and unpredictably across the working class (and indeed white collar groups) in response to the vagaries of economic and social policy and life circumstances'. A focus on multiple deprivation directs attention to the manner in which 'problem' groups emerge, the evolution of alternative value systems and the spatial concentration of poverty. In that context the big expensive policies relating to the disadvantages experienced by broad class and status groups – education and employment policies, taxation and welfare transfers – come to receive less attention.

Notes

1. These include Townsend (1979), Mack and Lansley (1985) and Gordon et al. (1995) with British data, Mayer and Jencks (1988) for the USA, Callan et al. (1993) and Nolan and Whelan (1996a, 1996b) with Irish data, (Muffels, 1993) with Dutch data, Hallerod (1996) for Sweden and Kangas and Ritakallio (1998) for Finland. For a comparative discussion see Andreß (1998).
2. For an approach that focuses more specifcally on longer-term accumulation of disadvantages, see Layte and Whelan (2002).
3. As will be apparent from an examination of the range of analyses included in our previous publications to which we have referred, our conclusions relating to income-deprivation relationships are not dependent on the particular poverty line chosen.
4. For further discussion, see Whelan et al. (2002a).
5. For recent discussions of this literature see Friedrichs (1998), Glennerster et al. (1999), Kleinman (1998) and Nolan and Whelan (2000).
6. A more comprehensive treatment of these issues is provided in Layte et al. (2001).
7. The discussion in this section draws on Whelan et al. (2002b, 2003). The findings presented have been reported previously in Chapter 7 of Giorgi and Verma (forthcoming).

References

Andreß, H.J. (1998), 'Empirical poverty research in a comparative perspective', in H.J. Andreß (ed.), *Empirical Poverty Research in Comparative Perspective*, Aldershot: Ashgate.

Atkinson, A.B. (1998), 'Social exclusion, poverty and unemployment,' in A.B. Atkinson and J. Hills (eds), *Exclusion, Employment and Opportunity*, London: London School of Economics.

Bane M. J. and D. T. Ellwood (1986), 'Slipping in and out of poverty: the dynamics of poverty spells', *The Journal of Human Resources*, **12**, 1–23.

Bane, M.J. and D.T. Ellwood (1994), *Welfare Realities: from Rhetoric to Reform*, Cambridge, MA: Harvard University Press.

Berghman, J. (1995), 'Social exclusion in Europe: policy context and analytical framework,' in G.J. Room (ed.), *Beyond the Threshold*, Bristol: Policy Press.

Callan, T., B. Nolan and C.T. Whelan (1993), 'Resources, deprivation and the measurement of poverty', *Journal of Social Policy*, **22** (2), 141–72.

Duncan, G. (1984), *Years of Poverty, Years of Plenty*, Ann Arbor, MI: Institute for Social Research, University of Michigan.

Esping-Andersen, G. (1990), *The Three Worlds of Welfare Capitalism*, Cambridge: Polity Press.

Friedrichs, J. (1998), 'Do poor neighbourhoods make their residents poorer? Context effects of poverty neighbourhoods on residents', in H.J. Andreß (ed.), *Empirical Poverty Research in Comparative Perspective*, Aldershot: Ashgate, pp. 77–100.

Gallie, D. and S. Paugam (2000), 'The experience on unemployment in Europe: the debate', in D. Gallie and S. Paugam (eds), *Welfare Regimes and the Experience of Unemployment in Europe*, Oxford: Oxford University Press.

Gallie, D., S. Paugam and S. Jacobs (2003), 'Unemployment, poverty and social isolation: is there a vicious circle of social exclusion?', *European Societies*, **5** (1), 1–31.

Giorgi, L. and V. Verma (2003) *Income, Poverty Risk and Social Exclusion in the European Union – Second European Social Report*, Report compiled in the framework of the contract No. 200036300002 Lot 3 for EUROSTAT.

Glennerster, H., R. Lipton, P. Noden and A. Power (1999), *Poverty, Social Exclusion and Neighbourhood: Studying the Area Bases of Social Exclusion*, CASEpaper 22, London School of Economics.

Goldthorpe, J.H. (1997), 'Current issues on comparative research', *Comparative Social Research*, **16**, 1–26.

Goodin, R.E., B. Headey, R. Muffels and H.J. Dirven (1999), *The Real Worlds of Welfare Capitalism*, Cambridge: Cambridge University Press.

Gordon, D., C. Pantazis, P. Townsend, G. Bramley, J. Bradshaw, H. Holmes and B. Halleröd (1995), *Breadline Britain in the 1990s: A Report to the Joseph Rowntree Foundation*, Bristol, Department of Social Policy and Planning: University of Bristol.

Gordon, D., A. Adelmann, K. Ashworth, J. Bradshaw, R. Levitas, S. Middleton, C. Pantazis, D. Payne, P. Townsend and J. Williams (2000), *Poverty and Social Exclusion in Britain*, York: Joseph Rowntree Foundation.

Hallerod, B. (1996), 'The truly poor: direct and indirect measurement of consensual poverty in Sweden', *Journal of European Social Policy*, **5** (2), 111–29.

Heath, A. (1981), *Social Mobility*, London: Fontana.

Hills, J. (1999), 'Social exclusion, income dynamics and public policy', Annual Sir Charles Carter Lecture, Belfast: Northern Ireland Economic Development Office.

Kangas, O. and V.-M. Ritakallio (1998), 'Different methods – different results? Approaches to multidimensional poverty', in H.J Andreß (ed.), *Empirical Poverty Research in Comparative Perspective*, Aldershot: Ashgate.

Kleinman, M. (1998), *Include Me Out? The New Politics of Place and Poverty*, CASEpaper 11, London School of Economics.

*Layte, R., B. Maître, B. Nolan and C.T. Whelan (2001), 'Explaining deprivation in the European Union', *Acta Sociologica*, **44** (2), 105–22 (*EPAG Working Papers*, **12**).

*Layte, R. and C.T. Whelan (2002), 'Cumulative disadvantage or individualisation? A comparative analysis of poverty risk and incidence', *European Societies*, **4** (2), 209–33 (*EPAG Working Papers*, **21**).

Mack, J. and S. Lansley (1985), *Poor Britain*, London: George Allen and Unwin.

Matsaganis, M and P. Tsakoglou, (2001), 'Social exclusion and social policy in Greece', in D. Mayes, J. Berhgman and Salais Roberts (eds), *Social Policy and European Policy*, Cheltenham, UK and Northampton, MA, USA: Edward Elgar.

Mayer, S. and C. Jencks (1988), 'Poverty and the distribution of material hardship', *Journal of Human Resources*, **24** (1), 88–114.

Muffels, R. (1993), 'Deprivation standards and style of living indices', in J. Berghman and B. Cantillon (eds), *The European Face of Social Security*, Aldershot: Avebury.

Nolan, B. and C.T. Whelan (1996a), *Resources, Deprivation and Poverty*, Oxford: Clarendon Press.

Nolan, B. and C.T. Whelan (1996b), 'Measuring poverty using income and deprivation indicators: alternative approaches', *Journal of European Social Policy*, **6** (3), 225–40.

Nolan, B. and C. Whelan (2000), 'Urban housing and the role of "underclass" processes: the case of Ireland', *Journal of European Social Policy*, **10** (1), 5–21.

Paugam, S. (1996a), 'La constitution d'un paradigme', in S. Paugam (ed.), *L'Exclusion: L'État des Savoirs*, Paris: Editions La Decouverte.

Paugam, S. (1996b), 'The spiral of precariousness: a multidimensional approach to the process of social disqualification in France', in G. Room (ed.), *Beyond the Threshold: The Measurement and Analysis of Social Exclusion*, Bath: Policy Press.

Paugam, S. and H. Russell (2000), 'The effects of employment precarity and unemployment on social isolation', in D. Gallie and S. Paugam (eds), *Welfare Regimes and Unemployment in Europe*, Oxford: Oxford University Press.

Portes, A. (2000), 'The hidden abode: sociology as analysis of the unexpected', *American Sociological Review*, **65**, 1–18.

Ringen, S. (1987), *The Possibility of Politics*, Oxford: Clarendon Press.

Ringen, S. (1988), 'Direct and indirect measures of poverty', *Journal of Social Policy*, **17**, 351–66.

Room, G. (1995), 'Poverty and social exclusion: the new European agenda for policy and research', in G. Room (ed.), *Beyond the Threshold*, Bristol: Policy Press.

Room, G. (ed.) (1999), 'Social exclusion, solidarity and the challenge of globalisation', *International Journal of Social Welfare*, **8** (3), 166–74.

Sen, A. (2000), *Social Exclusion: Concept, Application and Scrutiny*, Manila: Asian Development Bank.

Townsend, P. (1979), *Poverty in the United Kingdom*, Harmondsworth: Penguin.

*Whelan, C.T., R. Layte and B. Maître (2002a), 'Multiple deprivation and persistent poverty in the European Union', *Journal of European Social Policy*, **12** (2), 91–105 (revised version of *EPAG Working Papers*, **19**).

*Whelan, C.T., R. Layte and B. Maître (2002b), 'Persistent deprivation in the European Union', *Schmollers Jahrbuch (Journal of Applied Social Science Studies)*, **122**, 31–54, (*EPAG Working Papers*, **23**).

*Whelan, C.T., R. Layte, B. Maître and B. Nolan (2001), 'Income, deprivation and economic strain: an analysis of the European Community Household Panel', *European Sociological Review*, **17** (4), 357–72.

*Whelan, C.T., R. Layte, B. Maître and B. Nolan (2003), 'Persistent income poverty and deprivation in the European Union: an analysis of the first three waves of the European Community Household Panel', *Journal of Social Policy*, **32** (1), 1–32 (*EPAG Working Papers*, **17**).

* Direct output from EPAG's *DynSoc* research programme (see page 268)

11. Conclusion: Micro-dynamics and Public Regulation

Jonathan Gershuny

(with contributions from Richard Berthoud, Maria Iacovou and Antonio Schizzerotto)

This book is a study of comparative social 'micro'-dynamics. By this, we mean the processes by which individuals move between key social positions, especially in the 'domains' of family, employment and income. There is a recursive process of acquisition or accumulation of individual characteristics in various life domains through the life-course. What has happened to us so far, changes us, and influences what happens to us next. Individual trajectories are affected by previous circumstances, but similar prior individual circumstances can have different consequences in different environments. It is these environments which provide the 'macro' influences on people's behaviour. Policy 'regimes' are, in the most general sense, sets of public regulations and provisions by the political authorities of the state. The comparative study of regimes, as we have been engaged with it in this book, concerns the differences that particular sets of provisions and regulations make to these relations between individual-level causes and consequences.

Consider the everyday story told by Figure 11.1, which relates the family, employment and income experiences of a couple as they form, and then perhaps dissolve, a union. The man starts with a good job and a high income, and the woman, also with a good job, enjoys perhaps not so high an income. They meet and become partners. Combining their previous incomes and sharing household expenses, they both enjoy prosperity. Then she falls pregnant, and, in accordance with convention, quits her job to care for the child full-time. Their joint income falls. Then he leaves the marriage and returns to his previous high-income status. She keeps the child, and with neither a job nor recent work experience, she and the child fall into poverty.

Most of the links in this sequence of events can be identified among the research findings reported in previous chapters. The sequence is of course strongly influenced by conditions and processes well beyond the couple's individual lives. General economic conditions, social norms and expectations,

Figure 11.1   *Illustration of the family, employment and income experiences of a couple over time*

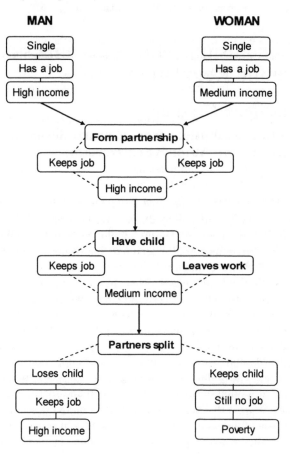

all make their contributions. But of particular importance are various actions or inactions of the state. Consider the wife's decision to leave work when her baby was born. If, as in some EU countries, there had been a battery of policies to encourage mothers to remain in the labour market (including, perhaps, paid parental leave in the early months after childbirth, free high-quality childcare and appropriate tax and benefit provisions), then the couple would not have had to make a decision about who would leave the labour force. The woman could have kept her job. If the husband then quit the partnership, she would still have a moderately well-paid job and the child would not have been brought up in poverty. And of course there are other lines of consequentiality on which we might speculate. Would he have left his partner had she remained in employment? A different regime context might have led perhaps to the persistence of the partnership and more children in due course – or alternatively to the woman running off with one of *her* colleagues.

We are, of course, not in the business of speculating on these sorts of counterfactuals in individual cases. But when we find differences in the aggregate outcomes of these sorts of micro-dynamics in different countries, the explanation must to some degree reflect such differences in the effects of particular national regimes.

Figure 11.2 repeats part of the analytical framework outlined in Chapter 1, showing the links and interactions between family structure, employment and income – the 'FEI nexus'. As before, the figure illustrates the 'macro'-environmental factors – institutions and policies, social norms and economic conditions – which influence the 'micro'-behavioural decisions made by individual men and women. Since a particular concern of this book is to understand the effects of the activities of the state, whether acting as regulator, or as a provider, the emphasis in this version of the model is on the influences that the state's institutions and policies exert on all the other sectors of the nexus.

The figure illustrates the existence of five types of direct effect of state activity. Arrow 1 indicates the effect of national policy on the level of economic activity through fiscal regulations and monetary management. Arrow 2 indicates its effect on the family (such as the legal arrangements surrounding marriage and divorce). Arrow 3 represents the effect of the state on employment and earnings through regulations concerning working conditions, job security and minimum wages. Arrow 4 shows the effect of the state on the distribution of income through taxes and social security benefits. And in principle quite distinct is the direct effect on living standards indicated by arrow 5, where the individual spending choices of private households are supplemented by the direct provision of free or subsidised cultural, educational, medical and other services by the state.

Our empirical analysis has focused in the first instance on the 'micro'-dynamic elements of the model – studying the processes affecting individual family, employment and income events within and between countries. It is the 'macro' comparison between countries that provides the base for policy interpretation. We have not studied the policies themselves. Nor can we directly distinguish the effects of specific public policies in different countries, since these policy differences coincide with differences in other national cultural and historical characteristics. But nevertheless we can make some progress in the direction of suggesting which lines of public policy intervention are associated with which sorts of outcomes in individuals' life-courses.

Figure 11.2   Influences of public policy on the family-employment-income nexus

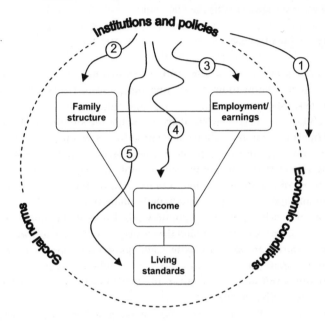

Themes from the Research Programme

The most general finding is, simply, variety. The underlying social and economic processes affecting the life-course may be broadly in common across the European Union (EU) (compared with societies in other continents and/or in other centuries), but we nevertheless find major national differences in outcomes.

Many of these differences can be summarised in terms of the political, geographical or cultural characteristics of countries, though there are almost always exceptions to the rules. This section reviews some of our key results in relation to the each of the three main life-course domains, and concludes with a review of the evidence on the role of 'welfare regime' as an explanatory factor.

Family dynamics

The analysis of household structure and family status offers a strong and simple hybrid typology of countries (Chapter 2). It consists of three groups rather than the four discussed in Chapter 1 – and indeed may be viewed as something of a continuum from north to south. The observed groupings are as follows:

- a 'Nordic' grouping, consisting of Scandinavia and the Netherlands;
- a 'northern/Protestant' grouping consisting of the continental European corporatist regimes, plus the UK; and
- a 'southern/Catholic' grouping consisting of the 'residual' welfare regimes plus Ireland.

Household size increases substantially from north to south. There are similar dramatic contrasts in age of first independent household formation, with, for example, young men first leaving home in Nordic countries on average about five years earlier than in southern/Catholic countries. First childbirth occurs relatively soon after partnering in southern countries, with timings more widely separated in the northern groups. And symmetrically, at the opposite end of the age range, older people are more likely to be living alone in northern countries, less likely to do so in southern, while those in the south are much more likely to live with their children.

We conclude that a mixture of cultural and economic factors explains the differences. So, for example, we find that young people from well-off families in Nordic countries are *more* likely to leave home than poorer young people, indicating a preference for 'family privacy', while similarly placed young people in southern/Catholic countries are *less* likely to do so, indicating a preference for family 'togetherness'.

In other cases, we are able to attribute national differences to interactions between culture and regulatory provisions. Thus, in northern/Protestant countries, giving birth as a teenager has substantial and negative effects on a woman's subsequent access to the labour market, but the effect is much weaker in both the Nordic and the southern/Catholic groupings. This may be attributable to the combined consequences of strong employment protection together with provisions for working parents in Nordic countries, and women's more frequent withdrawal from the labour market in southern/Catholic countries. This in part reflects the balance between 'informal' family-based provisions and the availability of state-provided services. Grandparents (particularly grandmothers) in southern/Catholic countries are much more likely to provide coresident childcare services than their Nordic counterparts. And the same gradients apply to elderly parents themselves receiving coresident care from their children.

Chapter 3 looks in more detail at the timing and, more particularly, the sequence of events in early adulthood: the ending of full-time education, finding a full-time job, establishing a stable cohabiting union, and becoming a parent. The median age of attainment of highest school qualifications has risen consistently for successive birth cohorts through the 20th century in every country.

Observed inter-country differences approximately fit the hybrid three-category profile, with these events happening later in the north and earlier in the south. Absolute differences between the country groups have declined as the southern group has increased its level of tertiary educational provision rather faster than the northern groups. The southern group also shows a distinctively extended transition from the end of full-time education to the start of the first job, which may be explained by high levels of unemployment in these countries, and the relatively non-vocational structures of their educational systems. Thus, Spain, Italy and Greece, in particular, with earlier median ages of the end of school education, also have the latest median age of job-start. The extended length of the school-to-work transition may also go some way to explain the strikingly higher levels of heterogeneity in career sequences at particular ages in Spain and Italy, as compared to the UK, Germany, France and Denmark.

The traditional life-course sequence from formal educational qualification to job to marriage to childbirth seems to be maintained throughout the EU. The median age of first marriage in all countries and in each birth cohort is higher than that of first job. And, in turn, in each country, despite the continuing moves away from traditional family patterns, the median age of first childbirth is everywhere later than that of first marriage.

Employment dynamics

Chapter 4 turns from the consideration of family patterns in themselves to the effects of family life on employment. There are clear and familiar individual-level regularities independent of country: adult men below retirement age are generally attached to the labour market irrespective of their family status, as are single women, whereas women in formal marriages, and particularly those coresiding with their own children, are less likely to be so. But beyond these, we immediately discover a substantial national variation.

Only a relatively small part of this variation appears to be related to the welfare-regime typology set out in the introductory chapter. Among the Scandinavian countries, for example, a majority of couples with young children both have full-time jobs – but they share this characteristic with Belgium (normally placed within the corporatist group) and Portugal (classified as a southern European residual regime). To choose another example, Ireland shows a pattern of women's withdrawal from employment associated with care-giving responsibilities that is more characteristic of the residual regime than of the liberal group in which it is usually placed.

For mothers, it appears that, rather than the general regime type, it is one particular field of state provision that is most strongly associated with the relationship between family status and employment: the level of provision of childcare. Simply and unsurprisingly, the higher the level of public provision of daycare for young children, the less the reduction in women's working hours after childbirth.

Chapter 5 focuses on non-standard employment, which again is clearly an issue where gender is important: nearly two-thirds of non-standard work across Europe is done by women. Here, a subset of five countries (Denmark, the UK, the Netherlands, Germany and Portugal) are used as representatives of the different regime types. We see clearly that varying welfare state settings may result in different outcomes in terms of women's labour market participation – but also that very different welfare state settings may result in very similar outcomes, for different reasons.

In social-democratic Denmark, institutions encourage a high degree of equality for men and women in the labour market. In the liberal UK and the social-democratic/corporatist Netherlands, institutions show some features of modernisation, but their performance in terms of gender equality is less successful than that of Denmark. Institutions in corporatist Germany display a much lesser degree of modernisation, and support the continuation of a male-breadwinner regime. In all these countries, female labour market participation appears to be linked to the institutional framework, and to some extent mirrors the aims of different welfare state regimes. However, Portugal is an exception. Although institutions in Portugal show some features of 'catching-up' modernisation, this process is well behind those of the other countries considered. However, Portuguese women participate in the labour market at similar levels to Danish women. To explain this, one must look beyond the welfare state setting, to explanations such as low wage levels and the availability of relatives to look after children.

Chapters 6 and 7, dealing with employment and unemployment respectively, show that there is a marked degree of commonality between European countries, as well as differences between countries and regime types. Similarities are represented, first, by the low outflow rates, measured over a three-year period, from the states of employment, self-employment, retirement and out of the labour force. Throughout the EU, the proportions leaving their respective states were very low during the three-year observation window (Chapter 6).

A second homogeneous feature of EU labour markets is made up by the remarkable proportion of individuals who remained permanently employed between 1993 and 1995 (Chapter 6). Across all groups of countries, immobility in this state varies with age, being much higher among adult workers (those aged 25–49) than among their younger and older counterparts.

Education is a further individual attribute that exerts quite homogeneous effects on labour market mobility across EU countries. Everywhere, highly qualified people enjoy a greater opportunity of being permanently employed and lower risks of unemployment compared to poorly educated individuals. However, the labour markets of EU countries are also characterised by remarkable differences in their functioning.

Chapter 6 demonstrates that, despite its shortcomings for the analysis of family/employment patterns, the standard regime typology still works reasonably well for the analysis of many of these differences. In particular, the proportion of people escaping from 'exclusion' – defined as being out of work over a 12-month period – is higher in the residual regimes. The social-democratic regimes have the lowest rates of 'downward mobility' into full labour market exclusion. But this is bought, in part, at the cost of lower rates of upward mobility into the fully employed category: liberal regimes have the highest rates of this sort of upward mobility, followed closely by the corporatist, then by the social-democratic, and then at some distance by the residual state regimes.

In Chapter 7, which deals with unemployment and job search, differences between welfare regimes are found in terms of general levels of unemployment, with the social-democratic and liberal regimes having lower levels of unemployment than the corporatist and particularly the residual regimes. However, there are outliers within most regime types, and apart from measures of the incidence of unemployment, there are few marked patterns which suggest that welfare-regime typology is useful in this area.

Precise definitions of unemployment were found to be important in nearly all countries, with significant differences between a definition based on self-reported status, and one based on standardised criteria. Among those who fail to qualify as unemployed on formal criteria, there are also important differences between those who may be defined as outside the labour market, and those who retain some attachment to the labour market – a 'hidden labour force'. However, these differences appear to be common across (nearly) all countries, with no systematic welfare-regime effects.

The same is true when the factors associated with job search are considered. The proportion of people searching for a new job varies widely between countries, but no patterns are observable between welfare regimes for any group of people – the unemployed, the securely employed, or those on temporary contracts. Among the unemployed, people who are more optimistic about finding a job are more likely to search for one. Among the employed, those on temporary contracts, and those who feel their current income is insufficient, are more likely to be engaged in job search. Again, these findings are common to many countries across all welfare regimes.

As far as job search is concerned, the only discernible pattern across welfare regimes is that active search seems to be more strongly related to finding a new job in the social-democratic and residual regime types than in the liberal and corporatist regime types.

Income dynamics and standards of living

Since Esping-Andersen's theory of welfare regimes was framed mainly in terms of the varying role of social security benefits, this typology should be especially relevant to an analysis of the distribution of income. We found evidence in favour of the regime-type classification, but also evidence contradicting it, dependent on the particular issues under consideration.

Chapter 8 analyses the distribution of household incomes. Countries representing the liberal and residual regimes have the widest range of inequality, and the social-democratic regime the lowest. These conclusions, directly in line with predictions, are visible in a single year's income distribution, but are more robust if a sequence of several years is taken into account.

It is clear that market incomes are largely responsible for inequality, but transfer incomes, especially pensions, may also contribute to inequality because they are linked to previous earnings. The impact of pensions varies, especially between pay-as-you-go systems and capital-funded systems.

It appears that the various welfare regimes are more consistent in terms of the distribution of *state* transfers. All regimes tend to target their welfare benefits to the low-educated, lone-parent families and the (long-term) unemployed. Many of the hypotheses concerning regime-type differences in the redistributive impact of the taxes and benefits seem to be confirmed, although the pattern of differences between countries is less clear-cut than expected.

The ECHP makes it possible for the first time to examine the processes of poverty dynamics across a number of countries (Chapter 9). Poverty (often defined as a household income less than 60 per cent of the national median) is experienced by up to twice as many people over a five-year period than face it in any one year. But those poor in one year have a much higher risk of being poor in subsequent years, and this leads to a polarisation between the persistently poor and the never poor. Countries with social-democratic and employment-centred corporatist regimes are less polarised than liberal and residual regimes, and this reduces the impact of persistent poverty.

Demographic characteristics such as being a single parent, or being in a household with larger numbers of adults and children, all contribute to an increased risk of repeated or persistent poverty. However the greatest risk is associated with socio-economic characteristics such as the employment status and level of education of the individuals in the household.

The limited run of data in the ECHP confirms that the chance of exiting poverty reduces as the duration of the spell increases. Social-democratic states have higher exit rates than liberal or residual states, but this patterning is not as strong as in other analyses.

These conclusions relate to 'poverty' defined simply in terms of households with a low income. The 'social exclusion' perspective has focused attention on the processes leading to exposure to multiple disadvantage and social isolation, and this is the theme of Chapter 10. Persistently poor individuals clearly constitute prime candidates for exposure to multiple disadvantage. However, our analysis showed that even when deprivation is measured in terms of items of daily living which people cannot afford (where we might expect relationships to be most straightforward), the poor are not always deprived, and vice versa. In other aspects of life, such as living in high-crime areas, or social isolation, there is virtually no association between poverty and deprivation. The observed pattern does not conform to one of systematic multiple disadvantage.

Persistent poverty is, though, more closely associated with *persistent* deprivation. But it is clear that a great many factors, other than persistent income poverty, play a role in determining deprivation, and that these factors will vary across dimensions. Understanding deprivation cannot simply focus on a cleavage between a multiply deprived and excluded minority and a comfortable majority. The concept of multiple deprivation directs attention to the manner in which disadvantaged groups emerge, the evolution of alternative value systems and the spatial concentration of poverty.

A major lesson drawn from our studies of income, poverty and deprivation relates to the added value of longitudinal data at the micro level. Whereas cross-sectional studies can only tell us who is in poverty, or deprived, at a single point in time, panel data allow us to show how far these disadvantages are long-term and persistent experiences rather than temporary situations. Being able to understand what factors influence the probability of experiencing a long spell of disadvantage is crucial both for an academic understanding of how different individual and household characteristics interact with varying socio-economic systems and institutions, but also for the development of more effective social policy interventions.

Do 'regimes' summarise the variations between 'countries'?
The quest for a synthesis of knowledge, for a simplified interpretation of complex information, for generalised patterns from the mass of the particular, forms a fundamental part of human nature – and comparative social researchers are no exception to this rule. In this book, cross-national variations and similarities in people's lives have been documented in detail – and out of the mass of detail, each chapter has looked for unifying patterns.

The starting point in this investigation has mainly been the fourfold welfare-regime typology outlined in Chapter 1, adapted from the typology proposed by Esping-Andersen (1990, 1999). This typology proposes a 'social-democratic' regime, found in the Scandinavian countries plus the Netherlands; a 'liberal' regime in the UK and Ireland; a 'corporatist' regime in Belgium, Luxembourg, France, Austria and Germany; and a 'residual welfare' regime represented by Portugal, Spain, Italy and Greece.

In many respects, this typology fits observed patterns rather well. When employment dynamics are considered, the flexible labour markets in liberal regimes, together with relatively less generous levels of out-of-work benefits, are related to rather speedy exits from unemployment and relatively low levels of aggregate unemployment. By contrast, the combination of active labour market policies plus higher out-of-work benefit levels in the social-democratic countries leads to low levels of unemployment and social exclusion, but lower rates of movement into full employment from an unemployed or partially employed situation. Even in the case of employment, however, where there is a generally good fit between welfare-regime typologies and observed outcomes, there are important outlying examples which are not well explained by these typologies. For example, labour markets in the Netherlands and Portugal are strikingly different from other members of their respective groups as far as the participation of women is concerned.

When the distribution of household incomes is considered, countries representing the liberal and residual regimes have the widest range of inequality, and the social-democratic regimes the lowest. The incidence of poverty – in particular, persistent poverty – follows a related pattern, with social-democratic and corporatist regimes having the lowest levels of poverty, and liberal and residual regimes the highest. Moreover, in the liberal and residual regimes, which have higher rates of poverty to begin with, there is a stronger relationship between income poverty and material deprivation than in other regime types. Again, the link between social policy and poverty is clear, with the high levels of decommodification in social-democratic and corporatist regimes closely related to the lower incidence of poverty and deprivation in these countries.

However, in other domains, typologies based on welfare regimes fit much less well with observed variations between countries. Certain aspects of family life (for example living arrangements, the sequencing of transitions to adulthood, and the way people combine caring responsibilities with their engagement in the labour market) seem to vary less along the lines of welfare-regime typology, and more with other factors, such as the structure of education systems, or the level of childcare provision. In many ways, this is not surprising: typologies based on welfare regimes are good at explaining variations which are more or less the direct outcomes of welfare regimes themselves – and less good at explaining variations in outcomes which may depend on a wide range of national-level policies.

Thus, we may conclude:

- that despite the striking and important cross-country differences observed in almost all aspects of the lives across the EU, there is a high degree of commonality across countries in terms of many of the processes involved, which should not be overlooked;
- that welfare-regime typologies form a useful starting point for thinking about cross-national differences in a range of outcomes – although for the vast majority of outcomes, the fit is far from perfect;
- that typologies based on welfare regimes are less useful in categorising cross-national variations in areas – such as family patterns, or many aspects of employment – which depend on details of social policy other than those captured by the broader characteristics of welfare regimes; and
- that new ways of looking at cross-country variations will continue to emerge as social policy and other national-level characteristics change and evolve. In particular, the accession of new countries to the EU, with very different socio-economic and political histories from those of the existing members, will pose new challenges to social scientists seeking to understand similarities and differences between countries.

Life-course Social Mobility as an Approach to the Empirical Investigation of Social Justice

Besides addressing the substantive questions summarised in the previous section, the book has attempted to tackle some theoretical and methodological problems regarding the processes by which individuals arrive at different social positions. What do we mean by social position? Most fundamentally, we mean individuals' power to control their 'destiny' – their capacity to determine their own life chances. Social position, in this sense, reflects our control over economically salient resources – precisely those resources, the forms of human, social and cultural 'capital', accumulated in a recursive fashion throughout the life-course.

This sort of power is essentially relational. The personal characteristics that constitute the individual's accumulated capital are only of importance in so far as they determine the individual's relation to particular economic and social institutions. Human capital, for example, gives individuals access to the institutions of the labour market. Social capital provides access to social networks and agencies (clubs, churches, voluntary organisations) which provide frameworks for experiencing sociability, informal production and consumption. Responding to the micro-characteristics that we are able to study from our repeated measurements of individuals through their life-courses, are the macro-characteristics – and in particular the institutional rules and structures – of nation-states.

Longitudinal analysis of the various processes and interactions between the key spheres of life offers a new approach to one of the central questions of social science, concerning the 'fairness' of social arrangements for the distribution of well-being. In fact, research into the distribution of social outcomes might be undertaken for purely 'positive' reasons alone (for example, the distribution of income in a society may be of interest in so far as it influences the level of aggregate demand, as well as on grounds of equity). But in general we do this sort of research for primarily normative reasons. We are concerned about the extent of poverty or deprivation or exclusion, or the degree of polarisation between social classes. Most economists and sociologists have interests that lead them to consider societies in terms that relate in some degree to the core questions of social justice posed by John Rawls (1971). Are advantageous positions in society fairly competed for by all of its members? Are the disadvantages suffered by the losers in such competitions unavoidable in so far as other arrangements would lead to worse consequences for other members of society?

Our book has tried to answer these questions mainly by paying attention to the life-course movements experienced by citizens of contemporary EU countries in the three crucial social structures, or 'life domains' mentioned at the beginning of this chapter: namely, family, labour market and the distribution of economic resources. More precisely, we have studied variations between individuals and across cohorts of inequalities – generated by institutional and personal factors – in the chances of arriving at different positions in these life domains. From this point of view, one might say that our analyses are very similar to the analyses of intra-generational class mobility, or career mobility. The main difference between our study and standard career-mobility analyses is that we have been concerned with a wider set of social destinations other than simply occupation. In fact, there are good arguments and empirical evidence to sustain the view that class position affects destinations in many different domains of social life. However, it is also true that the chances of arriving at some positions are influenced not only by the occupational structure and the related fluidity of the employment regime, but also by national institutional arrangements as well as individual positions in the educational hierarchy, the family, the labour market, the income distribution and so on. So we would maintain that our approach can be viewed as a fruitful enlargement of career-mobility and social inequality studies and, especially, to the comparative version of these studies.

There is a further reason to claim that our approach represents a productive widening of the classical comparative approach to career-mobility studies and analyses of social inequality. Social disparities do not refer only to individuals' or groups' origins and destinations in the class structure or in other dimensions of social stratification. Inequality consists also of heterogeneity in the trajectories linking the positions of departure and arrival of men and women in the various social domains. In turn, the heterogeneity of trajectories refers to both their shape and their duration. Hence, this crucial aspect of inequality can be studied only by means of really dynamic data, covering individual experiences at several points in time, not just two points as in most career mobility studies (or even only one, as in inequality analysis based on cross-sectional surveys).

It is the longitudinal element that needs to be emphasised. Some aspects of these questions (though a surprisingly small proportion of them) can be answered by considering the distribution of advantages as they are seen at a single point in time. But, underlying everything in this book are three specific concerns that lead us to be dissatisfied with the simple analysis of cross-sectional evidence that has been the tradition for empirical social science throughout much of its history, and to analyse, instead, repeated measurements over time.

The aperture of observation

Cross-sectional observations are seldom if ever genuinely instantaneous. As Walker and Ashworth (1994) have observed, many more people experience empty bank accounts at some point in a given month than might appropriately be considered poor. Pockets progressively empty as pay-day approaches, but this clearly does not imply cyclical poverty in any meaningful sense of the word. Every cross-sectional survey, even those which most determinedly avoid the use of all retrospective measures, necessarily collects information whose reference period has some extension in historical time. The appropriate observation window varies. For some purposes, a week may provide an appropriate aperture, for others a year, But in all cases, studying income, poverty, deprivation or whatever, involves the selection of an appropriate period of observation. Many of the phenomena that concern us are in this way inherently longitudinal. Of course these inherently longitudinal phenomena can often be observed cross-sectionally, by asking survey respondents to recall information for the whole of a given reference period. But clearly, the longer the reference period, the more unreliable the recall, and the stronger the argument for repeated measurements.

Long-term accumulation of capital

Social science models incorporate a very powerful conceptual division between (on the one hand) the *structural characteristics* of individuals or households, and (on the other) their *personal behaviours*. (Though it can be argued that this distinction is not always made as explicit as it should be.) Structural characteristics are the determinants of social position, the characteristics which establish the relativities or relationships – of material advantage, prestige or authority – amongst the members of the society. Structural characteristics are, as we put it in the Introduction to this book, the assets and liabilities accumulated by the individual through the life-course. In sociologists' as well as economists' models of individual behaviour, we often find structural characteristics on the right-hand side of equations, and behavioural variables on the left. Structure determines behaviour.

But it is too easily forgotten that conversely the structural characteristics are also the consequence of behaviour. We do (or do not) experience various things, and as a consequence we become particular sorts of people. When we do things repeatedly we become accustomed to them, experienced, skilled – and we do them better. (Or in the case of a negative characteristic, such as poor health resulting from deprivation, our response is increasingly negative.) At the limit the behaviour involved in the acquisition of a structural characteristic can be completely passive and un-self-motivated, as where the mere experience of being born into a rich family leads to subsequent personal wealth. But we do not need to look far to find a less tautological and much more interesting application of the principle that one's current position in the social structure is a reflection of past behaviour or experience.

In short, structural characteristics are acquired through recursive processes over time. To understand how social-positional advantages and disadvantages are accumulated (and dissipated) we need repeated measures of individuals' behaviour.

Interaction among different spheres of life

Finally, accumulated characteristics in one sphere of life have consequences for others. Just consider the brief life history discussed in Figure 11.1. Clearly, activities in one sphere this year have consequences in other spheres next year, which in turn have consequences in the original sphere the year after that. The birth of a child (in other words a change in the family sphere) leads to a withdrawal from employment, which has immediate negative consequences for the household's income, and longer-term negative implications for the woman's human capital.

These three interconnected reasons for wishing to move forward from the study of conditions at a particular point in time, to the study of the sequences of events and durations in states, lie at the heart of longitudinal research. We study individuals' trajectories between different social positions, which is the essence of 'social mobility'.

A panel survey conducted within a single country enables us to study how the life-courses of a sample of the national population interact with that nation's economic and social institutions. We can discover, for a given society, how actions and incidents in one part of life impact on subsequent outcomes – given the particular institutions of that society. And we can make judgements about the fairness or justice of the arrangements within that society, directly from that evidence. We can conclude that a country's income is too polarised between rich and poor, or that the stability of household income provides insufficient incentive for human capital investment or individual entrepreneurship – or, conversely, that the instability of income over time provides insufficient rewards.

But all the variation available to us, in such an approach, is at the individual level. National studies provide no counterfactuals. What is the alternative to the current arrangements? We do not have two alternative versions of Spain, with different public policy regimes, to compare with each other. So we cannot do empirically what is demanded by Rawls' Theory of Justice. And it is certainly true that cross-national comparisons cannot provide good counterfactuals. Germany is not Spain. We cannot conclude that social and economic arrangements that work in a particular way in one country will work in the same way in another country. Nevertheless, cross-national comparisons provide the best empirical comparators we can expect to find.

This ultimately is the contribution of the sort of comparative research that is discussed here. By focusing on country differences, and by attempting to summarise them in terms of welfare regimes, we may hope to abstract from the specifically national experience of particular countries. To the extent that, say, the social-democratic group of countries have different histories, and distinct cultures, the similarities we find among them relate to that common approach to social policy that led us to group them in this way. Of course in reality these particular countries share too much history to allow us to place too heavy a weight of causal responsibility on the shared lines of social policy. Ultimately, to establish regime effects, we will need regime types constructed from countries with more historically diverse geography and history, to set against the shared line of public policy. Hence the importance, as this general approach to policy research goes forward, of integrating panel studies from other broadly comparable countries: Poland and Hungary, the USA, Canada, and Australia all have materials suitable for this purpose, though in the longer term we will have to look much wider still, to acquire the requisite international variability.[1]

We are still in the first stages of cross-national comparative longitudinal research. Some precursor data sets have provided harmonised panel data for a small number of countries. And there are already some distinguished books in this area (Goodin et al., 1999; Headey et al., 2000; Bradbury et al., 2001). But much international comparative research has suffered from the restriction of a small number of countries for comparison, leading to a requirement for concentration on national-level analysis, or at best the use of nations as exemplars of regime types. Only when we get to a data set with a coverage as wide as that in the ECHP can we even think of serious regime-level analysis – and this work will be even more powerful once the geographical base is widened beyond Europe.

On the basis of what is written here we might conclude:

- there is an important future for comparative cross-national longitudinal research, investigating issues that lie in the traditional heartland of the social sciences, but with new and powerful techniques to match the new data; and
- within the general field of comparative cross-national longitudinal research, there is an important role for the sorts of data sets – of which ECHP is for the present the primary example – that have sufficient national variation to allow us to abstract to some degree from national characteristics to investigate the effects of public policy regimes.

This book is a member of the first category, but contributes especially to the second. The foregoing chapters give a taste of what is possible in this field. Now that we are properly started along this line, and as all eight waves of the ECHP data become available for analysis, we hope that many more members of the European research community will be encouraged to follow into this new and very promising area of enquiry.

Notes

1. See page 13 for references to the CHER data set combining 18 countries, and to the EPUNet service to ECHP users.

References

Bradbury, B., S. Jenkins and J. Micklewright (2001), *The Dynamics of Child Poverty in Industrialised Countries*, Cambridge: Cambridge University Press.

Esping-Andersen, G. (1990), *The Three Worlds of Welfare Capitalism*, Cambridge: Polity Press.

Esping-Andersen, G. (1999), *Social Foundations of Postindustrial Economies*, Oxford: Oxford University Press.

Goodin, R., B. Headey, R. Muffels and H.-J. Dirven (1999), *The Real Worlds of Welfare Capitalism*, Cambridge: Cambridge University Press.

Headey, B., R. Muffels, B. Goodin and H.-J. Dirven (2000), 'Is there a trade-off between economic efficiency and a generous welfare state? A comparison of best cases of "The Three Worlds of Welfare Capitalism", *Journal of Social Indicators Research*, **50** (2), 115–157.

Rawls, J. (1971), *A Theory of Justice*, Cambridge, MA: Belknap Press of Harvard University Press.

Walker, R. and K. Ashworth (1994), 'Measuring claimant populations: time, fractals and social security', in N Buck, J Gershuny, D Rose and J Scott (eds), *Changing Households*, Colchester: ESRC Research Centre on Micro-Social Change.

Appendix: Working Papers of the European Panel Analysis Group

1999

1 *Longitudinal Poverty and Income Inequality: a comparative panel study for the Netherlands, Germany and the UK*, Ruud Muffels, Didier Fouarge and Ronald Dekker

2 *Education, Employment and Gender Inequality in the Family: a comparative analysis of the British and the German household panel data*, Malcolm Brynin and Juergen Schupp

3 *The Distribution of Income and Relative Income Poverty in the European Community Household Panel*, Brian Nolan and Bertrand Maître

4 *Income Mobility in the European Community Household Panel Survey*, Bertrand Maître and Brian Nolan

5 *Income, Deprivation and Economic Strain: an analysis of the European Community Household Panel*, Richard Layte, Bertrand Maître, Brian Nolan and Christopher T. Whelan

6 *Young People in Europe: two models of household formation*, Maria Iacovou

2000

7 *Exits from Unemployment Spells in Germany and the United Kingdom*, Lutz C. Kaiser and Thomas Siedler

8 *Health, Wealth and Progeny: explaining the living arrangements of older European women*, Maria Iacovou

9 *The Living Arrangements of Elderly Europeans*, Maria Iacovou

10 *Poverty Dynamics: an analysis of the 1994 and 1995 waves of the European Community Household Panel Study,*Richard Layte, Bertrand Maître, Brian Nolan and Christopher T. Whelan

2003

39   *The Impact of Children on Women's Labor Supply in Europe: a re-
     assessment of the role of institutions*, Wilfred Uunk, Matthijs
     Kalmijn and Ruud Muffels

40   *Welfare State Regimes and the Economic Consequences of
     Separation: evidence from the European Community Household
     Panel survey, 1994–1998*, Wilfred Uunk

41   *The Role of European Welfare States in Explaining Resources
     Deprivation*, Ruud Muffels and Didier Fouarge

42   *Immigrants' Economic Performance Across Europe: does
     immigration policy matter?*, Felix Büchel and Joachim R. Frick

43   *Female Partners' Income Contribution to the Household Income in
     the European Union*, Bertrand Maître, Christopher T. Whelan and
     Brian Nolan

44   *The Ageing Workforce and Labour Market Mobility: do mobility
     patterns differ between age groups and welfare regimes?*, Trudie
     Schils and Ruud Muffels

45   *Work-rich and Work-poor Couples: Polarisation in 14 Countries in
     Europe*, Maria Iacovou

46   *Unemployment and Income Inequality in Denmark: a decomposition
     approach*, Mette Deding and Peder Pedersen

47   *Duration of Poverty Spells in Europe*, Didier Fouarge and Richard
     Layte

48   *Poverty, Deprivation and Time: a corporate analysis of the
     structuring of disadvantage*, Christopher T. Whelan, Richard Layte
     and Bertrand Maître

2004

49   *The Transition into Work: specialities for the hidden labour force in
     comparison to other economically inactive persons*, Elke Holst and
     C. Katharina Spiess

50   *Area Variations in Income, and in Poverty, across the EU*, Richard
     Berthoud

51   *Social Position in Europe*, Karen L. Robson and Jonathan Gershuny

Index